Resisting Occupation

Decolonizing Theology

Series Editor: Jione Havea

This series aims to demonstrate the character and shape of the future of theology, which is a diversity of theologies 'decolonized' of Western captivity and influence. Each volume of the series, as such, will highlight and explore indigenous expressions of Christian theology from a thickly contextual perspective. At the heart of the project is the goal of providing readers an array of theologies from around the globe, many unknown or often overlooked by Western audiences, as a way of demonstrating the availability of non-Western Christian development and de-centering the study and methods of Christian theology from Western domination and standards.

TITLES IN THIS SERIES

Cuban Feminist Theology: Visions and Praxis, by Ofelia Ortega

Resisting Occupation: A Global Struggle for Liberation, edited by Miguel A. De La Torre and Mitri Raheb

Theologies on the Move: Religion, Migration, and Pilgrimage in the World of Neoliberal Capital, edited by Joerg Rieger

Theological and Hermeneutical Explorations from Australia: Horizons of Contextuality, edited by Jione Havea

Resisting Occupation

A Global Struggle for Liberation

Miguel A. De La Torre
and Mitri Raheb

LEXINGTON BOOKS/FORTRESS ACADEMIC
Lanham • Boulder • New York • London

Published by Lexington Books/Fortress Academic
An imprint of The Rowman & Littlefield Publishing Group, Inc.
4501 Forbes Boulevard, Suite 200, Lanham, Maryland 20706
www.rowman.com

86–90 Paul Street, London EC2A 4NE, United Kingdom

Copyright © 2022 by The Rowman & Littlefield Publishing Group, Inc.

All rights reserved. No part of this book may be reproduced in any form or by any electronic or mechanical means, including information storage and retrieval systems, without written permission from the publisher, except by a reviewer who may quote passages in a review.

British Library Cataloguing in Publication Information Available

Library of Congress Cataloging-in-Publication Data

ISBN: 9781978711372 (cloth)
ISBN: 9781978711396 (paper)
ISBN: 9781978711389 (electronic)

This book was made possible
through the kind contribution
of the Council for World Mission

Contents

Illustrations   ix

Introduction   1
   Miguel A. De La Torre and Mitri Raheb

PART ONE: OCCUPYING MINDS

1. Toward an Ethics *para Joder*: Decolonizing Minds by Transgressing Academic Borders   7
  Miguel A. De La Torre

2. "Imagined Occupation" and the Occupation of the National Imaginary: Scottish Stories in the Face of Brexit Britain   19
  John McNeil Scott

3. City Gate and Homeland Imagination: The Theology of Image in Post-Modern Taiwan   37
  Su-Chi Lin

4. Toward a Cross-Border Imagination: Another World Is Possible!   51
  Junghyung Kim

5. The Occupation of Theological Minds: The End of Innocence   61
  Mitri Raheb

PART TWO: OCCUPYING BODIES

6. The Construction of Religious Hybrid Identities: Resulting from Colonial Occupation   79
  Wanda Deifelt

7	The Boys in the Mirror *Luciano Kovacs*	95

PART THREE: OCCUPYING SPIRIT

8	The Devil that Occupies US: Social Sin and Sacred Silence in a Trumped Era *Stacey M. Floyd-Thomas*	105
9	The Motherly Spirit: A Geotheological Power of Life in Papua *Toar Hutagalung*	117
10	Resistance and Reconciliationthrough the Arts *Volker Küster*	131
11	Beauty in the Rubble?: Genuine Encounter, Self-Transformation, and Transnational Community in Activism for Palestine *Marthie Momberg*	153

PART FOUR: OCCUPYING LAND

12	Occupation in North America: States, Rule of Law, Language, and Indians *George "Tink" Tinker*	175
13	From Empire to Independent Composite Successor States: Postcolonial Political Theology in Melanesia *Richard A. Davis*	195
14	Palestine, Zionism, and Global Struggle: A Jewish American's Journey *Mark Braverman*	211
15	The Re-Reading of the Exodus Narrative: An African Perspective *Sindiso Jele*	227

Conclusion 239
   Mitri Raheb and Miguel A. De La Torre

Index 243

About the Contributors 249

Illustrations

Figure 3.1.	*Outside of North Gate*, Courtesy of National Central Library, Taiwan.	39
Figure 3.2.	Ishikawa Toraji, *Japanese Troops Occupy Taiwan* (台灣鎮定). Fresco, 1923. Meiji Memorial Picture Gallery in Meiji Jingu Gaien, Tokyo. Courtesy of National Central Library, Taiwan.	40
Figure 3.3.	*Taiwan Temple* (台灣神社). Courtesy of National Central Library, Taiwan.	42
Figure 3.4.	*Governor Baron Kodama Gentaro and His Official Residence* (台灣總督官邸和總督兒玉男爵). Courtesy of National Central Library, Taiwan.	43
Figure 3.5.	The unfolding of the Taipei city story from the 19th century to the present is projected on the surface of the North Gate (Bei Men) in 2017 Taipei Lantern Festival (See https://www.youtube.com/watch?v=T1GbfkKMZN0). Photo by Agi Chen Studio with permission.	45
Figure 10.1.	Hong Song-Dam, *Kwangju*, 1980s, courtesy of the artist.	135
Figure 10.2.	Hong Song-Dam, *The Twenty Days in Water* 1, 1999, courtesy of the artist.	136
Figure 10.3.	Hong Song-Dam, *The Twenty Days in Water* 4, 1999, courtesy of the artist.	137

Figure 10.4.	Hong Song-Dam, *The Twenty Days in Water* 8, 1999, courtesy of the artist.	138
Figure 10.5.	Paul Stopforth, *The Interrogators*, 1979, courtesy of the artist.	140
Figure 10.6.	Paul Stopforth, *Biko Series*, 1980, courtesy of the artist.	141
Figure 10.7.	Paul Stopforth, *Biko Series*, 1980, courtesy of the artist.	141
Figure 10.8.	Paul Stopforth, *Biko Series*, 1980, courtesy of the artist.	142
Figure 10.9.	Paul Stopforth, *Freedom Dancer*, 1993, courtesy of the artist.	142
Figure 10.10.	Paul Stopforth, *African Spice*, 2014, courtesy of the artist.	143
Figure 10.11.	Donatus Moyen, detail of murals, Cathedral of Jayapura, photo by the author, by permission of the artist.	144
Figure 10.12.	Donatus Moyen, detail of murals, Cathedral of Jayapura, by permission of the artist.	145
Figure 10.13.	Donatus Moyen, mural, Hawaii-Chapel, photo by the author, by permission of the artist.	146
Figure 10.14.	Donatus Moyen, mural, Hawaii-Chapel, photo by the author, by permission of the artist.	147

Introduction

Miguel A. De La Torre and Mitri Raheb

Occupation signifies more than just oppression; it signifies ignominy and indignity. To be occupied facilitates the erasure of personhood, the denial of self-determination. Occupation is more treacherous than simply controlling the land of others, for it encompasses the domination of one's very sense of being. To be occupied is a radical denial of human flourishing, a suppression of indigenous stories, a rejection of the other's humanity. And yet, for the vast majority of those who inhabit two-thirds of the world's land mass, occupation has historically been a way of being. Even long after the colonizer sailed away and their flags which were replaced by those home-grown, existing external neoliberal structures, coupled with the internalization of centuries of oppression, make the residual consequences of occupation as real and damning today as they were in past centuries. As satanic as it is occupying what has never rightly belonged, we are dumbfounded as to how Christian-professing empires justified pillage and plunder. To occupy requires a religious worldview that rationalizes the stealing of other's land, the raping of their bodies, and the massacring of their children. Such a Christianity was—no doubt—damning to those abused by occupation; but it also left a perpetual scar upon those who embraced the religion of occupation. To live in the shadows of Eurocentric empires frustrates the ability of both the occupied and the occupiers to faithfully live life abundantly. The occupied are denied their humanity by the very act of occupation, while the occupiers lose their humanity in the process. Both are victimized by the act of occupation, both require liberation and salvation.

The contributors to this book gathered at Yilan, Taiwan, in 2019 to engage in a conversation concerning occupation, a subject that has touched the skin and scorched the soul of many of us. Thanks to a generous grant from the Council for World Mission, to whom the coeditors of this manuscript are deeply grateful, leading Christian scholars and activists from around the world entered into a dialogue attempting to understand the many facets of occupation—the occupation of our minds, the occupation of our bodies, the occupation of our spirits, and of course, the occupation of our lands. We quickly discovered that the colonial venture to subjugate and dominate the land of others for the economic purpose of extracting raw materials and cheap labor required more than simply the necessary brute force required to control land. Controlling land solely through physical strength soon proves insufficient. Minds, bodies, and spirits also require colonization so as to make oppression appear not only normal and legitimate, but also desirable and beneficial. The colonized, in every aspect of life, must come to believe and support the mission of their own civilization and christianization. They must be taught to want, to yearn for, to embrace occupation. In effect, the colonized must learn to see and define themselves through the eyes of their colonizers.

But what would happen if those on the margins made a conscious decision to see themselves through their own eyes? What would those at the margins say if they had an opportunity to speak back to the colonial center? Would the subaltern even be heard? This book attempts to answer these questions. With the unifying theme of occupation, scholars from around the globe seek to unpack and uncover the colonial tentacles that historically have suffocated the liberative breath of the world's disenfranchised and dispossessed for centuries. Gathering voices from the four corners of the planet, this book examines the consequences of occupation from divergent social contexts, discovering that, regardless of our different experiences, we share common scars—the stigmata of occupation—not only on our bodies, but on our psyches.

To that end, we have divided the book into four sections. Essays in part one focus on *Occupying Minds*. The first chapter, by Miguel A. De La Torre, titled "Toward an Ethics *para joder*," argues that Eurocentric theological thought requires rejection from the colonized because it was never intended for them; it undergirds white supremacy; it serves as the precursor to and justifier of land occupation; and it erases the colonized's theological contributions. He instead calls for a decolonizing *ethics para Joder*, based on indigenous trickster figures which "screws" with the power structures. The second chapter, "'Imagined Occupation' and the Occupation of the National Imaginary," by John McNeil Scott, explores how the British state, the former seat of imperial power, now constructs a narrative of external oppression to justify Brexit. The occupier's false consciousness of being occupied is then challenged with counternarratives from their margins. Su-Chi Lin's third chapter, "City Gate and Homeland Imagination," examines Taipei's North Gate (Bei Men) to develop, through the connection of art and theology, a gateway to the island's public memory. The beauty and suffering signified by this doorway create a space to lament loss and contemplate the divine. Chapter four, by Junghyung Kim, "Toward a Cross-border Imagination," is influenced by the biblical call for reconciliation and looks to the popular 2013 movie *The Snowpiercer* to imagine a world other than the current divided Korea. The fictional character Namgung Minsu, contrary to the other train passengers, signifies that another way of being and existing is possible rather than that imposed by the current demilitarized zone (DMZ). And finally, "The Occupation of Theological Minds" by Mitri Raheb, explores how Christian theology, consciously or subconsciously, played a major role in aiding the ongoing colonization of Palestinian land and people, failing to see how the so-called Promised Land is but confiscated land. Fear of accusations of being called anti-Semitic contributes to the occupation of Christian scholars' minds.

Part two, *Occupying Bodies*, starts with Wanda Deifelt's chapter, "The Construction of Religious Hybrid Identities Resulting from Colonial Occupation." This essay focuses on religious pluralism in Latin America and the Caribbean, and specifically how, in spite of the predominance of Roman Catholicism among the enslaved and colonized, religious practices served as forms of resistance and means for survival to European colonialism and occupation. Luciano Kovacs's short story "The Boys in the Mirror" artistically addresses the paradox of how historical occupiers of others' lands now use the rhetoric of invasion to curb those fleeing situations to which occupiers contributed, whether by colonial rule, enslavement, economic pillaging, support of dictatorial regimes, proxy conflicts, or wars waged to plunder so-called natural resources.

Part three, *Occupying Spirit*, starts with a chapter by Stacey M. Floyd-Thomas titled "The Devil that Occupies Us." This chapter not only explores the U.S. utopian/nihilistic impulse of creating a fair and equitable society, but also how our present angst represents the dilemma of a nation which has the world held hostage in its claims of being the "great experiment" in human flourishing and governance for nearly two and a half centuries—a process which required conflating white patriarchal supremacy with God and the divine is what can be identified as "American eminence." Toar Hutagalung's chapter, "The Motherly Spirit," seeks a decolonization of geontopower in Papua by employing a pneumatological perspective. Geontopower, a concept derived from Elizabeth Povinelli's work, is an evil structure which rests upon colonization, mining, and racism. In response, geotheology is proposed, aimed to decolonize and reconstruct geontopower. The next chapter, "Resistance and Reconciliation through the Arts," by Volker Küster, looks to the arts as a non-verbal discursive instrument to resist occupation, overcome trauma in post-conflict situations, and negotiate reconciliation. The intersection of class, race, ethnicity, gender, religion, culture, militarism, globalization, and empire is explored through artistic case studies from South Korea, South Africa, West Papua, and Nagaland in India. Finally, Marthie Momberg's chapter "Beauty in the Rubble?" discusses the meaning and power of relational and aesthetic experience in Palestinian activism and how this experience is part of a global community's shared struggle.

The final section, part four, *Occupying Land*, focuses on the outward expression of the inward oppression of one's mind, body, and spirit. The section begins with George "Tink" Tinker's analysis of occupied territory in the chapter titled "Occupation in North america." Tinker attempts to hold white liberals accountable for not seriously examining their complicity with settler occupation, specifically how this is a Eurochristian and not a European occupation. The next chapter, "From Empire to Independent Composite Successor States," by Richard A. Davis, explores how the 1970s and 80s decolonization of the Pacific left in its wake a colonial legacy of new mini-empires masquerading as independent composite states. For a full decolonization of nations and minds to occur, a call is made for anti-statism. Mark Braverman's next chapter, "Palestine, Zionism and Global Struggle," explores how, in spite of the role churches played in the struggles for liberation during the twentieth century, when it came to Palestine, the biblical text was used to justify the erasure of Palestinian history and identity. And finally, the last chapter by Sindiso Jele, titled "The Re-reading of the Exodus Narrative," re-reads the Exodus story showing how Africans, as the new Canaanites, are destined to occupation based on the traditional Eurocentric reading of the text.

These fifteen chapters, emanating from different parts of the Earth, share a similar story concerning the consequences of occupation, demonstrating a unity in the struggle for liberation from said occupation. What these stories hold in common are the negative physical and psychological impacts of occupation. They may have arisen from different contexts; nevertheless, they have a similar impact on minds, bodies, spirits, and lands. These phenomena indicate a need for more conversation on the how those who have experienced occupation are spiritually and intellectually bound together. And, just maybe, the only hope for full liberation from consequences of colonization comes as stories are shared with each other in search of a unified cooperation. Maybe the first step in any liberative process is to see with our own eyes—a process manifested through the telling of our stories and the defining of our beings. To this task of lifting the voices and perspectives of the occupied, this text now turns its attention.

Part I

OCCUPYING MINDS

Chapter One

Toward an Ethics *para Joder*

Decolonizing Minds by Transgressing Academic Borders

Miguel A. De La Torre

Occupation of our minds is more insidious than the occupation of our lands, for if our minds are occupied, then the very physical and metaphysical essence of our being becomes subjugated to domination. Since childhood, the colonized have been taught to see and interpret reality through Eurocentric eyes. Eurocentric thought specializes in sustaining and maintaining a way of thinking which at best ignores its complicity with advancing the neoliberal goals of empire, and at worst, justifies empire. Academic rigor becomes a constructed discourse, legitimized and normalized by those who have the ways and means to make their subjectivity objective for all; determining who represents academic excellence, and who provides an interesting perspective but lacks scholastic rigor. The triumph of the colonizing process is best demonstrated when the colonized consciously or unconsciously define themselves and their communities through academic paradigms that historically and continuously have contributed to their marginalization. Constantly forced to demonstrate intelligence, the colonized at times seek their own voice through the use and application of Eurocentric paradigms incapable of liberating colonized minds. Consequently, the particularity of Eurocentric scholarship poses a clear and present danger to the colonized.

EUROCENTRIC THOUGHT NEVER MEANT FOR THE COLONIZED

To maintain the institutional violence that furthers the occupation of our minds, a Eurocentric way of philosophizing is required that was never intended to liberate the colonized. Among Eurocentric Christians, a theology of hope is constructed which may sound liberative but rather, I argue, reinforces the oppression of the colonized. Eurocentric hope is not some wishful optimistic desire, but a joyful expectation that God will bring about God's perfect purposes. Jürgen Moltmann, the prophet of hope, argues for a hope based on a God who keeps promises, a God one step ahead of humanity, a God making all things new (1967: 20–21). Moltmann's hope is especially attractive to the colonized because in spite of the trials and tribulations they face, they can hope in God's promises which validate Good News, assure an eternal afterlife, provide meaning and purpose to the future, fortify a sense of security, provide tranquility of the mind, and secure a sense of peace in the midst of the vicissitudes faced by the colonized.

But what do you do when this God of liberation fails to liberate from centuries of oppression and enslavement?—When God's promises fall short in the face of genocide? A Eurocentric theology must be created to limit who is called for liberation and, by extension, salvation. Eurocentric theology and politics must be formulated to exclude and blame the colonized for the liberative promises not kept by God. Think of the French Revolution's slogan *Liberté, Egalité, Fraternité*, whose lofty ideals were never meant for France's colonies in Haiti, Vietnam, or Algiers. Or Hegel's entire endeavor to create ahistorical truths resting on the presupposition of Teutonic superiority over and against the inferiority of non-Europeans. As his 1824 book *Lectures on the Philosophy of History* demonstrates, Northern Europe, specifically central Germany, is the Spirit of the new world whose purpose becomes the realization of absolute Truth as the unlimited self-determination of freedom (1824: 103, 341). Such a freedom was never meant for the colonized in need of civilization and Christianization. Even the U.S. rhetorical end to its daily oath of "liberty and justice for all" was never intended to include those from African descent, or those hailing from south of the border.

Eurocentric philosophical and theological thought just meant whites, not her colonies nor those among the colonized who followed their stolen raw material and cheap labor to the center of empires. Abstract philosophical and theological thoughts are constructed to tickle the cerebrum in a vain attempt of reconciling the quest for liberty and equality among whites who purposefully exclude those whom they deem inferior from the equation. This is not an issue of hypocrisy by colonizers spewing rhetoric about freedom; instead, it is an attempt to philosophically and theologically justify oppression through liberty-based platitudes. Moving philosophical and theological thought to the abstract obscures the economic need of dispossessing and disenfranchising the colonized and their descendants. Universal Eurocentric celestial concepts of rights blinds the colonized to the concrete feet-on-the-ground reality of oppression at the hands of such freedom-voicing whites. I am convinced, and thus argue, all Eurocentric philosophical and religious thought is detrimental to the lives of the colonized and oppressive to the world's disenfranchised. Our only hope of salvation is the total rejection of Eurocentric thought designed as the precursor to and justifier of the occupation of our minds.

If philosophical and theological thought is a construct of a particular type of culture, then those born into and/or raised within a Eurocentric culture are a product of a society where white supremacy and class privilege have historically been interwoven with how whites, for centuries, see and organize the world around them. How they "see" has been normalized and legitimized as universal. This racist and classist underpinning contributes to the metanarrative of how those within the Eurocentric culture developed their way of thinking. A worldview is constructed in which complicity with Eurocentrism is deemed normal and where those who benefit from white supremacy usually accept the present order of things, failing to consider the racialization of how they see and organize their world. Regardless how alluring Eurocentric philosophy and/or theology might appear to the colonized, most of it remains embedded within white supremacy and is thus potentially incongruent with any gospel message of liberation.

EUROCENTRIC THOUGHT DOMESTICATES THE COLONIZED

One of the unexamined assumptions of Eurocentric Christianity is a theology based on *esperanza*, on hope. "All things work for the good of those who love God, and who have been called according to God's purpose" (Ro. 8:28). Those who "hope" in English expect or wait for something good. But for those of us who read the biblical text in Spanish, the word *esperanza* is derived from the word *esperar*: to wait. The usage of the Spanish word connotes a negative dimension, implying apprehension for what is being awaited. To wait does not always imply happy endings, especially if the waiting drags on for centuries, as in the case of Hebrew slaves in Egypt or today's Latinxs residing in the belly of the empire. History and my existential experiences problematize this hope which Eurocentric theology seeks to sell. Claiming hope is somewhat naïve, especially if, as Latinxs, we are perceived as perpetual foreigners. We relate to King David's pronouncement, "We are foreigners and strangers before the eyes of God, just as were all our ancestors. Our days on earth are like a shadow, without hope" (1 Ch. 29:15). With Job, we cry out to a deaf God, "where then is my hope and who can perceive any hope for me?" (Jb. 17:15).

Hope reduced to the personal might provide false comfort; but what about the eventual hope in the triumph of justice? Hope, as a product of salvation history (either metaphysical or material-dialectic), can be optimistically believed. Thus, Martin Luther King, Jr. would be right in asserting that the arc of the moral universe bends toward justice (1986:52). But I am not convinced this is so. The existence of such an arc is nothing more than a statement of faith believed and accepted without proof. No doubt, hope, as a statement of unfounded belief, serves an important middle-class purpose, becoming an excuse not to deal with the reality of injustice. Those struggling to survive are keenly aware how destitution and death usually await the disenfranchised. Waiting for the colonized, all too often, leads to nothingness. The world's colonized occupy the space of Holy Saturday, the day after Friday's crucifixion, and the not yet Easter Sunday of resurrection; a space where some faint anticipation of Sunday's Good News is overpowered by the reality and consequences of Friday's violence; a space where hopelessness is the companion of used and abused people.

The hopelessness I advocate rejects quick and easy solutions which temporarily soothe the conscience; but it is no substitute for bringing about more just social structures. This hopelessness is not incapacitating; rather, it is a methodology which propels toward praxis. All too often, advocating hope interferes with listening and learning from the oppressed. To sit in the reality of Saturday is to recognize the semblance of hope as an obstacle serving as a mechanism which maintains rather than challenges prevailing social structures. The hopelessness in vanquishing injustices is never an excuse to do nothing. Yes, we may be living in the Saturday, but that's no justification to submissively wait for Sunday (De La Torre 2010:92–93). The colonized have few options. For many, their only option is to continue their struggle for justice regardless of the odds against them. To only hope becomes counterproductive. The virtue and/or audacity of hope become a class privilege experienced by those not fully exposed to Friday's realities or an opium used to numb this same reality until Sunday rolls around. Regardless of the optimism professed, the disenfranchised, their children, and their children's children will probably continue living in an ever-expanding oppression. Sunday is so far away. Waiting, *esperar*, is so tiresome. The situation remains truly hopeless.

I fear philosopher Walter Benjamin might have been closer in understanding historical progression (or the lack thereof) when he quipped: "There is no document of civilization which is not at the same time a document of barbarism" (1969:256). What if our creation of history and our remembrance of the past simply justifies the values and social power of those who get to write history, literally writing their privileged space into the national epic? What if no historical movement exists which leads toward some religious heavenly paradise or secular utopian based on enlightenment and reason? When Benjamin gazes upon Paul Klee's painting,

Angelus Novus, he sees "an angel looking as though he is about to move away from something he is fixedly contemplating. His eyes are staring, his mouth is open, his wings are spread. . . . This is how one pictures the angel of history. His face is turned toward the past. Where we perceive a chain of events, he sees one single catastrophe which keeps piling wreckage upon wreckage and hurls it in front of his feet" (1969:257). There is no teleology to history, nothing inevitable or meaningful concerning the passage of time, nothing but a game of random chance. History is chaos, with no rhyme or reason, because the events, like humans, are unpredictable and contradictive. Hegel, through the Eurocentric imagination, imposed his systemized privilege upon chaos and called it a progressive dialectical march toward a better human existence.

Eurocentric modernity teaches salvation history; we are moving toward utopia; we claim either capitalism (a rising tide will raise all ships) or communism (the eventual withering away of the state). We can hope in a future which will be more liberative and egalitarian than our past, thanks to science or human ingenuity or God. But what if salvation history is but a Eurocentric imaginary embraced by the colonized, thus reinforcing their minds' occupation? What if premodernity (history made by God) and modernity (history made by the human subject) are Eurocentric creations? What if Hegel's historical dialectic moving humanity in a progressively upward spiral is but an optimistic hypothesis imposed on a selective and disconnected set of historical events? For Benjamin, a storm is blowing from Paradise which caught the Angelus Novus wings with such violence that the angel no longer can close them. "The storm irresistibly propels him into the future to which his back is turned, while the pile of debris before him grows skywards. This storm is what we call progress" (1969:257). History at times may seem to move upwards; but ages of ignorance can just as easily follow spans of enlightenment, also creating downward spirals.

Michel Foucault argued that history does not exist as an internal and necessary unfolding dialectic flow, progressing in linear discourse. Instead he proposed historical discontinuation (1984: 81). A history not defined by triumphant metanarratives; instead, history is a kaleidoscope comprised of contradictory and complex untold stories and struggles of the unnamed least among us. The norm leans more toward stories of immorality vanquishing virtue, brutality crushing peace, and vulgarity winning elections. We presently live in a world neither improving nor becoming more secure for the colonized. Instead, due to the ever-widening global wealth gap, life is noticeably getting worse. Billions are born into poverty and die to its consequences so the privileged few can enjoy First World redemption. "Vanity of vanities," the teacher reminds us. "Absolute futility. Everything is meaningless" (Eccl. 1:1). If all this is true, what role then is played by religious hope?

EUROCENTRIC THOUGHT DWARFS RESISTANCE AND UNDERGIRDS WHITE SUPREMACY

Hope becomes the means by which the minds of the colonized become occupied and an excuse for the colonizers to ignore injustices. I first developed this theology of hopelessness when taking a group of predominately white students to the squatter villages of Cuernavaca, Mexico, in an attempt to listen to and learn from the world's wretched. We spoke with families living in horrific conditions, in roach-infested shacks constructed of discarded wood, cardboard, and plasterboard. That evening, as we processed the day's activities, one student stated that in spite of the miserable conditions witnessed, she still saw "the hope in the eyes of the little girls." Suffering an epistemological meltdown, I responded that these same little girls with supposed hope in their eyes would within a few years be turning tricks to put food on the table or trapped in abusive marriages attempting to survive the prevailing classism and sexism. I refused to let this student disconnect the neoliberal connection between how the same global economic structures which privilege her are responsible for the real-life suffering these little girls face. I refused to let the excuse of hope liberate my student from any responsibility for the sufferings these little girls experience. I refused to let her participate in the colonizing process of imposing First-World hope on these Third-World bodies so she could simply wash her hands of the realities that benefited her, at the cost of these little girls' torments. I instead demanded praxis, not optimistic sentiments.

Among those suffering global disenfranchisement, I find an ethos where hope is not apparent. Since this encounter, I have been wrestling with the realization that for many of the world's ultra-poor, hope seems to be mainly claimed by those in the Global North who are protected by economic privilege, a means to distance them from the unsolvable consequences of colonialization. As long as I have hope, I am persuaded to keep my head down, not rock the boat, not make trouble in a vain attempt to survive and overcome. But when it is truly hopeless, when I embrace the futility of the moment, then I am the most dangerous, most inclined to engage in radical revolutionary praxis because I have nothing else to lose.

How then do I create (in my case) an indigenous Latinx theological response? Over 125 years ago, the Cuban revolutionary José Martí, while living—as he originally wrote—"in the belly of the beast" (*OC* 2001:168), saw the danger of adopting a Eurocentric worldview detrimental to the existential intellectual space occupied by the colonized. He called the oppressed of the world to create a new way of thinking based on our indigeneity, writing: "*El vino, de plátano; y si sale agrio, ¡es nuestro vino!* (*OC* 2001:20). Allow me to translate: "Our wine from plantains; and if it turns out sour, it's our wine!" To build liberative edifices on Eurocentric philosophical and theological foundations reproduces the same consequences as pouring new wines into old skins.

The guardians of white supremacy normalized and legitimized a way of thinking and being that occupies minds while creating the illusion of freed bodies, because if the mind can be colonized, then those whom society is constructed to benefit don't need to worry about resistance to oppression. Unfortunately, liberative inclinations have, more often than not, looked to our oppressors for means of defining and expressing our thoughts. We seek to explain how to liberate dark bodies through white thoughts. We attempt to simply add some token color to white ideals as we attempt to humanize those same Eurocentric thinkers who dehumanize us. When the colonized seek a liberative methodology that rests upon Eurocentric philosophical paradigms, we construct resistance on shifting sand, contributing to and continuing our own oppression. And worse, elucidating resistance through Eurocentric thought, regardless how loud, fearless, and passionate we may sound, undermines our ability to bring about substantial change. But to create new wine becomes the means by which we can begin to decolonize our minds. The difficult task before us is to imagine and think new thoughts of our own accord, instead of as a response to Eurocentric ways and beliefs, an indigenous radical worldview different from the normative philosophies that have historically justified our subservient place within society.

The task in deoccupying our space begins by working with one's own hands and thinking with one's own head. No person can serve two masters, for they will love one and despise the other. Any colonized person who serves and loves the Eurocentric philosophical thought which excludes them, or the white Gods and Jesuses bent on their subservience, will despise the philosophical and religious wisdom emanating from their own culture. Martí called upon the oppressed of the world to create a new way of thinking, a new way of being, a new way of contemplating the metaphysical based on their indigeneity, by making their own wine out of plantains. In other words, even if our own plans and projects turn out sour, they are still better. Why? Because they are ours, made from our indigenous ingredients. For our survival, for our sanity, for our liberation, Martí calls us to become winemakers who harvest liberative grapes grown and nurtured in our own vineyards. We are called for more than simply understanding the Eurocentric world. We are called to seek its rejection.

TOWARD AN ETHICS PARA JODER

For the oppressed to rely on Eurocentric thought in the "messiness" of colonization is somewhat problematic. Much can be learned from U.S. slave religion. To steal during antebellum America was (and still is today) defined as immoral. A slave who steals a chicken from the master's coop is—by definition—unethical and non-virtuous. And yet, it was Eurocentric thought, constructed by the masters, that defined what is moral, ignoring that they stole black bodies to begin with. Within this oppressive structure, slaves understood they had a higher moral responsibility to feed their families than to honor and respect the master's chicken. So, to steal from the master, and do as little work as possible—even if it meant being stereotyped as shiftless or lazy—was a moral imperative (Sanders 1995:14–15). Any obligation to engage in practices defined by slaveholders and colonizers as ethical is immoral because it contributes to the occupation of our minds and the enslavement of our bodies.

Rejecting Eurocentric thought, by moving beyond the mythology that truth can somehow be arrived at objectively, leaves us with a clear realization that whatever we call truth has more to do with our social location than discovering any particular so-called "objective" universal truth. To hope against all hope requires a turn toward our own social locations, to making our own wine from plantains, by searching for the cultural signifiers which serve as a response to our embodied occupied locations and our occupied minds. Mirta was my mother, an illiterate country girl from the hills of Santa Clara, Cuba. After the arrest of her father, convicted of murder during a bar fight, her all-female family became poverty-stricken, unable to provide food for themselves. The solution they chose was to sell her, during her preteen years, to a family in the city to work as their domestic maid, where she faced physical and sexual abuse. Mirta, a devotee of Santería, taught me the ways of the African Yoruba orishas, specifically the ways of my *ori*, my head, Ellegúa—the trickster. Mirta's Christian faith, forged through her cultural symbols of the *orishas*, developed a trickster-based morality which served her well on the cold and mean streets of New York City when she became a refugee. From Mirta's life experiences, and the life experiences of all the Mirtas of the world, I developed what I have been calling "an ethics *para joder*."

Joder is a Spanish verb, never to be used in polite conversation, whose English equivalent is a certain four-letter word which begins with "F" and ends with "K." To decolonize our minds and de-occupy our space, I am calling for a praxis that "screws" with the established social structures. Note: I'm not calling to screw Eurocentrism, but to screw with Eurocentrism, an important difference in semantics. The word connotes an individual who is a pain in the rear end, purposely is causing trouble, constantly disrupting the established norm, shouting from the rooftop what those in power prefer be kept under wraps, audaciously refusing to stay in his or her place. And if you object to my use of profanity, you miss the point of the truly profane:

the death-dealing conditions in which the colonized are forced to live (De La Torre 2010:92).

The colonized, who stand before the vastness and unbearableness of a neoliberalism that offers little hope for radical change in their lifetimes, are left with few practical alternatives. Regardless of the good intentions of Eurocentric colonizers, or of praxis employed to paternalistically save and rescue the colonized, the devastating consequences of empire will worsen as the few get wealthier and the many sink deeper into the despair of stomach-wrenching poverty. Eurocentrism, including that of progressive liberal scholars, may be quick to offer charity and stand in solidarity, but few are willing to dismantle the very global structures designed to privilege them at the expense of the world's majority. But when the colonized start to *joder*, it literally creates chaos and instability. Any praxis which upsets the prevailing Eurocentric social order, which is designed to maintain empire, is an ethics which arises from the colonized and disillusioned, frustrated with normative Eurocentric values and virtues. While Eurocentrism insists on social order, the colonized must call for social disorder, a process achieved by *jodiendo*. Perhaps this might lead some with Eurocentric hope and privilege to share in the hopelessness of overcoming the global forces of neoliberalism. If so, it may be the only way progress is forged.

A liberative ethics *para joder* is frightening to those accustomed to their power and privilege because hopelessness signals a lack of control. Because those who benefit from the present social structures insist on control, sharing the plight of being vulnerable to forces beyond control will demonstrate how hope falls short. To *joder* is to refuse to play by the rules established by those, for example, who provide a space for orderly dissent, which pacifies the need to vent, but is not designed to change existing power relationships. If the goal of praxis is transforming society, then it is crucial to go beyond the rules created by the dominant culture, to move beyond the expected, to push beyond universalized experiences. If, indeed, ethics is a second act, a reflection of praxis, then allow me to provide an illustration of what this first act might look like.

During the late 1950s on the streets of Chicago, in a Puerto Rican bárrio called Lincoln Park, a street gang was formed, calling itself the Young Lords. Originally it was a turf gang providing protection for Latinxs from other ethnic gangs. But the Division Street Riots of June 1966, in response to the shooting of a Puerto Rican by the Chicago Police, changed the Young Lords' purpose and direction. The shooting revealed a continuous trend, mired in a history of police brutality against Latinxs. Add to this powder keg the frustrations over systematic evictions of Latinx families due to gentrification, including the families of gang members. Among the incarcerated who participated in the riots was gang member José "Cha Cha" Jiménez. While in prison, he and other gang members read books by revolutionary thinkers and leaders, contributing to their conscientization and leading to their evolution into a political social movement committed to fighting for and demanding basic human rights and better social services (Ortega-Aponte 2009:583–85).

As Presbyterian ministers convened in Texas for a national conference in April 1969, the Young Lords staged a sit-in at one of their schools—McCormick Seminary—occupying their building for a week. The Young Lords voiced their grievances, specifically the seminary's complicity with the displaced Puerto Ricans from the Lincoln Park community. They demanded funding, to the tune of $600,000, for low-income housing in the neighborhood where the seminary resided; a children's center; a legal assistance program for residents; and a cultural center for Latinxs. The occupation of the seminary ended when it agreed to the demands. *Jodiendo* bore fruit.

The New York chapter of the Young Lords launched the East Harlem Garbage Offensive on July 27, 1969. The Offensive consisted of sweeping the streets and neatly stacking the garbage up on the corners for pick-up. But the sanitation department historically ignored the accumulation of waste in communities of color, providing poor waste collection services. In response, the Young Lords moved the garbage bags to Third Avenue, where they built a five-foot-tall barricade across the avenue and set bags ablaze. Fighting broke out with the police when they attempted to stop the fire, arresting those responsible. This led to over 1,000 people marching to the 126th street police station to protest the norm of police brutality. In spite of the crackdown by the police, the protests, due to negative publicity, prompted the city to be faithful to its responsibilities of picking up the garbage in Spanish Harlem. Change came about by creatively screwing with the system. Soon, the organization focused its energies on other institutions that failed to respond to the needs of the people they were supposed to serve, specifically the church, which had moral responsibilities to protect poor and disenfranchised communities.

La Primera Iglésia Metodista Hispana (First Hispanic Methodist Church), located at Lexington Street and 111th Avenue in the Spanish Harlem bárrio, was visited by a delegation of the Young Lords, who requested to use available space in the church to provide children in the neighborhood with a breakfast program and residents with a clothing drive. Even though the church was empty most of the week, the pastor and the church board refused, referring to the Young Lords delegates as satanás—demons. When the Young Lord delegates attempted to address the congregation on Sunday, December 7, 1969, the church called the police, who showed up and proceeded to brutally beat the Young Lords. On December 28th, over one hundred Young Lord activists and sympathizers successfully took possession of the church building, sealing the door with six-inch railroad spikes and raising a wooden sign with red letters renaming it *La Iglésia de la Gente*—The People's Church, under the premise that the first responsibility of the church is to the people. During the eleven days of occupation, over three thousand people came to church. The People's Church briefly developed childcare for working parents, established breakfast programs for children, conducted clothing drives, provided opportunities for political education, fought police brutality, and made a concerted investment in social services (like health clinics). By January 7, 1970, the police retook control of the church, arresting 105 occupiers—at which time the church ceased being the people's church (De La Torre 2010:89–92).

Unfortunately, due to FBI infiltration and political infighting, the Young Lords disintegrated in the early 1970s. But for a brief moment in time, an indigenous Latinx-based methodology of *jodiendo* was en-fleshed. The Young Lords were concerned that institutions, specifically religious ones, that play a vital role in the lives of Latinxs, were abdicating their Christian mission. By playing the role of the trickster and turning away from Eurocentric-based ethical methodologies, they demonstrated the failings of Christianity and of United States political and religious institutions. In effect, by implementing services that should have been occurring, the Young Lords shamed these institutions for failing to live up to their supposed mission. This was not civil disobedience, but rather civil initiative—forcing governments and institutions to live up to their own rhetoric, a concept developed during the Sanctuary Movement of the 1980s (Fife, 2009: 170-75). Although the Young Lords was not a Christian organization, nor was it practicing a pacifist ideology, it did demonstrate, more so than most Eurocentric thinkers, that the implementation of the Gospel is a subversive and radical venture which literally disrupts, undermines, and challenges those who have become complicit with the status quo of oppressive structures. Their *jodiendo* in the streets is foundational to the Latinx decolonized ethical paradigm that I seek to construct.

Obviously, the term "an ethics *para joder*" did not exist when these events unfolded. I am cognizant I am imposing on history a term I have coined. Still, I will argue these events were led by individuals who refused to follow the rules that usually ensured subjugation to white supremacy. We have evolved into a society that requires obtaining a permit from the police department to picket the police department for the police brutality of the police department. We can drive to a march and exercise the freedoms to protest, as long as it does not disrupt the social equilibrium demanded by those privileged with power, and a social equilibrium morally justified by Eurocentrism, which benefits those same structures of power. I will argue that the best way for the powerless and marginalized to radically counter the prevailing status quo is to *joder*.

Although it may be tempting to end this chapter on a note of hope, the fact remains the dispossession, disenfranchisement, destitution, and death awaits way too many who live with minds which are occupied with Eurocentric thoughts. Billions are born into poverty and die to its consequences so that those living in the empire can maintain and sustain the privileges of First World status. The marginalized offer up their lives as living sacrifices so those closest to Eurocentrism can have life, and life abundant. And yet, the only salvation available to whites is for them to learn how to stand in solidarity with the hopelessness of the colonized of the world seeking the decolonization of their own minds, a goal that, if achieved, will occur by *jodiendo*. Then maybe, just maybe, we might be able "to hope against all hope" (Rom. 4:18).

BIBLIOGRAPHY

Benjamin, Walter. "Thesis on the Philosophy of History." In *Illuminations*. Trans. by Harry Zohn. Ed. by Hannah Arendt. New York: Schocken Books, 1969 [1940].

De La Torre, Miguel A. *Latina/o Social Ethics: Moving Beyond Eurocentric Moral Thinking*. Waco, TX: Baylor University Press, 2010.

Fife, John. "Civil Initiative." In "Trails of Hope and Terror: Testimonies on Immigration." Edited by Miguel A. De La Torre. Maryknoll: Orbis Books, 2009.

Foucault, Michel. "The Foucault Reader." Edited by Paul Rabino. New York: Pantheon, 1984.

Hegel, Georg Wilhelm Friedrich. "The Philosophy of History." Translated by J. Sibree. New York: Colonial, 1900 [1824].

King, Martin Luther, Jr. *A Testament of Hope: The Essential Writings and Speeches of Martin Luther King*. New York: HaperCollins, 1986.

Martí, José. *Obras Completas de José Martí, 26 Volúmenes*. La Habana, CU: Centro de Estudios Martinanos, 2001. Herein referred to as *OC*.

Moltmann, Jürgen, "Theology of Hope: On the Ground and the Implication of a Christian Eschatology." Translated by James W. Leitch. New York: Harper & Row, 1967.

Ortega-Aponte, Elias. "Young Lords Party." *Encyclopaedia on Hispanic American Religious Culture*. Vol. 2. Ed. by Miguel A. De La Torre. Santa Barbara, CA: ABC-CLIO, 2009.

Sanders, Cheryl. *Empowerment Ethics for a Liberated People: A Path to African American Social Transformation*. Minneapolis, MN: Fortress Press, 1995.

Chapter Two

"Imagined Occupation" and the Occupation of the National Imaginary

Scottish Stories in the Face of Brexit Britain

John McNeil Scott

> This may be the last stage of imperialism—having appropriated everything else from its colonies, the dead empire appropriates the pain of those it has oppressed.
>
> —Fintan O'Toole[1]

INTRODUCTION

Perhaps the most culturally revealing and theologically significant feature of life in Britain during the referendum campaign for the United Kingdom to leave the European Union in 2016 and since, is the re-emergence of language celebrating the British Empire and the application of concepts of vassalage, occupation, and liberation to describe 21st-century Britain. Brexit, the name commonly used to describe the policy, is often suggested to be a mere local instance of a rising "populism" or "nationalism" (negatively conceived); however, I argue that a fuller theological understanding of this phenomenon is to be found elsewhere. Unless we take account of the nature of the British state as an imperial project—both in origin and now—it is impossible to understand the depth, reach, and power of Brexit culture or to account for the quietude and confusion of British churches in the face of these developments. I maintain that the churches have been unable to react prophetically primarily because they have not adopted and disseminated a deep repentance for the British imperial project. The extent of British cultural disorientation and spiritual amnesia is revealed through unashamed misappropriation of discourses of occupation, colonisation and victimhood.

In the three and a half years that followed the 2016 referendum the Brexit crisis brought down two Prime Ministers. Unceasing political turbulence resulted in two parliamentary elections. The first of these demonstrated early popular confusion as the Brexit-prosecuting government was deprived of a majority. The withdrawal agreement negotiated between the British government under Theresa May and the European Union was repeatedly rejected. Successive extensions to the treaty-mandated withdrawal period were requested and granted. A leader of the Brexit referendum campaign, Boris Johnson, who came to office as a result of intra-party manoeuvrings, immediately suspended parliament illegally in order to avoid scrutiny of his revised agreement. His apparent purpose was to 'crash out' of the European Union through curtailing the legislature's ability to prevent such an outcome. Finally, in the last month of 2019, the United Kingdom's first-past-the-post electoral system granted Johnson a secure majority[2] under the grim slogan "Get Brexit Done," and the United Kingdom ceased to be a member state of the European Union on 31 January 2020.

"Get Brexit Done"—while the formal end of Union membership has come about, Brexit is far from done, and its work far from over. The unresolved contradictions in British political and ecclesial culture that have led to Brexit will remain—and return—until they are named and faced. The malign nature of the British imperial project—whose deep wickedness has long been better understood overseas than at home—now poisons the polity which formed around it. If the churches are to be faithful to their vocation, they must discern the truths of these times and, rejecting the fake mythologies of an unregretted empire, gather the peoples of their contexts around new, more truthful and life-giving narratives.

Such a movement begins with a recognition that Brexit is at root an ethical and theological matter. The constitutional stresses of these times have revealed neo-imperial attitudes and policies towards the smaller nations that neighbour England. Notably, the delicate and hard-won political settlement in Northern Ireland has been undermined by a careless and cynical British government. Viewing Brexit from a Scottish perspective,[3] we are led to ask what is revealed about the continuing nature of the state we are in, and what stories might guide both church and society to a better place.

FANTASIES OF EMPIRE AND IMAGINED OCCUPATION

While social alienation, inequality, regional economic imbalances and policies of austerity are all implicated in the project, Brexit could not have come to exist as a viable political enterprise without an unresolved and unrepentant culture of Empire to nurture it. This is the "deep truth" behind Brexit, whose most revealing manifestation is provided by the strange discourse through which Brexit was advanced and is still expressed. This discourse combines neo-imperial delusion, Empire nostalgia and the wholesale misappropriation of the language of victimhood and occupation.

People of faith—committed to telling the truths of history—must question how it can be that the majority population of an imperial centre, whose place in the world order is the result of capital and influence accumulated through colonisation and exploitation of other lands, came—without irony or shame—to describe (and experience) itself as a place *under occupation*. Brexit could only exist in a situation of historical amnesia, facilitated by imperial fantasy and a shamelessly casual use of moral language, in which truth was turned on its head.

Fintan O'Toole suggests that behind Brexit there was a necessary "structure of feeling," a mentality characterised by "a strange sense of imaginary oppression."[4] This, O'Toole says, relied on two apparently incompatible sentiments: a deep sense of grievance and a high sense of superiority. Nationalism has tended to exist in two antagonistic forms, we are reminded: One seeks to dominate the world and the second to escape such domination. However, "the incoherence of the new English nationalism that lies behind Brexit is that it wants to be both simultaneously."[5] It is fuelled by *fantasies of empire*. At the same time, since the naked language of Empire as mere re-statement is self-evidently impossible this yearning needed to be framed as a struggle for liberation. However, this struggle was fought in the absence of concrete conditions of oppression as an insurgent revolt against an *imagined occupation*. If the structure of meaning behind Brexit is here accurately discerned, and the British polity has been captured by fantasies of empire and imagined occupation, such circumstances ought to be religious and spiritual concerns to be recognised and addressed by people of faith.

The Fantasy of Empire

The longing for Britain's imperial past finds one expression in the objective voiced by the British government to build a "new global Britain," contrasted with the "constrained" status of being a "mere" member state of the European Union. Robert Gildea, whose *Empires of the Mind* describes the ways in which Britain's past continues uniquely to determine present attitudes, reminds us that the British Empire is a constant point of discursive reference for Brexit.

In February 2016, during the run-up to the British referendum on Europe, former Mayor of London Boris Johnson boasted, "We used to run the biggest empire the world has ever seen," "Are we really unable to do trade deals?"[6]

The repeated emphasis on "making our own global trade deals" was linked with the status of imperial power; and "freedom" from the European Union would allow Britain to recreate a mercantile empire. This cultural sense is peculiar among the former imperial powers of Europe. In noting the uneven psychological withdrawal from empire of Europe's former imperial centres, Gildea contrasts Johnson's relaxed boast of empire with a contemporary example of political campaigning in France:

> A year later, in February 2017, French presidential candidate Emmanuel Macron visited Algiers and declared his country's colonialism "a crime against humanity, a real barbarity, it is a past we must confront squarely and apologise to those we have harmed."[7]

In Great Britain, the defenders of empire are not all right-wingers. For example, Gordon Brown, the last Labour Prime Minister, said:

> I've talked to many people on my visit to Africa and the days of Britain having to apologise for its colonial history are over. We should move forward. We should celebrate much of our past rather than apologise for it.[8]

A positive view of the British Empire seems to be an almost indispensable characteristic of British identity. In public discourse positive references to "Empire 2.0" are made without embarrassment or irony. A poll in 2014 reported that three quarters of the British population think the British Empire is something to be proud of rather than ashamed, and a third would like it still to exist.[9] The civic honour commonly bestowed by the crown and government for meritorious public service is styled the "Order of the British Empire" even now, and few people pause to think how astonishing or inappropriate this might be.

There are, of course, voices that speak truth about the British Empire. Tom Nairn, the Scottish thinker, recalls

> British imperialists were not simply the first, the biggest, and the most successful plunderers on the international scene; they were also the best at pretending that their empire was really something else.[10]

Fintan O'Toole remarks, "The English like to see their empire, not as a ruthless machine, but as an almost accidental side-effect of curious gentlemen wandering off the beaten track."[11]

Imagined Occupation

To misunderstand an unrepented past of shame and characterise it as one of glory and pride is one thing, with powerful continuing effects. However, Brexit also involves a misrepresentation of the present. It is characteristic of our times that the powerful adopt the painfully-birthed language of subaltern truth-telling and liberation. Through venal carelessness towards precious words, or indeed with cynical intent, great lies are spoken in prophetic tone and register. The speeches of Brexit-supporting politicians were seasoned with immoderate expressions of fake victimhood that *bear false witness* against friends and partners. British government ministers have compared the European Union to the Soviet Union, and the prime minister of a fellow member state has been likened to a "concentration camp guard." A particularly egregious episode saw the Brexit Party's Anne Widdicombe telling the European Parliament:

> There is a pattern consistent throughout history of oppressed people turning on their oppressors, slaves against their owners, the peasantry against the feudal barons, colonies against empires, and that is why Britain is leaving.[12]

Brexit weaves together wilful denial of the *real meanings* of British imperialism with the language of an imagined occupation. The Leave campaign slogan was "Take Back Control." Both during and since the referendum a trinitarian imperative was continuously reinforced: Britain must take back control of *our money*, *our borders* and *our laws*. An image is presented of a country that has been plundered financially, overruled legally and over-run by outsiders. In particular, ending "free movement"—the principle whereby citizens of EU member states enjoy a conditional right to live and work throughout the Union—was offered as a major reason to leave the EU.

The European single market has four pillars: "freedom of movement" for goods, services, capital and people. Instead of regarding the last of these as the most defensible, benevolent, humane and desirable of the four, the Brexit narrative regards ending free movement of people as a principle on which it is impossible to compromise. This can be seen as an extension of recent policies to create a "hostile environment" for immigration. Opposition to any rights-based migration whatsoever was a British "red line," a non-negotiable principle around which any future relations must be built.

Fintan O'Toole has described the correspondence between pro-Brexit and anti-immigrant sentiment, and how animosity towards the European Union represented a sublimated or displaced anger towards the outsider: "The black and brown Other fused with the European Other."[13] Akwugo Emejulu,[14] among other scholars, notes that 75% of voters of colour throughout the UK voted to remain in the EU despite many of the same people having been most adversely affected by the austerity policies of the United Kingdom government over the past decade.

A community that imagines itself as a colony escapes political responsibility for injustices committed in its name within and outside its borders. It does not need to comprehend why people migrate in this world, nor to reflect that much population movement finds cause in the British imperial project. Both serious structural injustices and minor irritations of cultural change can be projected onto an external scapegoat. For over four decades the European Union has served this purpose in British politics.[15]

In March 2019, Boris Johnson, one of the chief campaigners for Brexit, now prime minister, appropriated biblical language to assert that his predecessor in that role, Theresa May, should "channel the spirit of Moses in Exodus and tell the Pharaoh in Brussels—LET MY PEOPLE GO."[16] Confucius wrote that "the beginning of wisdom is to call things by their proper name." Narratives such as those employed by Johnson are cynical assaults on the situations of people who do really suffer in the world. The claim to victimhood in such words has no foundation and—more than that—is a shameful debasement of language. It is contemptible for a prosperous, nuclear-armed, West European country that enjoys unmerited, excessive and unjust privilege in the international order to appropriate words whose proper use is to express *real* pain and misery to the purpose of undoing multilateral institutions. This is a matter of truth and lies. Surely people of faith must challenge unequivocally the imagined occupations, invented humiliations and fantasy colonisations of Brexit.

THE CHURCHES IN THE FACE OF BREXIT

The crisis of Brexit exposes some uncomfortable realities about the nature of the British polity. It also brings lessons for the churches, uncovering some truths about our ecclesial cultures and societal assumptions. In face of Brexit, church leaders have, in general, been unable to discover and articulate a consistent response of any theological depth. The comments of church councils, committees and task groups have sometimes lamented intemperate political language, more consistently resisted the 'othering' of resident European citizens, and the tone of Brexit discussion. However, while church denominations raised corporate voices against the social and economic damage of a "no deal" Brexit, to date they have seldom addressed Brexit itself as a political programme and cultural phenomenon. As bodies, the churches have been somehow unable to name Brexit as *a theological and an ethical issue*. Instead, the churches' efforts have more usually focused on promoting an "understanding of different views." Official responses have concentrated on "bringing people together," "re-uniting the country," and moderating the tone of political debate. Public pronouncements almost universally address the *manner of implementation* or the *tone of debate*[17] but fail to identify the origins, the "deep truth" and meaning of Brexit, or to interrogate the nature of Britain as a state (either in the past or now). On the contrary, the present British polity is assumed as a theological good.

On the weekend that the United Kingdom was first supposed to have left the EU (before departure was postponed) the Church of England's Liturgical Commission produced resources encouraging "informal café-style meetings . . . to bring together people of all standpoints and encourage open discussion." While laudable on one level, this—it must be said—is far from the "ministry of public theological naming"[18] that would constitute a truly contextual response. It does, however, demonstrate an endearingly English confidence in the power of a cup of tea to smooth over great differences. We should not be surprised that the churches have struggled to respond prophetically and specifically to Brexit. Church membership—and, in England, belonging to the dominant Church of England—was a strong predictor of voting "leave." It is believed that United Reformed Church members followed the Anglican proportions (66 percent "leave"). Church of Scotland proportions were roughly 50/50, while Scotland as a whole voted by large majority to "remain."[19] The churches, I believe, have tended to miss the "deep truth" of Brexit because the churches themselves have not understood and named the ways in which Brexit is rooted in empire, and the degree to which empire continues unremarked in the hidden structures of the British state. And all of this is because the historic churches and their ecclesial cultures are themselves very largely formed by the experience of the British imperial project.

While many secular commentators have identified the impulse for Brexit in post-imperial longing, such an analysis has been absent from intra-church discussions. The churches have understood differing Brexit positions as expressions of (mere) "identity choices" whose alternatives are without theological or ethical significance *in themselves*. But if a yearning for a renewal of British imperial enterprise even if in different form—what Anthony Barrett calls *the lure of greatness*[20]—really underlies Brexit, then the choices involved and the positions taken are of unavoidable spiritual and ethical import.

In *Theologising Brexit*,[21] Anthony G. Reddie argues that the colonial Christianity that was exported during the days of the British Empire continues to provide both metanarrative and setting for church life in the United Kingdom, and that in these ecclesial contexts the meanings of empire have not been honestly faced (let alone rejected). Academically, systematic theology in Britain remains, as R. S. Sugirtharajah says, "complacently unwilling to confront the reality of empire and its postcolonial consequences."[22] Brexit is the most recent and clearest example of a spiritual condition in which, as John M. Hull insisted, "The theology of empire has outlived the empire. The empire has gone but its theology lingers on."[23] Because of this deeply-rooted empire theology, the churches are weakened and confused and uncertain attitudes to Brexit are a result. However, if Brexit poses a challenge to the churches (albeit so far a largely unrecognised one), then there is also in these circumstances an opportunity for renewed discernment and putting right. Here is the chance to lay to rest once and for all the dreams and theologies of empire. But this requires the churches explicitly to repent the *historical reality* of the British Empire and the power relations that persist in its wake. Only then will people of faith be able to join battle with "empire" in its continuing incarnations as a *contemporary theological reality*.

Churches that seek to be faithful to Christ and Christ's Kingdom must hold our discipleship to engagement with the *questions that are being asked* or *being ignored* in our own concrete social and historical circumstances. Contextualisation demands that we discern and face the *real challenges of history* when they come. Contextual commitment requires taking the uncomfortable holy chance of discernment and naming clearly what is seen. And then to *risk* our living and our reputation on our reading of the deep truths of our context.

Brexit as "A Story without an End in View"

The Irish theologian Terence McCaughey writes of "stories without an end in view."[24] Such stories are dreams that cannot be satisfied, that seek not *future-oriented* transformation towards kingdom values but an *impossible return* to an imagined past. Once Brexit is understood as the outcome of misguided and unfounded expectations, it will follow that as a project built on an imagined occupation and a fantasy of imperial return it cannot deliver its promises but will only bring destruction and disappointment. An *imaginary occupation* can never result in a *real liberation*.

"Britain, Especially England"

I have suggested that the political culture of Britain has not merely allowed, but fostered and encouraged, powerful ideas of a phantom and illusory occupation. In addition, the British state continues to celebrate rather than deprecate its former empire, thereby holding open a vital discursive space for imperial nostalgia. The churches are particularly implicated and weakened through theologies and ecclesial cultures that have not shaken off the stain of the British Empire. If there is any truth in these assertions, we cannot escape asking hard questions about the nature of the British state itself as a project. If British political culture is unique—or at least unusual—in incubating these phenomena, where are the causes to be found?

The 2016 Brexit referendum issued in a "leave" vote of 51.9 percent. However, while the proposal was supported by a majority of the English and Welsh populations, it was rejected by decisively larger margins in Scotland and Northern Ireland. Scotland voted against the proposal to leave the European Union by 62 percent.[25] Brexit, as the expression of a culture of imperial nostalgia with tales of imagined occupation, was rejected in Scotland. Anthony G. Reddie's *Theologising Brexit*[26] is a seminal work for considering Brexit theologically. Reddie comprehensively describes many postcolonial aspects of the Brexit phenomenon and the churches' implication in them. However, in common with almost all commentators on Brexit, Reddie does not tell us explicitly which socio-political context provides the best frame for analysis. He writes frequently of "Britain, especially England" without exploring the distinction upon which he simultaneously insists.[27] This self-questioning elision is an important theological clue. There is here a hint that unheard voices might have something helpful to say. It whispers of two possibilities: firstly, that the British project might *in itself* be theologically problematic and open to question; secondly, that insights from those parts of the British experience that are not English could provide a means through which all may better understand the signs of Brexit times.

BRITAIN AS CONTINUING IMPERIAL PROJECT AND THEOLOGICAL PROBLEM

For the churches to move beyond Brexit in any kind of theological shape, they must leave behind the socio-political world and the ecclesial cultures in which Brexit is possible. This means telling the truth about *the state we are in* in multiple ways—firstly, that we are not under fantasy occupation. But, further, if we are not to return here again under a different name, it also means telling another truth about *the state we are in*, that is, the truth of the British Empire *in history* and the truth of Britain as a *continuing imperial state*.

The Occupation of a National Imaginary

The malign effects of the British story are being uncovered daily. The present reality of the British state as a polity made for empire and resistant to re-founding on any other basis is being clarified in our times. Scotland requires a retelling of its national story that deals honestly, hopefully and usefully with what has been and might yet be. This can be a spiritual task and could involve weaving from the events of history a narrative that carries repentance for the British Empire, as well as cautioning against national presumption, toxic vanity and the "lure of greatness." We might populate those national stories with virtues—tell tales of equality, fairness, openness, kindness and welcoming—in tones of aspiration, rather than hubris, and as ideals that we wish were more completely true of our common life. These stories would be calls to action and bulwarks against, rather than facilitators of, national self-satisfaction.

"Union for Empire" and the "Lure of Greatness"

There is a reading of Scotland's history and current national situation that is both true and purposed. It is—or could be—an appropriate and revealing theological resource for reflection. It might even be thought of as "a Brexit morality tale." Such a spiritual re-telling of Scotland's stories would remind us that Britain is not a nation that came to have an empire, but that the United Kingdom was and is an imperial project. We might be helped to see again the deep truth that Britain and Empire are inseparable. The union of 1707, that created the state of Great Britain, was pressed on the commercial interests that dominated the Scottish parliament following the failure of the Darien Scheme, Scotland's chief project to build a foreign empire of its own.[28] In the Kingdom of Great Britain, Scotland's elite found an outlet for imperial ambition, but only as a part of an incorporating union. The history is complex, and involves both pressure from the English state as well as Scottish opportunism.

In Scotland, the legacy of participation in the British Empire is all around. The handsome merchant architecture of Glasgow and Edinburgh testify to imperial prosperity. The cities and towns of Scotland became wealthy in the Eighteenth and Nineteenth centuries through industry and commerce—tobacco, tea, and slaves were traded. This trading of commodities and human lives was supplemented as the decades unfolded by engineering and industrialisation. An expanding British Empire provided colonial raw materials to feed the engines of industrial development, secure and almost limitless captive markets for manufactured goods, as well as an outlet for Scottish talent. For wealthy landowners the colonies of settlement were a safety valve too, allowing them to force subsistence populations—often in the highlands—into exile, clearing the land of unprofitable people and replacing them with livestock. The empty highlands and deserted islands, no less than the handsome cities, stand in testament to centuries of deep involvement in the British Empire.

Scotland's relationship with coloniality is complicated. The nation sacrificed its own independent statehood enticed by the "lure of greatness." Imperial ambition came at the cost of political erasure. Scotland, as part of the

British imperial centre was an enthusiastic coloniser. However, the Scottish story is also—albeit not in a straightforward way—the tale of a nation subjected to colonization through near political obliteration and cultural domination. The Scottish settlers on other peoples' lands had often migrated because there was, actually or metaphorically, no place for them at home. This too was empire. Scotland's story tells where the greed of the powerful, as well as the desire for "significance" as a world power, led the country. The end of an overseas British Empire has led to a new narrative about the British Empire in Scotland. This retelling is often tinged with regret for what that historical empire meant overseas as well as at home. Likewise, the end of the British Empire has resulted in a steady decline in British identity among Scottish people. The aspiration of independence-supporting Scots is to be a "normal European country." For Scotland, participation in the British Empire is a story of a "will to power" gone wrong, of betrayal by "the lure of greatness."

The story of early Israel provides concrete resonances with the nation's own story, contextual counterpoints to remind the group of the folly of the "lure of greatness" and the worth of a smaller national society that provides "dignity and livelihood for all members of the community."[29] In Scotland the aspirations of nation and empire stand in opposition.[30] Using the resources of Scottish experience, we can also give voice to truth about the nature of Britain as an intrinsically imperial state, both in the past and now. From 1707 to 1999, Scotland possessed some of the institutions of a separate national life—distinctive systems of religion, law and education—as well as a distinct national culture, but no independent political competence. In 1999 a Scottish parliament was re-established as a body subordinate to the central government in London.

Since the Brexit vote, aspects of the constitutional settlement that had been guaranteed have been undone at the whim of the government in London. Competences being returned from the European level that constitutionally belong to the Scottish parliament have been arrogated to the British state. When Scottish parliamentary consent legally required to United Kingdom-wide legislation (including that needed to effect withdrawal from the European Union) was not forthcoming, the British government simply changed the law. In the absence of a binding codified constitution, a neo-imperial British state has been able to swat away inconvenient opposition. As most of the distant overseas empire is consigned to history books,[31] Scotland cannot claim to be blameless, nor conjure up fantasy oppressions and imaginary occupations. But the contemporary Scottish story tells truths of the enduring imperial nature of the British state that even "at home" allows self-government without a guarantee of self-determination. In the United Kingdom self-government is "devolved" and can be curtailed whenever inconvenient for the imperial centre. The power relations of the British Empire persist, albeit on a reduced scale. How else do we explain that the British state bases its nuclear weapons of mass destruction 36 kilometres from Scotland's largest city against the wishes of Scottish society, parliament and government? What, other than, imperial in nature are the British government's repeated refusals to allow a fresh referendum on independence in the light of the revolutionary change that is Brexit?

THE SCOTTISH NATION AS AN ETHICAL AND A THEOLOGICAL CHOICE

The churches, especially the historic "mainstream" Protestant churches, are among the "most British" institutions in the United Kingdom today. They are marked by the imperial theologies that John M. Hull and Anthony G. Reddie have described. These churches are also shaped by associations with centres of power in the military, monarchy, and government forged during the historic British Empire. A blindness to empire, born of intimacy, inhibits deep discernment about the *nature of the state* we are in. In Scotland, support for building a new state independent of the United Kingdom has grown from being the aspiration of an eccentric and tiny minority fifty years ago to the point where it represents the settled conviction of roughly 50 percent of the electorate (and a clear majority of those younger than 65 years old). However, the culture of Protestant churches and the political views of members has not changed with the country they inhabit. In the 2014 referendum on independence, there was a strong majority in favour of independence among self-identified Roman Catholics, as well as those of "non-Christian religion" or "No religion." Sixty-nine percent of Protestant Christians "saved the Union" by voting against independence.[32]

There are, I suggest, three dominant attitudes to the British state in our churches. For some, a British context for church life is commonly taken for granted as the natural state of affairs, uncoloured by any hint of an ethical dimension. Those who operate in this spiritual mode would be uncomprehending of any suggestion that the British state represents the reification of structural power relations that could or should be critiqued from a Christian point of view. A second perspective, common in the Scottish churches, views the option for a Scottish or a British context for political or theological reflection as another *mere* "identity choice" (rather like Brexit) and *in itself* without theological or ethical significance. Finally, there exists a sizeable group who are uncomfortable with the very idea of nation. This perspective tends to an incipient and easy universalism, usually understood and experienced as a Christian imperative. In this view, the true Christian believer eschews national belonging. A fatal theological and ethical weakness of all of these viewpoints is that they place the structures and power relations of the British state beyond question. They easily default to seeing the United Kingdom as an unquestioned first step to a supposed Christian universalism. All of these perspectives make theological reflection about the nature and legitimacy of the state impossible. All of them blind the churches, so that the power and theological significance of political cultures are put beyond the type of theological reflection that other nations and contexts take for granted. This is, I believe, theologically unsustainable and indefensible. It represents a flight from context.

The Scottish theologian Douglas Gay invites us to approach nations as "approximate, relative and provisional communities that resist both entire denial and exact definition of their existence,"[33] and encourages us in a tentative Christian sense of "nation as vocation."[34]

> Nations are coalitions and constructions assembled from resources both inherited and imagined, they are "texts under negotiation," a term applied by Walter Brueggemann to the Bible, whose meanings are continually subject to hermeneutical activity and conversation. They are "affective communities," characterised and identified by shared patterns of love that are continually evolving and that vary in intensity over time and across populations.[35]

Gay also argues that the stories of modern nations resemble biblical books in this respect also, they "are not unanimously and unambiguously anti-imperial or pro-imperial. They speak with different and sometimes ambivalent voices."[36]

If the churches in Scotland were to accept the challenge that starting from such an understanding entails, (and break free from the hitherto dominant perspectives I have outlined) they would seek to encourage those positive elements in the (re)emerging stories of Scottish nationhood. From such a starting point, churches would commit themselves without reservation to tasks of nation-building and seize eagerly the opportunity available to help determine what stories and values will be given significance in a new country. In the stories that the Scots tell about themselves, both historically and in the present moment, there are narratives that strengthen the good, articulating and consolidating aspirations to justice and social wholeness. There are also stories of empire that remember shameful episodes, to be recounted as warnings of how a nation can go astray.

Immigration and Occupation

While tiny fringe groups that espouse a "blood and soil" nationalism do exist, the contemporary movement for Scottish independence is overwhelmingly "civic nationalist" in character. "If you are here you are one of us," is often heard in political discourse. The description "New Scots" is commonly applied to recent arrivals in Scotland. It would be mistaken to suggest that racism and disadvantage is not present. The country has a continuing problem with historic sectarianism. However, there are powerful elements of discourse concerning Scottish identity that run counter to essentialist and racial conceptions of nation. These future-tending elements of story deserve to be developed and strengthened by faith communities committed to the nation's future. One of the anthems of the independence movement is a song, "*Scotland's Story,*" by The Proclaimers. The lyrics frame Scottish nationhood as ancient, but no less importantly, constituted by the arrival of ethnic groups from other places. The Scottish nation as a cultural and political community comprises not only the indigenous and adjacent—"the Gael and the Pict, the Angle and Dane"—but also people who have come more recently from all over the world, celebrating that "we're all Scotland's story and we're all worth the same."[37]

Stories with an End in View

The world has never needed stories more. In stories, nations rehearse who they think they are, which is often who they wish to be. That is an acceptable spiritual sleight of hand, with a long pedigree in the Bible—where Israel's civic aspirations find scriptural form in rehearsed laws of jubilee and welcome. In the current Brexit crisis, there are many stories that deal in exclusion, anxiety, and venal nostalgia. But there are also narratives to be heard and embraced that bring life and good news—and Good News. Times call forth stories. And the stories we tell in those times will determine how we will read the history that we must endure and that we must build. There are positive stories from Scotland, planted and watered and remembered in the shadow of the end of an empire. Scotland has stories of how an Empire began and from them the means to understand its situation now that the imperial British state is coming to an end.

Fintan O'Toole, in a piece published in July 2019, says what people of faith already know, that there are life-enhancing and death-dealing narratives. He further reminds that there are healthy and unhealthy ways to hold to stories.[38] However powerful our stories for Scotland, the end of *the* Empire does not mean *the end of empire*, the "power of oligarchies and markets and inequalities to restrict democratic choice" is not automatically overthrown.[39] In harnessing the power of stories, even stories with an end in view, Scotland and her churches must be wary of the self-delusion that claims and misidentifies aspiration as manifest destiny or, worse, some intrinsic quality of national nobility. And yet, O'Toole says, the act of building an independent nation is not without meaning, even amid the troubles of the contemporary world.

> Room to maneuver can be expanded. Democratic spaces can be opened up. The terms of the struggle between public and private interests can be renegotiated. Citizens can become more confident of their power to insist on decency and dignity . . . And the great constraints, and the more naked the power of unaccountable elites, the more vital it is that whatever collective freedom remains is grasped.[39]

At the same time,

> [what] a free country quickly discovers is that the better "us" of its imagination is not already there, fully formed, just waiting to blossom in the sun of liberation. It has to be created and to do so you have to genuinely decide that you want it.[40]

For O'Toole, and for all of us who have cause to be wary of the impulses that pass under the name of "nationalism"—perhaps also for those in our empire-born churches, if we can hear the call—

> what is actually most interesting about the possibility of Scottish independence is not that Scotland might become a new state, but that it might become a new kind of state. For independence to be meaningful, Scotland would have to start with an acknowledgement that many of the things to which it appeals—the power of government, the legitimacy of democratic institutions, the equality of citizens—are in crisis. They cannot be assumed; they have to be radically reinvented.[41]

The churches of Scotland—and of Britain as a whole—are struggling to live out our discipleship in circumstances that we struggle to understand. Our histories and complicities with empire have weakened our capacity to read the signs of Brexit. In Scotland and across the United Kingdom, ill-defined, and often misdirected, theologies of nation, culture and empire have become obstacles to discerning and participating in the stories of hope inherent in the narratives of a (re)emerging Scotland.

The history of these islands will unfold, and so will the Brexit story with which the British Empire finally ends. It yet remains to be seen whether the churches, in Britain or in Scotland, will continue to be merely distressed and confused by developments we are ill-equipped to comprehend, or if we can yet be among those able to make meaning of it all in the light of Good News. What remains unavoidably true, I suggest, is that all who inhabit the United Kingdom—the greater part of a small archipelago of windy islands on the Northwest edge of Europe—will not begin to work out what it means to live faithfully *in the face of empire* until we first understand the empire of which we have been a part, and reject its toxic imperial power relations in the past and the present. The contemporary stories that carry Scottish aspirations can provide at least some of the necessary tools to finally lay the British Empire to rest, and ready us to live and struggle for kingdom *stories with an end in view.*

NOTES

1. Fintan O'Toole. *Heroic Failure: Brexit and the Politics of Pain.* (London: Apollo, 2018), 21.
2. Johnson's Conservative Party won 56% of seats in the legislature on a 44% vote share. In Scotland, his party polled 25% and lost more than half of the seats they held. The independence-supporting, Scottish National Party had 45% support and won 81% of seats.
3. The author is an Irish person living and working in Scotland.
4. Fintan O'Toole. *Heroic Failure*, xvii.
5. Ibid., 3.
6. Robert Gildea, *Empires of the Mind: The Colonial Past and the Politics of the Present.* (Cambridge: Cambridge University Press, 2019), 1.
7. Ibid., 1.
8. *The Daily Mail*, 15 January 2005. http: //www.dailymail.co.uk/news/article-334208/Its-time-celebrate-Empire-says-Brown.html (Accessed 10 October 2019).
9. https://yougov.co.uk/topics/politics/articles-reports/2014/07/26/britain-proud-its-empire.
10. Tom Nairn, *The Left against Europe*. (London: Pelican, 1973), 20.
11. Fintan O'Toole, "The English love of eccentricity has turned sour" *The Irish Times*, 19 February 2019.
12. *The Guardian*, 4 July 2019. https://www.theguardian.com/politics/2019/jul/04/ann-widdecombe-likens-brexit-to-emancipation-of-slaves.
13. O'Toole, *Heroic Failure*, 17.
14. Akwugo Emejulu, *On the Hideous Whiteness of Brexit*. Verso Books Blog, 26 June 2016. https://www.versobooks.com/blogs/2733-on-the-hideous-whiteness-of-brexit-let-us-be-honest-about-our-past-and-our-present-if-we-truly-seek-to-dismantle-white-supremacy.
15. Some of the unrelenting diet of bizarre and negative misrepresentation of actual EU laws and policies in the British media is documented at the EuroMyths website. https://wayback.archive-it.org/11980/20200131183933/https://blogs.ec.europa.eu/ECintheUK/.
16. *The Telegraph*, 25 March 2019.
17. See, for example, the Methodist Conference President's 'Statement on the Political Situation': https://www.methodist.org.uk/about-us/news/latest-news/all-news/statement-on-political-situation/ (Accessed 10 October 2019).

18. Christine Smith, *Preaching Justice: Ethnic and Cultural Perspectives* (Eugene, OR: Wipf and Stock, 2008), 134.

19. Greg Smith and Linda Woodhead. "Religion and Brexit: populism and the Church of England," *Religion, State and Society*, 46, no. 3 (2018): 206–23.

20. Anthony Barnett. *The Lure of Greatness: England's Brexit and America's Trump*. (London: Unbound, 2017).

21. Anthony G. Reddie, *Theologising Brexit: A Liberationist and Postcolonial Critique*. (London: Routledge, 2019).

22. R. S. Sugirtharajah, *Postcolonial Reconfigurations* (London: SCM Press, 2003), 148.

23. John M. Hull. *Towards the Prophetic Church* (London: SCM Press, 2014), 199.

24. Terence McCaughey, *Memory and Redemption: Church, Politics and Prophetic Theology in Ireland* (Dublin: Gill & Macmillan, 1993), 40.

25. The Brexit referendum in 2016 followed a plebiscite less than two years before, in which Scotland rejected independence with a vote of 55 percent. Ahead of the 2014 vote, the British government and supporters of the British union deployed—to great effect—an argument that a sovereign Scotland would cease to be part of the European Union.

26. Anthony G. Reddie, *Theologising Brexit* (2019).

27. Unlike Reddie, most scholars fail even to acknowledge different national experiences in Britain.

28. David Armitage, "The Scottish Vision of Empire" in John Robertson (ed.). *A Union for Empire: Political Thought and the Union of 1707*. (Cambridge: Cambridge University Press, 1995), 114–120.

29. Norman Gottwald, "Early Israel as an Anti-Imperial Community" in Richard Horsley, *In the Shadow of Empire: Reclaiming the Bible as a History of Faithful Resistance*. (Louisville, KY: Westminster John Knox, 2008), 9.

30. Alan Bissett's video poem "Vote Britain" exemplifies the anti-imperial tenor of pro-independence discourse. With deliberate irony, Scots are urged in the 2014 Independence Referendum to "Vote Empire," "Vote tradition" and "Vote for our proud shared history of enslaving other nations and stealing their natural resources." Available at https://youtu.be/HIgP4gPTENI Accessed 1 August 2019.

31. At least in its explicit political manifestations.

32. British Religion in Numbers (British Academy Research Project) http://www.brin.ac.uk/scottish-independence-and-other-news/ (Accessed 10 October 2019).

33. Douglas Gay, *Honey from the Lion* (London: SCM, 2013), 139.

34. Ibid., 71.

35. Ibid., 141.

36. Richard Horsley, *In the Shadow of Empire* (Louisville: WJK Press, 2008), 7

37. The Proclaimers Official webiste http://the.proclaimers.co.uk/ (Accessed 20 October 2019).

38. Fintan O'Toole, "The Art of Leaving and Arriving: Brexit, Scotland and Britain" in *Scotland the Brave*, edited by Gerry Hassan and Simon Barrow (Edinburgh: Luath Press, 2019), 326.

39. Ibid., 325.
40. Fintan O'Toole, "The Art of Leaving and Arriving," 325.
41. Ibid., 326.
42. Ibid., 327.

BIBLIOGRAPHY

Akala. *Natives: Race and Class in the Ruins of Empire*. London: John Murray, 2018.

Barnett, Anthony. *The Lure of Greatness: England's Brexit and America's Trump*. London: Unbound, 2017.

Gay, Douglas. *Honey from the Lion: Christianity and the Ethics of Nationalism*. London: SCM Press, 2013.

Gildea, Robert. *Empires of the Mind: The Colonial Past and the Politics of the Present*. Cambridge: Cambridge University Press, 2019.

Hassan, Gerry, and Simon Barrow, eds. *Scotland the Brave: Twenty Years of Change and the Future of the Nation*. Edinburgh: Luath Press, 2019.

Horsely, Richard. *In the Shadow of Empire: Reclaiming the Bible as a History of Faithful Resistance*. Louisville, KY: Westminster John Knox, 2008.

Hull, John M. *Towards the Prophetic Church: A Study of Christian Mission*. London: SCM Press, 2014.

McCaughey, Terence. *Memory and Redemption: Church, Politics and Prophetic Theology in Ireland*. Dublin: Gill & Macmillan, 1993.

Nairn, Tom. *The Left against Europe*. London: Pelican, 1973.

O'Toole, Fintan. *Heroic Failure: Brexit and the Politics of Pain*. London: Head of Zeus, 2018.

Reddie, Anthony G. *Theologising Brexit: A Liberationist and Postcolonial Critique*. London: Routledge, 2019.

Robertson, John, ed. *A Union for Empire: Political Thought and the Union of 1707*. Cambridge: Cambridge University Press, 1995.

Smith, Christine. *Preaching Justice: Ethnic and Cultural Perspectives*. Eugene: Wipf and Stock, 2008.

Smith, Greg, and Linda Woodhead. "Religion and Brexit: populism and the Church of England." *Religion, State and Society*, 46, no. 3 (2018): 206–23.

Sugirtharajah, R. S. *Postcolonial Reconfigurations*. London: SCM Press, 2003.

Chapter Three

City Gate and Homeland Imagination

The Theology of Image in Post-Modern Taiwan

Su-Chi Lin

INTRODUCTION

Over the past four centuries, Taiwan has been occupied and ruled by the Dutch, the Manchurian Qing Empire, the Japanese, and finally the Chinese Nationalist regime. In 1628, the Spanish occupied the northern part of Taiwan, establishing Fort San Domingo. In 1642, the Spanish were expelled by the Dutch. Shortly after the Dutch occupation, Cheng Ch'eng-kung (鄭成功, 1624–1662) of Late-Ming China arrived in Taiwan. Cheng's force was defeated by the Qing dynasty and the island was integrated into the Qing Empire in 1683. After Japan won the first Sino-Japanese War (1894–1895), the island was ceded to Japan and became the empire's first formal colony. When Japan was defeated at the end of World War II, Taiwan was once again transferred back to China, this time as a province of the Republic of China (ROC) led by Chiang Kai-shek and the Chinese Nationalist Regime (Kuomintang or KMT). When the KMT was driven out of Mainland China by the Chinese Communist Party (CCP) in 1949, they fled to Taiwan and set up the nationalist central government on the island, turning it into the remaining territory of the ROC. Under martial law executed by the KMT regime, Taiwanese people experienced subordination through an imposed assimilation policy toward Chinese culture and Mandarin language, which threw Taiwanese people's identity into confusion and incoherence. By 1947, tens of thousands were killed or imprisoned due to the February 28 massacre and the subsequent White Terror. By 1987, martial law was finally lifted, and Taiwan was transformed into a democratic society. Recovering traditions and rewriting national histories are the urgent tasks of the Taiwanese nativization movement.[1] According to Taiwanese theologian Shoki Coe (1914–1988): "Those who identified Taiwan, not China, as their homeland were severely censured and persecuted by the Nationalist totalitarian regime" (2011:ix–xii). Taiwan as "homeland" has been understood as a theological issue accompanied by the nativist movements in Taiwanese society.[2] Christ's incarnation as the contextualization of God's message of liberation can become the source of identity for Taiwanese churches and people, becoming a prophetic voice affecting social transformation.

In contemporary Taiwan, art and culture has given way to "post-modernism."[3] At the intersection between public architecture and political memory, Taipei North Gate (北門 Beimen) was recently transformed by a government-commissioned avant-garde installation. Through the installation of 3D light sculpture in the North Gate plaza, the combination of digital images with high technology reinvigorates public and professional interest in creating a new sense of common memory on the land. However, due to a lack of historical memory, Taiwanese people have long been in a state of ideological division. Professor of church history Cheng Yang-un observes: "Taiwanese people have not only lost their own history, nor they can have a common memory. Because they have long been ruled by foreign regimes and forced to instill in foreign history."[4] By exploring the visual representation of the gate, this chapter aims to explore the issues related to the theme of "homeland" through an approach of visual culture. I ask, whose beauty does the art speaks for? How can art help us to find the cultural voice of subjectivity? This chapter will reflect on the colonized legacy, working out a historical relation with the former colonizer. The process can be a painful process which involves the practice of self-rediscovery.

As the site of competing meanings and memories, as an in-between space of colonizer and the colonized, images of gates become the connecting points for the exploration of the relationship between art and theology. Through a number of artworks, from historical mural painting, propaganda postcards to contemporary installation, this chapter aims to propose a theology of image in which art could challenge us toward social justice through its transformative power and its ability to articulate this vision of justice. I argue that art can be considered as text for exploring struggles against any form of colonization. Images as cultural mediation open spaces for enriching theological expressions, while offering an opportunity to transcending our position for liberation.

CITY GATE IN THE HISTORICAL CONTEXT OF TAIWAN

For hundreds of years, the city gates of Taipei have silently witnessed various colonial regimes that have ruled over the island. Without doubt, the art, architecture and cultural imaginary of Taiwan are formed by the relationship of the people and their colonizers. In terms of its political context, the erected monument represents the government's authority. Every regime which has ruled the island re-modeled the gate as a symbol of possession of the territory. Taipei city gates were first established in 1884 in Qing dynasty (figure 3.1). By 1895, the first year of the Japanese colonial rule, the city's walls were destroyed as part of the city's restructuring plan. Four city gates in Taipei were all built on thick stone, connected to solid brick walls under the flying eaves. The fortress style with small windows was designed to resist foreign aggression. The original stone-based structure, with its arched doors framed by ancient cloud patterns, reflects the dynasty's prominent political and historical values. If we look closely, the monument with Chinese flying eaves creates and reinforces the primitive, exotic beauty that leads the contemporary viewers to the history of the land. It is clear the city gates were constructed in particular time and places contingent on the political, historical reality of the moment.

Worth noticing is the military aspect of the North Gate, seen in the mural painting (figure 3.2, 1923) by Ishikawa Toraji (石川寅治, 1875–1964) titled *Japanese Troops Occupy Taipei.*[5] The mural records the historical moment of Japanese occupation—June 11, 1895, when Imperial Prince Kitashirakawa Yoshihisa (北白川宮能久親王, 1847–1895) led Japanese troops into Taipei

Figure 3.1. *Outside of North Gate,* Courtesy of National Central Library, Taiwan.

city. Toraji visited Taiwan several times from 1917–1923 in order to depict the colony's scenery. As a war painter, Toraji's goal of visiting Taiwan was deeply related to several significant propaganda projects devoted to the Meiji emperor. The juxtaposition of city gate imagery and the Japanese military were subject matters of the work. In his first visit to Taiwan in 1917, Toraji wrote: "Particularly interesting things about traveling in the island [of Taiwan] were that the vegetation was verdant and thriving even in the hard winter, and I saw Chinese style edifices in a state of deterioration and ruin. Reddish flaking walls and broken eaves were all very interesting."[6] The metaphor of Chinese styled historic ruins clearly appears in this commissioned work to express the otherness of Taiwanese landscape.

In the center of the work, a procession of Japanese soldiers enters Taipei on a lonely stone road. On both sides of the line are ordinary Taiwanese men and women, elders and children, wearing Chinese traditional costumes. The red

Figure 3.2. Ishikawa Toraji, *Japanese Troops Occupy Taiwan* (台灣鎮定). Fresco, 1923. Meiji Memorial Picture Gallery in Meiji Jingu Gaien, Tokyo. Courtesy of National Central Library, Taiwan.

and white flags signify the Japanese state, decorating the arcades of the Chinese *minnan* style building. In the background, the vanishing point emphasizes the fortress-like North Gate, with mountains reaching up to the blue sky. No doubt, the historical mural painting demonstrates the significant moment of conquest. City gate imagery stands in the background of the performance of Japanese imperial victory. The representation of the Japanese colony of Taiwan, with its intense local colors and tones, became the metaphor for a modernity which Japanese artist wished to glorify.[7] Hence, the Japanese version of city gate determines interpretations of Taiwanese landscape and of the people's history through the lens of imperial ideology. Taiwan as the exotic South, with Chinese style city gate imagery, manipulates the Taiwanese people's perception of their homeland.

In 1906, Taiwan's Governor-General Office published a series of postcards for the commemoration of the tenth anniversary of colonial rule. In one particular postcard entitled *Taiwan Temple* a black and white half-length profile of Yoshihisa, the Governor-General of Taiwan, who led the first Japanese troops into Taipei on the date of occupation June 11, 1895, is depicted (figure 3.3). This image of the conquering of Taiwan shows Yoshihisa sitting on a horse with the power of imperial authority and a gesture of victory. Under the portrait of Yoshihisa is the photo of a Taipei Shinto shrine, built to consolidate Yoshihisa's power in the takeover of Taiwan and commemorating his death. The photograph records the Taipei Shinto shrine as the metaphysical embodiment of Japan's divine spirit.

In another postcard, the appropriation of the city gate imagery serves to promote imperial power in the colony (Fig. 3.4). The silhouette of the multilayered flying eaves sits against the vivid yellow background, apparently celebrating the cheerful spirit pervading the air. The postcard image clearly shows that the city walls still existed, connected with the city gate prior to its removal in 1900. In the middle of the postcard is a photograph of the residence of Taiwan Governor-General, Baron Kodama Gentaro (兒玉源太郎, 1852–1906). The Governor's official residence was located inside the East gate where only Japanese were allowed to live in the center of the city. At the bottom is a portrait of Kodama surrounded by a yellow floral pattern. During his tenure (1898–1906), Kodama did much to improve the infrastructure of Taiwan and to alleviate the living conditions of the inhabitants. The propaganda view of a modern cityscape featured in this postcard guarantees foreign tourists who visit Taiwan will see the quaint Chinese architectural feature as well as modern Western style cityscape. The contrast between the world of old and new, Chinese-style construction and Western-style colonial government residence, signifies the Japanese achievement of modernization in its colony.

Figure 3.3. *Taiwan Temple* (台灣神社). **Courtesy of National Central Library, Taiwan.**

Whether in historical mural or postcard images, the depiction of the city gate subtly indicates the territorial reach of Japanese control and the empire's victory. Taiwanese people, as ethnic Chinese, are portrayed as "others" for Japanese viewers, and Taiwanese cultural identities are framed by the imperial context. The antiquity of the city gate satisfies the Japanese

City Gate and Homeland Imagination 43

Figure 3.4. *Governor Baron Kodama Gentaro and His Official Residence* (台灣總督官邸和總督兒玉男爵). **Courtesy of National Central Library, Taiwan.**

desire to return to an ancient past. Whether the land of Taiwan is at peace or at war, studying the city gate enables viewers to start a journey of decolonization so as to free both the colonizing and colonized from the limits imposed by its colonial history.

CITY GATE IN THE CONTEMPORARY ERA

The image of the gate, without doubt creates discomfort and uneasiness. To underscore the relationship between public space and identity, Robert S. Nelson addresses the inclusion of architectural monuments erected by the empire as appropriations of the land. He writes, "the goal was to establish one's identity and possession in places where people gathered, such as crossroads, city squares, and prominent buildings."[8] Standing at its threshold, the gate was and is still located in the government center of the Taipei city. The sign of the gate in the past creates a boundary between colonizer and colonized under the Japanese occupation. In the modern era, Taiwan under the KMT regime was defined as the last fortress of recovering the Mainland China. Entering into the gate, we are invited to see the suffering of the world in front of the gate. The monument serves as the sign of Taiwan's struggle against colonialism, which is still active on the domestic and regional level. With the awakening consciousness of cultural subjectivity, Taiwanese people pay attention to the "ethnic conflict" which has unfortunately long remained a cause of political turmoil in the society.[9] In terms of the demographics of Taiwan, the small island is composed of four major ethnic groups.[10] We hope that different groups preserve the varieties of their traditional cultures and languages and make positive use of them as sources for contemporary cultural expressions. On the regional level, Mainland China continues to influence the international community into recognizing the "One China Principle."[11] Taiwan is still suffering from its political status as an international orphan.[12] The history of totalitarianism and colonialism only increases the contemporary critics toward the authority presented by the Taipei city gate.

Throughout history images of gates have served as symbolic passageways into new regimes. The monument has undergone a rapid transformation, reflecting the social and aesthetic contexts of the time since the modern era.[13] This provides an opportunity to reflect on this landmark toward the island's common memory. In the 2017 Taipei Lantern Festival, North Gate was transformed from a traditional monument to a fantastic light sculpture (figure 3.5), taking viewers on a journey through different eras of the city.[14] Made by the artist Chen Yi-chieh (陳怡潔), projection mapping was cast on the three sides of the architecture.[15] The installation with sound and lighting effects represented the life of old Taipei city which no longer exists. It was designed to bring back memory of the old book stores, camera shops, postage vendors and all business establishments in the surrounding area of the North Gate plaza. The plaza is surrounded by numerous historical structures which date back to the Japanese colonial era, including the Qing dynasty monuments. The invited public came thrilled at such a new spatial effect that aimed to

Figure 3.5. The unfolding of the Taipei city story from the 19th century to the present is projected on the surface of the North Gate (Bei Men) in 2017 Taipei Lantern Festival (See https://www.youtube.com/watch?v= T1GbfkKMZN0). Photo by Agi Chen Studio with permission.

transmit to the contemporary generation the stories of ordinary people and past events related to the founding history of the city.

The potency of the gate, derived from its previous political associations, is now used to advertise the communal memory of the city. All this is done through the addition of "simulacrum" on the architecture, including animation, sound, and music.[16] Apparently, the juxtaposition of the digital images and monument in building projection creates for the viewers a new relationship toward the gate. Through visual cultural of expression, Chen successfully communicates to the public the city's history of glory.[17] The appropriation of the monument, like myth, as Roland Barthes (1915–1980) explained, is a type of speech which refers to cultural value and belief conveyed through connotative meaning.[18] For Barthes, connotative meaning contains a set of hidden rules which belong only to a certain community and should be considered under certain social context. Building a projection becomes the signifier of Taiwan's memory which provides for the citizens of different social positions new contexts and imaginations toward the history.

Through the appropriation of the city gate, viewers have an opportunity to offer a new act of interpretation toward their cultural imaginary. According to art critic Gong Jow-Jiun, instead of repeating the metaphor of the colonial power dynamic, Chen's light sculpture could be the means by which to expose the darkness covered by the historical narratives of the empire.[19] Locating Taiwan under the context of oppression redefines the sign of the gate, suggesting a new direction of human liberation, whether individual or corporate. City gates which represented values of the colonial past are now discredited by the multiple interpretations with new reference created by the art installation. Here, the representation of the gate illuminated with simulacra calls for viewers to imagine the reality. The sign of the gate evokes viewers to enter into the common memory of the land; meanwhile, it offers opportunity to deconstruct the colonial cultural imaginary and identification. Art here brings us together to a shared community in ways that political or ideological design cannot.

CITY GATE AS TEXT FOR THEOLOGICAL REFLECTION

The gateway imagery becomes a theological text for the viewer to resist empire and build bridges between hostile powers. The city gate as a heroic icon celebrating political authority is now transformed into an ironic conceptual installation. The appropriation of the city gate challenges one to examine different ideological associations with the uncertainty of homeland identity. Engaging the problematic notion of identity manifested in this post-modern installation, viewers are invited to leave behind the colonial bondage and to imagine a new reality beyond the ambiguity.

The inclusive language of art thus opens and invites us to find solidarity with the people of Taiwan of the past and present. Between old and new, traditional monument and high technology, the sign of the gate standing on the crossroad confronts the viewer to enter into the memory of the past. At the same time, the past necessarily reenters the present shaped by the monument. The sign of the gate as cultural medium goes back and forth between the past and present and offers a future vision for imbuing reality with memories of one's homeland. Deconstructing the traditional monument and its colonial cultural imaginary enables the viewer to the multiplying identification of the site in new ways. Viewers are drawn to imagine reality and search for hope and justice for a better homeland to be free from the power of domination.

Viewers are made aware of their own context which influences them on seeing the ugly or beauty in the history of suffering.[20] Gateway image enables viewers from different cultural backgrounds to reflect upon what homeland means in their own stories, which is deeply rooted in their living environment. The city gate constructs a place for one to lament the loss of the one true story as well as to contemplate the divine. The belief that there is only one story which expresses the truth ignores the diversity of the many other stories. Michele Saracino argues that being "hybrid" means "being composed of many stories, some of which overlap or contrast with others."[21] Saracino understands God's larger story of salvation incorporates many other smaller stories. Hybridity becomes the way to share each other's story, acknowledging the fact that our life stories are somehow connected with other people's stories, no matter how different we are. The hybrid existence of city gates with old and new becomes the site of cultural contact or conflict, rather than of merely shared values of one story. The visual representations of city gates challenge the viewer to respond properly to "others" whose life stories are different from ours. A dynamic and multiple belonging of destiny hides behind the monument which provokes viewers to search for the higher beauty and justice of God and God's creation. When contemplating the gateway image in each one's homeland memory, the viewer is led to remember that which goes beyond worldly things. Through the articulation of things that cannot be seen with the physical eye, we imagine a land of justice where we can recover the vision of something better than humanity.

I have considered the gate imagery on which the new meaning of homeland memory is born. Neither the past nor its meaning are just one interpretation. God's love is the foundation to experience the beauty of the homeland and building up God's kingdom in this world. "The way we live as Christians—which is to live in mission—is constantly to live in dialogue with and discerning our context and correlating that context with the broader and older Christian tradition."[22] In this way, the theological engagement of the city gate in the post-modern Taiwan has contributed to a missiological dialogue in the wider context of a non-Christian world. God's vision manifested in the monument suggests itself as a basis for future action, that is, a response to God's kingdom constituted in sharing our stories and visions with others in a greater narrative of salvation. The hybrid beauty shown in the monument has challenged us to respond to all people whose life stories are different from ours. Through this process of transformation, art has enabled us to encounter God and find our true identities in God's beauty of wholeness.

NOTES

1. Chen Kuan-hsing argues that the Taiwanese nativization (*bentuhua*) movement and the Korean cultural revitalization movements have been the cultural and social basis of the political democratization movements (2010:9).

2. Theologian Wang Hsien-chih (王憲治,1941–1996) proposed that Taiwanese people should identify Taiwan as their homeland. To respond to Taiwan's political crisis, the Presbyterian Church in Taiwan (PCT) issued *A Declaration on Human Rights* upholding the universal principle of self-determination, advocating Taiwanese people have the right to seek an independent political status.

3. As Robert Schreiter emphasizes, the post-modern concept of culture "saw themselves more as a fragment of traditional cultures and emerging hybrids growing out of culture contact contested together to form new cultural configurations" (2017:93–97).

4. Cheng Yang-un 鄭仰恩.《歷史與信仰：從基督教觀點看台灣和世界》 *History and Faith: Looking at Taiwan and the World from a Christian Perspective,* (Tainan: Zen-Guan, 1999).

5. Yen Chuan-ying 顏娟英.《風景心境, Feng Jing Xin Jing—Tai Wan Jin Dai Mei Shu Wen Xian Dao Dou, *Landscape Moods: Selected Readings in Modern Taiwanese Art* (Taipei: Xiongshi Meishu, 2001), 71.

6. Translations mine (from the Chinese version). Besides native flora, nostalgic ruins become popular painting subject matters that Toraji was interested in exploring (Yen 2001:71).

7. Katsumi, Miyake. "Impressions of Taiwanese Journey." Feng Jing Xin Jing—Tai Wan Jin Dai Mei Shu Wen Xian Dao Dou, *Landscape Moods: Selected Readings in Modern Taiwanese Art*, (Taipei: Xiongshi Meishu, 2001), 60.

8. Nelson, Robert. "Appropriation," in *Critical Terms for Art History.* Ed. Robert Nelson and Srichard Shiff. (Chicago: The University of Chicago, 1996), 160.

9. According to Chen, unlike gender, class, or race, "ethnic conflict" or "provincial register contradiction" (*shengji maodun*) in local term is not an analytical but living concept, politically constructed in the concrete historical process of everyday life. The years 1945–1949 are a dividing line. *Bensheng* and *waisheng* refer to those who came to Taiwan from China before 1945 called *bensheng* (native), and those who came after labeled *waisheng* (newcomer) (2010:124).

10. There are four major ethnic groups in Taiwan: Minnanese (the largest population), Hakka people, Mainlander, and indigenous groups.

11. In 1971, the permanent seat of Taiwan at the United Nations, officially known as the Republic of China (ROC), was replaced by the People Republic of China (PRC). The political status of Taiwan became ambiguous. Taiwan suffered further international isolation as its allies the United States formally recognized the "One China Principle" advanced by Mainland China in 1979. The PRC government claims itself as the legitimate ruler of China and Taiwan is a sacred, inalienable part of its fatherland. According to Lo Kong-hi: "All the peoples of both sides of the Taiwan Strait are the same descendants of the one ancestor and, therefore, Taiwan cannot separate from China and the unification of the ancestor's country must be done even with the military power" (2018:179).

12. The government of Taiwan is denied international access to many international political, professional and academic organizations (Hsu 2018:142).

13. Young, James E. "Memory/Monument." *Critical Terms for Art History.* Ed. by Robert Nelson and Srichard Shiff, (Chicago: The University of Chicago, 1996), 234.

14. Chen Yi-Chieh, "West Street Party: Projection Mapping Show Featuring the North Gate (Beimen)" https://www.agichen.com/copy-of-something-red-in-phuket).

15. The history of projection mapping, or spatial augmented reality in an academic term, was originally a searchlight technology developed from the lighthouse in the 17th century. It could be used as the metaphor that the position of light is equal to the position of speech (Chen 2014).

16. According to Baudrillard, a simulacrum is a reproduction of an object or event characteristic of a specific stage in the history of the image or sign. In the post-modern world, simulacra have no relation to reality whatsoever, and are their own pure simulacra or imitations of imitations (Macey 2001:353).

17. Visual culture can be defined as practices shared by a certain group, community, and society and through it the meaning is created from the world of visual or textual representation (Sturken and Cartwright 2013:11).

18. Roland Barthes, *Mythologies* (New York City: Hill and Wang, 1972), 169.

19. Gong Jow-Jiun 龔卓軍. "Haptics of Architecture: 3D Mapping Projection and Architecture in *Translation of Animation*, Agi Chen" (建築的觸視：動畫轉譯中的建築投影－陳怡潔). *Art Critique of Taiwan* (藝術觀點 ACT) Vol. 66 (April 2016).

20. As St. Augustine reminds us, "it is not just the art object that determines its spiritual power. It is also the spirituality and discernment of the beholder that determines how illuminating the work will be" (Brown 2003:123).

21. Michele Saracino, *Being about Borders: A Christian Anthropology of Difference* (Collegeville: Liturgical Press, 2011), 15.

22. Stephen B. Bevans and Roger P. Schroeder, *Prophetic Dialogue: Reflections on Christian Mission Today* (New York: Orbis Books, 2011), 63.

BIBLIOGRAPHY

Bart, James E. "Memory/Monument." *Critical Terms for Art History*. Ed. by Robert Nelson and Srichard Shiff. Chicago: The University of Chicago, 1996.

Barthes, Roland. *Mythologies*. New York City: Hill and Wang, 1972.

Bevans, Stephen B., and Roger P. Schroeder. *Prophetic Dialogue: Reflections on Christian Mission Today*. New York: Orbis Books, 2011.

Brown, Frank Burch. *Good Taste, Bad Taste, and Christian Taste*. Oxford: Oxford University Press. 2003.

Chen, Kuan-Hsing 陳光興. *Asia as Method: Toward Deimperialization*. Durham: Duke University Press, 2010.

Chen, Kuan-Yu 陳寬育. "Screen and Light on the Gable: Architectural Projection and Chen Yi-Chiehs Cross-Domain Experience" (屏幕與山牆上的光：建築投影與陳怡潔的創作跨域經驗). In Journal of National Culture and Arts Foundation (國藝會線上誌), March 2014.

Chen, Nan-jou陳南州 (ed.). 《台灣鄉土神學-王憲治牧師文集》 *Taiwan Hsiang Tu Shen Hsueh. Wang Hsien Chih Mu Shih Wen Chi (A Testament to Taiwan Homeland Theology: The Essential Writings of Wang-Hsien Chih)*. Taipei: Yeong Wang, 2011.

Cheng, Yang-un 鄭仰恩. 《歷史與信仰：從基督教觀點看台灣和世界》 *History and Faith: Looking at Taiwan and the World from a Christian Perspective*. Tainan: Zen-Guan, 1999.

Gong, Jow Jiun 龔卓軍. "Haptics of Architecture: 3D Mapping Projection and Architecture in the Translation of Animation, Agi Chen" (建築的觸視：動畫轉譯中

的建築投影—陳怡潔). *Art Critique of Taiwan* (藝術觀點 ACT) Vol. 66 (April 2016).

Hsu, Victor. "Taiwan's International Status: An International Orphan." *Taiwan Ecumenical Forum 2018 November Meeting Handbook (second edition)*. Taipei: PCT, 2018.

Katsumi, Miyake. "Impressions of Taiwanese Journey." *Feng Jing Xin Jing——Tai Wan Jin Dai Mei Shu Wen Xian Dao Dou (Landscape Moods: Selected Readings in Modern Taiwanese Art)*. Ed. by Yen Chuan-ying. Taipei: Xiongshi Meishu, 2001 (1914).

Lo, Kong-hi. "A Taiwanese Critical Perspective on the Primordialistic Nationalism in the PRC's Official Documents and in the Deuteronomistic History." *Taiwan Ecumenical Forum 2018 November Meeting Handbook (second edition)*. Taipei: PCT, 2018.

Macey, David. *The Penguin Dictionary of Critical Theory*. London: Penguin Books, 2001.

Nelson, Robert. "Appropriation." *Critical Terms for Art History*. Ed. by Robert Nelson and Srichard Shiff. Chicago: The University of Chicago, 1996.

Saracino, Michele. *Being about Borders: A Christian Anthropology of Difference*. Collegeville: Liturgical Press, 2011.

Schreiter, Robert. "Trajectory in Intercultural Theology." *Interreligious Studies and Intercultural Theology*, Vol 1, No.1 (2017): 93–97.

Sturken, Marita, and Lisa Cartwright. *Practices of Looking: An Introduction to Visual Culture* (觀看的實踐: 給所有影像世代的視覺文化導論). Taipei: Cheng Ban, 2013.

Yen, Chuan-ying 顏娟英. 《風景心境》 *Feng Jing Xin Jing——Tai Wan Jin Dai Mei Shu Wen Xian Dao Dou (Landscape Moods: Selected Readings in Modern Taiwanese Art)*. Taipei: Xiongshi Meishu, 2001.

Chapter Four

Toward a Cross-Border Imagination
Another World Is Possible![1]//
Junghyung Kim

DREAMING OF A NEW WORLD

Jesus invites and challenges us to dream of a new world. Jesus himself dreamed of a world filled with life and peace, ruled by the God of love. Jesus proclaimed that such a reign of God would soon come on earth. Christians accept the gospel that Jesus proclaimed, and believe that God is still alive and working. For them, therefore, the future is a reservoir of infinite possibilities, since it is always open to God's new works.

The God the Bible testifies is the One who does ever new things every day. The God promises us a new life and a new world. For Christians who believe in God's promises, the future can never be a simple repetition of the life of past or present. The future contains in it the possibility of a new life that transcends, and thus is totally different from, the life of past or present. So Christians dream. They dream of another world. They are convinced that another world is possible that is completely different from the present world. They live in the hope for such a new world. They believe that this dream would not befool them, since this is God's dream and God will surely make it come true. Hence, Christians experience a transcendence of this world by dreaming of another world different from this world. They also experience a presence of the transcendent by fore-tasting the new world.

Meanwhile, dreaming of another world requires extraordinary imagination. Jesus proclaimed the gospel of a new world in which the God of love rules by justice and peace and the fullness of life brings about great joy. However, such a wonderful world has never existed in history. Therefore, one cannot draw the picture of the new world of God's reign simply by studying the history of humankind. Once the reign of God is completed on earth, the new world will operate in a totally different way from the present world ruled by the powers of sin and death.

Therefore, without an extraordinary imagination to draw the picture of another world in our minds, our commitment to the gospel of the reign of God would remain superficial. We need a bold imagination that goes beyond our experiences. We need a resolution to boldly put down the things that have sustained our lives so far. In this regard, biblical writers help us with exciting visions, such as children playing with wild beasts and gentle animals, overflowing water in the desert, and the revival of dry bones in the valley of death. Assisted by those visions of the Old Testament prophets, we must develop imagination of a new world, one that is totally different from the present one.

IMAGINATION BLOCKED BY A BORDER

Under the Constitution, the territory of the Republic of Korea (South Korea) extends north to the Amnok (Yalu) and Tuman (Tumen) rivers, bordered by China and Russia.[2] However, the actual north territory of South Korea is bordered by the military demarcation line (MDL), which divides the Korean peninsula into two Koreas. In other words, the MDL is not a constitutional border, but is actually considered a national border. Besides, since the adoption of the Inter-Korean Basic Agreement and simultaneous joining of the United Nations in 1991, the two Koreas have officially recognized each other. Still, many South Koreans are reluctant to recognize the MDL as a legitimate national border, for such recognition implies justifying North Korea's inhabitance in the northern peninsular.

Many South Koreans wish that the Korean peninsula be unified under the banner of liberal democracy. They are looking forward to the day when the blue wave from the South runs across the MDL and reaches the Tumen River and the Yalu River. At the same time, they also fear that the red wave from the North may run over the military frontier and cover the whole peninsula. On the one hand, they hope for the MDL to disappear; on the other hand, they are afraid that the disappearance of the MDL may lead to an unexpected result against their wish. Perhaps many North Koreans under the communist regime hold similar hopes and fears, though the situation is the opposite. On the one hand, they wish that the divided nation be re-unified under the red flag of communism; on the other hand, they are afraid that the annihilation of the MDL would bring about the collapse of their communist system.

The MDL is a line agreed upon by both North Korea and the United Nations Command in the Korean Armistice Agreement in 1953. However, in order to better understand the significance of the MDL, it is necessary to recall the year of 1945 when the Korean peninsula was liberated from Japanese imperialism. Soon after the national independence, the Korean peninsula was divided into South and North by US and Soviet forces. The dividing line was centered on the 38th parallel. Originally, this boundary line was only provisionally drawn until a unified government was established on the Korean peninsula. However, as separate sovereign governments were established respectively in South and North and then the Korean War broke out, the national division was fixed and perpetuated. In the early days of the Korean War the front line moved across the entire Korean peninsula, and soon it was formed around the present MDL. Then it became the military front of large and small battles that killed thousands of casualties before the Armistice Agreement was signed (and intermittently even after that). Compared with the 38th parallel in 1945, the MDL at the time of the armistice in 1953 is slightly lower to the South in the West (the North calls it "New Liberation District"), and slightly upwards to the North in the East (the South calls it "Restoration Area"). It is important to remember that thus far a great number of lives have been sacrificed to keep or move this boundary. In the process, and as a result, massive military power has been concentrated around the MDL. It is still one of the most armed and tense areas in the world. In this regard, the MDL, the sole legacy of the Cold War that still remains even in the 21st century, is a symbol of military conflict, confrontation, war, and violence.[3]

To make matters even worse, the MDL is a symbol of no peace, because it blocks our imagination for a new peaceful world. Those who feel safe and thus believe they are enjoying "peace" thanks to the border can never dream of a genuine peace or a universal and greater peace across the border. Their imagination is blocked by the border.

THE SNOWPIERCER AND TWO BOUNDARIES

In 2013, the movie *The Snowpiercer*, directed by Bong Jun-ho, was released. Based on a science fiction French graphic novel, *Le Transperceneige*, its story is "set in a future where a failed climate-change experiment kills all life on the planet except for a lucky few who boarded the Snowpiercer, a train that travels around the globe, where a class system emerges."[4] Briefly speaking, the technological civilization has accelerated the global warming, in order to cope with which the human community once again relies on a new technology. This counteract, however, pushes the entire planet into the ice age. As a result, all life has disappeared from the earth, except for those aboard the Snowpiercer, a globe-circulating train with its own perpetual-motion engine. The plot of the movie focuses on class conflicts symbolized by strict discrimination between train cars in the Snowpiercer, the only surviving community on Earth.

Two different kinds of boundary play an important role in the progress of the film. The first boundary is one between the inside and the outside of the train; and the second boundary is one between the front and the tail section. The former symbolizes an issue of life and death, whereas the latter symbolizes discrimination, oppression and exploitation between different classes.

There are doors (hatches) to the outside of the train in each car, but people do not think they can be opened so that they can pass through. They believe that once they leave the train, they all freeze and die. So they have locked all the doors to the outside of the train, so that nobody can open them. Those who ran out of the train were all frozen on the hill, which was later named as "the Seven Frozen's Revolt." This event became a decisive moment for everyone in the train to take even more seriously the boundary between the inside and the outside. Not only those who enjoyed a relatively comfortable life in the front cars, but also those who lived in a miserable condition of the tail section believed that one can survive only on the train. As a result, people came to regard those doors to the outside of the train as a wall or barrier that no one can pass through.

Meanwhile, as all the doors to the outside of the train were closed and no energy exchange between the inside and the outside was made possible, there emerged the problem of limited resources within the "closed system" of the train. As regards the resource depletion over time, the engine constantly moved to produce its own energy; as regards the distribution of limited resources, clear boundaries were drawn between different cars and the ecosystem within the train was thoroughly and carefully controlled. However, as the engine was hallowed as a god due to its production of all the energy consumed in the train, the sacrifice of children was justified for the engine's uninterrupted driving and those in the tail section were forced to live in misery. Eventually this becomes a crucial issue that heightens tensions between different cars, which forms the background of the entire storyline of the movie.

THE KOREAN REALITY IN LIGHT OF *THE SNOWPIERCER*

If we look at the situation of the Korean peninsula in light of the movie *The Snowpiercer*, it seems that different interpretations are respectively possible from the perspectives of South and North Korea.

First, from the perspective of South Korea, the film is interpreted as follows: The frozen globe represents the communist dictatorship in North

Korea threatening to overthrow South Korea, the permanent motion engine symbolizes the liberal democracy and the capitalist ideology of continuing economic growth, and the train divided into several cars depicts class conflicts in the South Korean society marked by the increasing gap between the rich and the poor. In today's South Korean society it has become very difficult for anyone to move from one class to another, primarily due to the bequeathing of both wealth and of poverty. Although various policy efforts, including welfare budget expansion, have been made to redistribute wealth, citizens feel that the boundary lines between different classes are increasingly clearer and thicker. But there is an even bolder and much clearer borderline than that between classes, which is drawn between South Korea and North Korea. Many people who are still afraid of North Korea's provocation think that no one is allowed to open the door to North Korea. For them it is like a wall or barrier. To our regret, it is still a minority in South Korea who believe that dialogue, communication, exchanges, and cooperation with North Korea can help make an even richer future.

From the perspective of North Korea, on the other hand, the film may be interpreted differently. The ice age represents South Korea as well as the US-centered international community under the ideology of liberal democracy, which threaten the North Korean regime; the uninterrupted engine symbolizes the communist dictatorship grounded on Juche ideology; different cars in the train refer to the hierarchy in the North Korean society. It has been over 50 years since North Korea lagged behind South Korea economically. In the mid-1990s, extreme famine and plagues killed a number of North Koreans. In the meantime, leaders of the regime and citizens of Pyongyang remain relatively safe. Despite the fact that the gap between classes is bringing many people to death, the North Korean regime has sealed and controlled the door to the outside, and instead asked the residents for self-regeneration. I suspect that there might be some North Koreans who believe that the North Korean society should open the door to the outside world and create a new and richer future through dialogue, communication, exchange, and cooperation with South Korea and the international community. However, in fact, it seems that few people can publicly express such beliefs or put them into practice.

Interestingly, the two views of South and North Korea have one thing in common. Both societies build robust barriers to protect themselves in the context of hostile threats, and seek sustainable survival strategies within the barriers. In other words, each of them draws a boundary line dividing the inside and the outside of its system, justifies the boundary on the basis of its own security ideology, and then brainwashes it to all residents, thereby making it an opportunity to justify the internal boundaries between classes within the system. Of course, South and North Korea hold on to different ideologies which are in conflict with each other. This is why the boundary between them forms an impenetrable barrier that blocks any communication or exchange between them.

THERE IS NO ALTERNATIVE?

In my view, modern physics may help us interpret *The Snowpiercer*. According to the thermodynamic theory, "an open system" refers to one in which there is an exchange of matter and energy between the system and the surroundings, whereas "a closed system" refers to one in which there is no exchange of matter or energy between the system and the surroundings. In the movie, most people firmly believe that the train is a closed system which cannot receive any energy from the outside. However, since in an isolated system its entropy (disorder) tends to increase, a sustainable life is impossible (the second law of thermodynamics). Now one can understand why the engine, which is the only source of energy in the train, is worshiped as a divine entity. To use a theological language, the world within the train creates and sanctifies the idol of the engine while struggling to survive by its own strength.

Meanwhile, let's turn our eyes from people struggling for survival within the train and look at the globe outside the train. At first glance it seems that no life could survive because of the ice age. But the Sun has continued to supply energy to the earth even after the coming of the ice age. With the constant supply of energy from the sun, the snow of the globe has already began to melt and the ice age is heading toward an end. Most people, however, think of the train as a closed system and pay little pay attention to the outside world. In fact, however, the globe outside of the train is an open system receiving energy from the outside (the Sun). The globe has kept accumulating energy.

What if passengers in the train had had time to watch outside carefully? What if they had taken into serious account the possibility of bringing into the train the energy accumulated in the outside? What if they had recognized that the train is in fact an open system that can exchange energy with the globe outside the train? If so, then their way of life on board would have been completely different from that described in the film. If passengers had known that there is another source of energy besides the train engine and that the energy source supplies much abundant energy even for free, they would have chosen to open the doors to the outside and receive energy from the outside—rather than making an idol of the engine and closing the doors to secure their own safety. If those aboard the train had made such a decision, both the boundary between the inside and the outside of the train and the boundaries between different train cars might have come to have a quite different meaning and function.

The analogies of the closed and open system provide a very useful insight both in diagnosing the reality of Korea as a divided nation and in envisioning the future of the re-unified Korea. The history of the national division began with the trusteeship of the United States and the Soviet immediately after the national independence, and then was consolidated through the Korean War. Not until a great number of casualties had occurred, did the Korean War end with both parties' agreement on the establishment of a cease-fire line (MDL) to prevent additional sacrifices. Perhaps at that time, both Koreas might have seen the line only as a provisional one, and dreamed of a unified world in which this provisional boundary line disappeared. The problem, however, was that the two parties had very different visions regarding the system of the unified Korea. As a consequence, the MDL has become an area of constant military confrontation between the two. But now, more than sixty years later, whether Korean people recognize it or not, the MDL is regarded as an almost permanent border between two Koreas. Most residents in the Korean peninsula have also accepted it as a solid barrier that no one is allowed to pass. South Koreans have acquired their own survival strategies within their boundaries—that is, in the South Korean society is understood as a closed system. Likewise, North Koreans have also acquired their own survival strategies within their boundaries—that is, in the North Korean society is understood as a closed system. In this situation both of their imaginations for the future of the Korean peninsula are curtailed by the armistice line. The genuine imagination for a new world across the border has been lost.

ANOTHER WORLD IS POSSIBLE!

Let's go back to the story of *The Snowpiercer*. The basic plot of the movie flows as passengers in the tail section struggles to move forward to the engine at the front of the train. I find the following four lines worthy of special attention—each by Wilford, kindergard teacher, Curtis, and Namgoong Minsoo.

First, the ingenious inventor and leader of the train, Wilford, says, "Everyone has their preordained position." There is a hierarchy within the train. It is fixed like a fate; therefore, no one can change it. Otherwise, the fined-tuned ecosystem of the train may be destroyed and all the passengers annihilated. "This train is a complete ecosystem which must respect the balance. Air, water, food, people. Everything must be regulated. For this, it was sometimes necessary use more radical solutions," Says Wilford.

Next, the kindergarten teacher in charge of children's ideological education stresses how hollow the engine is. "What happens if the engine stops? We all freeze and die. But will it stop, oh will it stop? No, no. Can you tell us why? The engine is eternal. Yes! The engine is forever." Here the engine of the train is exalted as something sacred and absolute. This ideology of a divine engine justifies even the sacrifice of young children on behalf of engine accessories. For everyone believes that this is the only way everyone else can survive: There is no other alternative.

Third, Curtis is the leader of the revolution in the tail section. Before he embarks on the revolt, Curtis expresses his determination to his mentor Gilliam. "We take the engine, we control the world." At the end of several twists and turns, Curtis eventually reaches the door to the engine and takes control of the sacred engine. Curtis, however, feels desperate in reluctant agreement to Wilford's saying that radical measures are inevitable for the sustainable ecosystem within the train. Curtis too could not find any alternative.

Fourth, and finally, it is Namgoong Minsoo's gaze that has attracted me most in the movie. The gaze of Curtis, who was dreaming of overthrowing the hierarchy in the train, was directed all the way to the front engine. However, Minsoo's gaze was always oriented through windows to the outside of the train. "The door that I really want to open is not the door to the engine, but the door that leads out of the train." About thirteen years ago Minsoo's wife jumped out of the train with her fellows, but became an ice pillar not far from the railroad tracks. Minsoo must have long chewed on this tragedy of the past. Then, he dreamed of a new life outside the train and sought to find how to get out of the train. On the other hand, he waited until the temperature of the earth cooled down enough for life to survive. Unfortunately, his wife and her fellows hastily escaped and were frozen in the hill. Nonetheless, Minsoo was convinced that the day would surely come. So once a year he carefully observed changes in the global environment, checking the rate of the snow's melting. In other words, he carefully watched out and awaited the end of the ice age. Everyone on the train, including Curtis, believed it was impossible to survive outside the train. However, Minsoo was determined to start a new life outside the train someday, and prepared himself for the day. He assumed that another world, different from the oppressive and violent world within the train, would be possible outside the train. Eventually, the train exploded and two surviving children could witness a living creature (bear) on a snowy hill. This last scene is a marvelous symbol of the beginning of a new life in a new land.

Minsoo dreamed of another world in which people could enjoy infinite resources of the globe. The new world was quite different from the old world of the train in which there was a competition for survival due to limited resources. Wilford was a conservative who wished to maintain *status quo*; Curtis was a revolutionary who sought to overthrow the present structure of power. But Minsoo was a sort of radical, different from both of them. Minsoo's vision of a new world was much more radical than Curtis'.

TOWARD A BORDER-CROSS IMAGINATION

Today many people in the global village see the world as bounded by various boundaries, and struggle for their survival within the closed system. But what if all people on Earth turn their eyes to a completely new world that transcends all the current boundaries? Would it be possible? How is it possible? Still many Koreans' imagination of the future of the Korean peninsula is blocked by the MDL. Could we imagine a new world order that goes beyond the MDL? Could we imagine a new future in which the MDL disappears? The story of Minsoo, who dreamed of a new life outside the train, challenges all the inhabitants of the Korean penisula to imagine and dream of a new world, or a new future that transcends the MDL currently dividing Korea into two.

Here one needs to carefully distinguish between a world in which the MDL is "transcended" and a world in which the MDL is "annihilated." The idea of the MDL's "annihilation" may give an impression that only one of two systems in North and South Korea predominates, whereas the other disappears. In this regard, a premature emphasis on "unification" can be understood as self-centered and oppressive. Rather, it seems more desirable to emphasize "peace" as a process of respecting the other's system, communicating with each other, learning from each other, resembling each other, and creating a totally new world that has never existed in the past history.

Over the past year rapid changes in the geopolitical situations surrounding the Korean peninsula have encouraged many citizens to hope for the final end of the Korean War and the subsequent arrival of a new era of peace in East Asia. Though the new future still looks far from us, no one would doubt that it is time to prepare for the new era after the end of the Korean War. Once it is declared that the Korean War has indeed come to an end, the current MDL would no longer be a "cease-fire line." Then, the line ought to be reborn with a new name and a new definition. How one renames it and identifies its primary function would be of decisive importance for creating a new world order in East after the end of the Korean War.

Once the Korean War ends and a peaceful system is established on the Korean peninsula, one may expect that the demilitarized zone (DMZ) around the MDL, which is now filled with land mines and heavy weapons, will turn into a land filled with life and peace. Then the current DMZ and MDL will gain new names, for they would be the forefront of bringing life and peace to East Asia.

Of course, when one redefines the current DMZ in the future, one should be careful not to erase all the memories of the past bloody history entangled in it. With those memories kept alive the DMZ will give the next generations an invaluable lesson that no more violence should be allowed. Besides, the DMZ will be born again to be a milestone or a signpost for a different world of just peace. It will be the forefront that leads the entirety of Korea and East Asia to a completely new future, a little closer to the vision of the eschatological kingdom of God.

We have seen how the Berlin Wall, once a symbol of conflict, has turned into a symbol of peace ever since the reunification of East and West Germany. Switzerland, once a country of mercenaries for European powers, now functions as a buffer zone mitigating conflicts between European countries after having become a permanent neutral land. Though the MDL is still dividing the Korean peninsula into two different systems, there are an increasing number of citizens who dare to imagine and dream of a new world of peace across the MDL. Such a cross-border imagination is to be loved and encouraged.[5]

NOTES

1. This is an extended application to the context of the divided Korea of my earlier ideas which was published in *Yesunimeui Nunmul (Jesus' Tears)* (Seoul: *The Blessed People*, 2019) 70–83.

2. According to the Constitution of the Republic of Korea, "The territory of the Republic of Korea shall consist of the Korean peninsula and its adjacent islands" (Chapter 1 Article 3). https://www.wipo.int/edocs/lexdocs/laws/en/kr/kr061en.pdf (accessed October 6, 2019).

3. Bruce Cumings gives a helpful introduction to the Korean War: Bruce Cumings, *The Korean War: A History* (New York: Random House, 2011).

4. Official blog: https://snowpiercer-film.com/ (accessed October 6, 2019). Bong Jun-ho is one of the most influential directors in South Korea, whose recent movie *Parasite* won the Palme d'Or at the 2019 Cannes Film Festival.

5. In his contribution to a German newspaper, Frankfruter Allgemeine, South Korea's president Moon Jae-In asked for this cross-border imagination: "Die Bürgerinnen und Bürger Südkoreas konnten sich keine Vorstellung davon machen, wie es jenseits der Waffenstillstandslinie aussah. Wenn sich einfache Bürgerinnen und Bürger aber ein umfassenderes Bild machen können, wird damit auch eine Befreiung von Ideologien einhergehen." Moon Jae-In, "Die Großartigkeit des Einfachen," *Frankfurter Allgemeine Zeitung* (September 5, 2019).

BIBLIOGRAPHY

Cumings, Bruce. *The Korean War: A History*. New York: Random House, 2011.
Moon, Jae-In. "Die Großartigkeit des Einfachen," *Frankfurter Allgemeine Zeitung*, September 5, 2019.
Nunmul, Yesunimeui. *Jesus' Tears.* Seoul, The Blessed People, 2019, 74–78.
The Snowpiercer, Official Fan Page, https://snowpiercer-film.com/, accessed Oct. 6, 2019.

Chapter Five

The Occupation of Theological Minds

The End of Innocence

Mitri Raheb

In his book *Missionary Conquest: The Gospel and Native American Cultural Genocide*[1] George E. Tinker, A Native American Lutheran theologian, argues that Europe's colonial conquest of the Americas was largely fought on two separate but symbiotically related fronts. One front was relatively open and explicit; it involved the political and military strategy that drove peoples from their land to make room for the more "civilized" conqueror and worked to deprive Indian peoples of any continuing self-governance or self-determination. The second front, which was just as decisive in the conquest if more subtle and less explicitly apparent, was the religious strategy pursued by missionaries of all denominations. In this conquest, as in the European conquest of Indian peoples, theology becomes a crucial ingredient, and missionaries become an important strategic phalanx.[2]

My thesis in this chapter is that the colonization of Palestinian land by Israel is fought also on two fronts: the front of the Israeli military occupation and the front of theology, with one small difference: that the role that missionaries played in the colonization of the Americas is replaced in the case of Palestine today by theologians of all denominations.

Tinker doesn't imply colonial intentions among the missionaries, but rather a certain naïveté. He writes, "They surely did not intend any harm to Indian people, yet their blindness to their own inculturation of European values and social structures meant that complicity was unavoidable . . . it is clear that the missionaries were myopic regarding their own cultural biases."[3] This is also very true of many theologians in relation to Palestine: On the one hand they are naïve, and on the other there is an inherit bias towards "Israel" that sustains the continual colonization of Palestine. Christian theologians, in few cases consciously but in most cases subconsciously, keep using a "biblical" language and producing "theological" concepts whose "Sitz im Leben" is blunt colonialism. They might do this "innocently" because their minds are occupied with the Bible on the one hand and with a Western cultural narrative on the other.

For Palestinians, including the Palestinian Christian community, Palestine is a real land with real people; it is our homeland. For Christians in the West, Palestine is an imagined land, a land that they know mainly from the Bible. It has little if anything to do with the real Palestine. When Christian pilgrims visit Palestine, they want to reinvent the Holy Land of the Bible. They are excited about how the Bible comes alive in Palestine. Nineteenth-century archaeologists, while digging in Palestine, were looking for the Bible. This is true also for theologians. When Christian theologians write about Palestine, their minds are occupied with the Bible and a Western dominant narrative. They write about the Land as if it exists in a vacuum; they strip it from its socio-political context, from its real people, and they rarely think about how such a theology has been and is being used to enhance settler colonialism. These occupied minds reinforce the continuing occupation of Palestine. Here, I'm not talking about evangelical theologians or Christian Zionists alone, but I'm concerned about those who are well-regarded, mainline, and accomplished theologians of many denominations. In the last seventy years, many theological concepts were developed and occupied the minds of several generations of theologians worldwide. Many of these concepts might have been well intended at some point, but they mean something totally different in the current context of occupied Palestine. Theologians in their naiveté are still using a language and concepts that support current Israeli settler colonialism. In this chapter I shall highlight and expose only two of these concepts.

THE HARAM VERSUS TEMPLE MOUNT

A few years ago, I wanted to publish a book on Jerusalem. To that end, I approached a good friend, a theologian from the United States, to work with me on this book. When we met to discuss the table of contents and the topics to include in the book, it became clear to me that we had two very different perspectives on Jerusalem. For me, Jerusalem was a real city I used to visit as a boy on a weekly basis. I still vividly recall how I used to sit with my friends on the Ottoman walls of the Old City, visit the Church of the Holy Sepulchre, which dates back in part to the Byzantine Era, and walk to the Al-Aqsa Mosque and the Dome of the Rock, built during the Ummayyad Period in 7th century. A trip to Jerusalem was never complete without buying the famous Jerusalem "ka'ek," a local sesame bread, and eating it with za'atar, wild thyme. I had an aunt and many friends from the church youth who were living in Jerusalem. For me Jerusalem was a real, lively, and living city with real people.

My colleague from the United States didn't have the same connection to the city, and I soon came to realize that he was not particularly interested in what is there today. Rather, he was obsessed with ancient Jerusalem, with what once was; that and that alone occupied his imagination. He was intrigued by the remains of the Herodian walls and didn't pay enough attention to the existing Ottoman wall from the 16th century. His mind was occupied with the ancient roads on which Jesus walked rather than the current *Souq* with all its rich social and economic history. He was less interested in the city as it is and as it has developed over the centuries. His focus was clearly on the biblical Jerusalem; on the Jerusalem of the Old and the New Testament. He was interested in the Second Temple and was less interested in Al-Aqsa Mosque, which has been standing there since the seventh century. My friend was eager to reinvent the Jerusalem of the Bible and to bring it back to life for the potential readers of the intended book. I came to realize that his mind was occupied with the biblical past. This would not have been a problem if it would not have devastating consequences to the current realities in Palestine. My friend wasn't a Zionist or evangelical Christian, but rather a sophisticated theologian who was raised with liberal and historical-critical methods. My friend might have been innocent; however, he was unaware that what occupies his mind was, and is, one tool in the continuing colonization of Palestinian land and people.

I noticed how my friend kept referring to the area of Al-Aqsa Mosque and the Dome of the Rock as the Temple Mount. I asked myself, why would a Christian theologian keep calling this area "Temple Mount?" There hasn't been a temple there for the last 2,000 years. There are two major and ancient Muslim shrines from the seventh century that dominate the skyline of the old city of Jerusalem. I certainly can understand it if the phrase "Temple Mount" was used as a historical reference, to say that the Jewish Temple once stood there or as an archaeological reference to some of the remains of the Herodian wall. But to ignore and pretend not to see or reference two major Muslim Holy sites and to keep referring today, and in a volatile political context, to the whole area as the "Temple Mount" is not innocent, but very problematic, to say the least.

Imagine if theologians were to keep calling the Church of the Nativity "the Tammuz" or "Mithra Temple" because the church was built on the spot that most probably was earlier used as a temple for the gods Tammuz and Mithra. How would we feel as Christians?

One might say, "but people keep calling the Hagia Sofia in Istanbul with this name, even though it was transformed into a mosque." But the case of the Haram Al-Shareef is different than Hagia Sofia. Hagia Sofia was used as a church for centuries and stood there as a church when the Ottomans invaded and occupied Constantinople. The church was then transformed into a mosque with the attempt of eliminating all Christian symbols from the church.

In the case of the Haram, it was a totally different story. When the Caliph Omar took over Jerusalem, the platform referred to as the "Temple Mount" was a devastated place, a ruin full of garbage. The Romans had destroyed the temple and Jerusalem and left it in ruins, and the Byzantines weren't eager to build in that specific area due to their fear of Jesus' words that no stone will stay on another there. The Christian Patriarch donated that platform to the Muslim Caliphs and the Umayyads built there, toward the end of the seventh century CE, Al-Aqsa Mosque, and a few years later, under Caliph 'Abd al-Malik, the Dome of the Rock. These shrines were used by Muslims throughout the last 13 centuries, except during the time of the Crusaders, who transformed Al-Aqsa into a Palace "Templum Salomonis" and the Dome of the Rock into a Christian Sanctuary "Templum Domini."[4]

The consistent use of the "Temple Mount" for the Haram might be made innocently by Christian theologians, but this is theologically disastrous. Christian theologians are often unaware that behind this phrase "Temple Mount" often lies a Zionist political claim. Theologians who continue to innocently use the name "Temple Mount" instead of Haram are playing into the hands of radical Israeli settlers who are determined to occupy the Muslim shrines and transform them into a Jewish site. In the last five decades, Israeli settlers have been attempting to destroy or occupy the Haram in order to construct a Jewish temple there. This is the current "Sitz im Leben" of this phrase.

The use of the name "Temple Mount" is not innocent at all, but plays into the agenda of a radical (Christian)-Zionist ideology as well as settler colonialism. Following the Israeli occupation of East Jerusalem, an Israeli military officer, Gershom Salomon, founded an organization with the name "the Temple Mount Faithful" with the goal of "building the Third Temple on the Temple Mount in Jerusalem in our lifetime in accordance with the Word of G-d and all the Hebrew Prophets and the liberation of the Temple Mount from Arab (Islamic) occupation so that it maybe consecrated to the Name of G-d."[5]

On August 21, 1969, a Christian Zionist and Australian citizen, Michael Dennis Rohan,[6] set on fire the ancient pulpit commissioned by Salah ad-Din in Al-Aqsa Mosque, believing that he was called to burn the Muslim shrine so that the Jewish temple could be erected there. Rohan, a militant Christian Zionist, was declared insane and deported later to Australia. Nonetheless, Christian-Zionist groups are still obsessed with this idea of seeing the third temple constructed, Muslims defeated, and their shrines in Jerusalem destroyed, as a prerequisite for the second coming of Christ.

Starting in the late 1970s, Jewish terrorist groups attempted several times to blow up the Dome of the Rock. The first attempt, in 1978, was made by Yehuda Etzion,[7] who believed that the destruction of the Muslim mosque would trigger a Jewish national spiritual revival. He and another Israeli-Jewish terrorist and expert in explosives, Menachem Livni, studied the Haram in detail, stole explosives from an Israeli military base in the Golan Heights, and made 28 precision bombs to blow the Dome of the Rock into the air. For several reasons, the operation had to be aborted.

A second attempt to blow up the Dome of the Rock was made in 1980 by the American-Israeli rabbi and member of the Knesset, Meir Kahane,[8] followed by a third one in 1982 by Alan Goodman,[9] an orthodox Jewish American who opened fire on Muslim worshipers. By the mid-1980s, attempts to storm the Haram by Jewish settlers became a regular practice.

During the first *Intifada* (Uprising), Gershom Salomon, the leader of the Temple Mount Faithful, announced his intention to storm the Haram area and to lay there the foundation for the new temple. In 1996, Netanyahu's government authorized the opening of a tunnel underneath the Haram, giving new momentum to the Temple Mount Faithful movement. Gershom Salomon was proud to announce his goal: "We will liberate the Temple Mount, even if the political leadership doesn't want to. . . . Instead of the Dome of the Rock and mosques, the flag of Israel and the Temple! . . . It's the will of Providence that we struggle to remove the abominations from the mount."[10] On September 29, 2000, Israeli opposition leader Ariel Sharon,[11] guarded by Israeli soldiers and accompanied by members of the Israeli government, stormed the Haram, triggering the second *Intifada*. Such attempts have continued since then, almost on a weekly basis, provoking Muslim worshippers and authorities, leading to riots and the deaths of hundreds of Palestinian people so far. The last attempt was on June 2, 2019, coinciding with Eid al-Fitr, when Muslims were marking the end of the fasting month of Ramadan. Through these attempts, the Israeli settlers intend something very similar to what Crusaders did to the two Muslim shrines and analogous to what the Ottomans did to Hagia Sofia.

With such a history of Jewish settler colonialism that resembles Crusaders' behavior, how can theologians keep using the term "Temple Mount?" Are they so naïve? Can they claim innocence? How can we liberate the theological minds from this invisible "occupation?" Is it not time to wake up from using a language that only plays into the hands of Jewish Settler colonialism, Christian-Zionist ideology, and Islamophobic rhetoric? Indeed, it is high time to end this kind of theological innocence.

THE LAND

The second example I would like to highlight in this chapter has to do with the use of the phrases "The Land" and "the Promised Land" in relation to Palestine. In 1977, the well-known American Old Testament scholar Walter Brueggemann published his book titled *The Land*, a typical book about biblical theology which influenced a whole generation of American pastors and theologians. In this book, Brueggemann responded to an emerging American context where many people felt a "sense of being lost, displaced and homeless."[12] This existential and socio-psychological yearning for a secure place led Brueggemann to claim that the Land is the "central theme in biblical faith"[13] and is primarily concerned "with the issue of being displaced and yearning for a place."[14] In this book, Brueggemann talks about three important aspects of the land. He speaks of the land as a gift, a temptation, and a task, thus emphasizing the dialectic between landlessness and landedness.[15]

However, in the preface of the second edition of the same book, published in 2002, Brueggemann wrote about five major developments that were pressing in Old Testament studies that had not been on his horizon at the time of the initial writing in 1977. One of them was the following:

> the recognition that the claim of "promised land" in the Old Testament is not an innocent theological claim, but is a vigorous ideological assertion on an important political scale. This insight is a subset of ideology critique in the field that has emerged as a major enterprise only in the last decades. Perhaps the most important articulation in this matter is the recognition of Jon Levenson that Israel's tradition demonizes and dismisses the Canaanites as a parallel to the anti-Semitism that is intrinsic to the New Testament. That is, Israel's text proceeds on the basis of the primal promises of Genesis 12–36 to assume entitlement to the land without regard to any other inhabitants including those who may have been there prior to Israel's emergence . . . The shortcoming in my book reflects my inadequate understanding at that time, but also reflects the status of most Old Testament studies at that time that were still innocently credulous about the theological importance of the land tradition in the Old Testament. . . . Most recently scholarly attention has been given to the ongoing ideological force (and cost) of the claim of "promised land." On the one hand, this ideology of land entitlement . . . has served the ongoing territorial ambitions of the state of Israel, ambitions that, as I write (April 2002), are enacted in unrestrained violence against the Palestinian population.[16]

When Brueggemann wrote his first book on the Land, he was 46 years old. That book was his thirteenth. He was in the middle of his career. The second edition of Brueggemann's book came at a time when he was at the height of his career. The political situation had also changed dramatically between

1977 and 2002. The second edition was published in the context of the second *Intifada*, the Palestinian uprising. Israeli tanks had just invaded most of the Palestinian towns. The Church of the Nativity was under siege by Israeli troops. President Arafat was imprisoned in his compound. Yet, Brueggemann attributes the change in his perception to the emergence of ideology critique, although ideological criticism had emerged around the same time his first edition was published. That is, it took Brueggemann over two decades to realize the importance of ideological criticism for his topic.

Further, in his book on the land, Brueggemann was keen to be relevant to his *American* context and to relate the issues of land as gift, promise, and challenge to current issues within that context. What he failed to see, however, was how such a theology was used and misused *in the founding of his own country*, the United States, as exemplified by using the biblical land theology and ideology in the conquest of North America and the occupying of Native American lands. His mind was occupied with the Bible, and the Bible alone, which didn't help him in looking at biblical reception history. I don't want to question Brueggemann's innocence, and I'm glad to see him later confessing his earlier naïveté. But did that confession lead him to altering his theology in any radical way? Unfortunately, no; in my view, he continued to be what Hayes called a Liberal Christian Zionist.

In 2015, Brueggemann published a booklet under the title *Chosen?: Reading the Bible amid the Israeli-Palestinian Conflict.*[17] The opening of this book sounds promising, as Brueggemann is open about a change in his convictions. His connection to Palestinian Christian theologians and Jewish American Peace activists played a role in this conversion:

> My own convictions concerning this conflict, as those of many other people, have changed considerably over time, a change that I judge responsible in the face of changing political reality. Mindful of the long history of Christian anti-Semitism and the deep fissure of the Shoah, we have surely been right to give thanks for the founding of the state of Israel and the securing of a Jewish homeland. But the issues have altered dramatically as the state of Israel has developed into a major military power that continues administrative-military control of the Palestinian territories.[18]

But very soon after, one is shocked to read in the introduction to this booklet:

> In my own thinking, which is much influenced by my work as a Scripture scholar, I begin with a focus on the claim of Israel as God's chosen people. That conviction is not in doubt in the Bible. It is a theological claim, moreover, that fits with compelling persuasiveness with the reality of Jews in the wake of World War II and the Shoah. Jews were indeed a vulnerable people, whose requirement of a homeland was an overriding urgency. Like many Christians,

progressive and evangelical, I was grateful (and continue to be so) for the founding and prospering of the state of Israel as an embodiment of God's chosen people. That much is expressed in my earlier book entitled *The Land*. I took "the holy land" to be the appropriate place for the chosen people of the Bible which anticipates the well-being of Israel that takes land and people together.[19]

In this book, it is very troubling how Brueggemann unapologetically connects the biblical promise of the land with the notion of "God's chosen people," a phrase that doesn't even appear as such in the Bible (but is clearly important in Christian-Zionist ideology), then moves swiftly and uncritically not only to connect these biblical topoi with modern Judaism, but also then to speak about the state of Israel as "an embodiment of God's chosen people."[20] Brueggemann in his booklet thus confuses biblical Israel and Israel as a theological construct with the State of Israel of today.[21] Even when he seemed to be criticizing the occupational policies of the state of Israel, Brueggemann immediately felt a need to express his unshakable allegiance to that same state. He writes, "I have not changed my mind an iota about the status of Israel as God's chosen people or about urgency for the security and well-being of the state of Israel."[22]

At the end of chapter three, however, Brueggemann seems to contradict himself when he asks the question: Is Today's Israel Biblical Israel? To this, he answers:

Concerning any interpretive question, critical faith will resist a direct line from ancient text to contemporary claim. The land issue is no exception to that general rule for critical interpretation. Consequently, it is simply not credible to make any direct appeal from the ancient promises of land to the state of Israel. That is so for two reasons. First, much has happened between text and contemporary political practice that resists such innocent simplicity. Second, because the state of Israel, perhaps of necessity, has opted to be a military power engaged in power politics along with the other nation-states of the world, it cannot at the same time appeal to an old faith tradition in a persuasive way. Thus, the state of Israel can, like any nation-state, make its legitimate political claims and insist upon legitimate security. But appeals to the ancient faith traditions about land promise in order to justify its claims carries little conviction except for those who innocently and uncritically accept the authority of that ancient story.[23]

There seems to be a disconnect here. Brueggemann is not a naïve evangelical Christian. In fact, he doesn't connect biblical Israel with the state of Israel directly, but uses the Shoah and anti-Semitism as hermeneutical keys to bridge both entities. Brueggemann is not troubled at all with this kind of theology, but writes that he became concerned because "the state of Israel has developed into a major military power that continues administrative-military control of the Palestinian territories."[24]

Based on his biblical reading, Brueggemann doesn't question the use of the biblical narrative to colonize Palestine. Based on his theological understanding of the biblical issue of the land, Brueggemann doesn't question Israel's "biblical" and "unconditional" entitlement to the land, but he is troubled only with the way Israel is treating the Palestinians. To that end, Brueggemann finds the Israel of today to be in a similar context to that of biblical Israel at the time of Ezra. Those coming "back" into the land are developing exclusionist theologies about the other. As a result, Brueggemann sees "the question of the other" as "the interpretive key to how to read the Bible. The other can be perceived, as in Zionist perspective, as a huge threat to the security of the state and the well-being of the holy seed. Conversely, the other can be perceived as a neighbor with whom to work at shalom."[25]

In his endorsement of Brueggemann's book, Rabbi Michael Lerner, editor of *Tikkun* magazine, commends Brueggemann for his approach of loving "the stranger/the Other." This framing is troublesome, to say the least. By describing the Palestinians as the stranger or the Other, *even as they dwell in their ancestral land,* Rabbi Lerner's and Brueggemann's minds are occupied with the Bible so that they see the Anglo-Saxon or Russian-Israeli Settlers as the heirs of the land, and thus elevated. While both Brueggemann and Lerner are concerned about the discrimination against the Palestinians by the state of Israel, they themselves discriminate against the Palestinians theologically by calling them "strangers," while in fact they belong to the land and their history, culture, and identity is deeply rooted in the land, Palestine. As a Palestinian, whose roots are in this land, I hear the biblical call to be kind to the Israeli incomers, but I resist vehemently being called a stranger and being made an alien in my own homeland, or being discriminated against politically by Israel or theologically by Christians or Jews, all in the name of the Bible.

In chapter three, Brueggemann comes back to the issue of "Holy" land and reiterates what he wrote many years ago of the land as a "gift with strings attached."[26] He summarizes it here in this way: "Thus, the land is *given (unconditionally)*, the land is *taken (by conquest and force)*, and the land is *losable (if the Torah is not kept)*."[27] So Brueggemann doesn't question that it is God who gave Israel the land of Palestine, a promise he understands to remain in effect today, specifically with regard to the state of Israel; and he takes the militant conquest of Joshua as a biblical given, without connecting it to the history of colonization, ancient or modern. The only possible problem he sees, by implication, is that modern Israel doesn't keep the Torah, which he equates with the human rights charters of today.

My question is, how can a critical mind such as his write such a booklet in the year 2015, when the colonization of Palestinian lands had reached unparalleled dimensions as Israeli colonies spread all over the West Bank, thus transforming it into isolated *bantustans,* or (on another analogy) semi-native American reservations, while grabbing its land and resources and subjugating its indigenous population to Apartheid laws and a matrix of total control? Israel today occupies not only Palestinian land itself, but also everything under and above ground, including electromagnetic fields.

The international community at large is uneasy with the expansion of Israeli settlements, i.e., colonies in the West Bank. They oppose expansion because it violates international law, the Geneva Convention, as well as the UN Human Rights Charter. In such a context, the Israeli government refers to biblical entitlement to the land (of Palestine) as a last resort, in the apparent hope that "divine rights" would trump "human rights" and sugar-coat their violation. In April 2019, Danny Danon, the Israeli ambassador to the UN, was cornered at the United Nations Security Council by the international community regarding the expansion of Israeli settlement in the West Bank, and he couldn't escape the confrontation except through referring to the Bible. In a demonstrative and unapologetic way, he lifted a Bible and started waving it, declaring: "This is the deed to our land," before continuing:

> From the book of Genesis; to the Jewish exodus from Egypt; to receiving the Torah on Mount Sinai; to the gates of Canaan; and to the realization of God's covenant in the Holy Land of Israel; the Bible paints a consistent picture. The entire history of our people, and our connection to Eretz Yisrael, begins right here.[28]

How can an accomplished theologian of Brueggemann's caliber write about land theology while ignoring the reception history of land ideology in modern settler colonial history? This could only be explained by one phenomenon: Brueggemann's mind has been occupied by the Bible in a way that prevented him from seeing the reception history of biblical land theology and ideology. Brueggemann continues writing theology as if there was no colonial history that used biblical land theology at its foundation. Brueggemann only sees the Christian anti-Semitism that led to the Holocaust in the West, but doesn't see the colonial history of the Christian West.

Just as alarming is that a serious theologian like Brueggemann, who has a critical mind and who is politically aware, overlooks the reception history of the land theology in the context of the colonization of North America. Nowhere in the booklet do we see Brueggemann referring to the notion of colonialism and its connection to land theology. In his framework, which includes blacks, women, and gays and lesbians, the indigenous people are absent.[29]

Why is the theology of conquest not questioned? Is Brueggemann, a descendent of a settler community, blind to the troubling history of the colonization of North America, i.e., the use of the doctrine of discovery to seize Native American land? How can his mind be occupied with the Bible in such a way as not to take its use in history and today seriously?

Brueggemann is in no way an exception here. He represents many biblical theologians. Several "Christian Holocaust Theologians" were so much in awe of the State of Israel that they went on to emphasize a strong bond between God, land (Palestine), and people (Jewish),[30] while totally ignoring the rights of the Palestinian people to their land. This near-equation of "theological" Israel with the state of Israel is what Stephen Hayes describes as "liberal Christian Zionism."[31]

It is incomprehensible to me when the occupation of Palestinian land is not seen as part of modern European colonial history, but as part of biblical and thus salvation history. It is very disturbing when theologians ignore the ways in which biblical ideology is used as a political claim with major colonial consequences. How can somebody like Brueggemann keep ignoring the current context in which the land theology is used to continue the colonization of Palestinian land?

In contrast to Brueggemann's land theology, I would like to look briefly at another "Western theologian" almost the same age as Brueggemann, who was able yet to reach a different reading and conclusion. Norman C. Habel, a Lutheran Australian Old Testament scholar, published a book in 1995 titled *The Land is Mine: Six Biblical Land Ideologies*. As the title implies, Habel was already aware that land theology is always an ideology "which employ[s] theological doctrines, traditions, or symbols to justify and promote the social, economic and political interests of a group within society."[32]

In his 2018 booklet *Acknowledgement of the Land and Faith of Aboriginal Custodians after following the Abraham Trail*,[33] Habel went a step further. He was aware that most of the land theologies are utilized by colonizers and are never concerned with the perspective of the colonized. This wasn't a mere theoretical observation, but rather a biographical experience. In the preface, Norman writes:

> I am a descendant of a Prussian migrant who can be compared to Abraham who moved from his homeland, Ur of the Chaldees, to the host country of Canaan. And the Aboriginal people of Canaan can be compared to the Aboriginal Peoples in the land of Australia and other countries. . . . Recent generations of colonial readers have viewed the promised land tradition of the narrator of the

Abraham trail as a divine justification for entry into so-called uncivilised lands of the New World: lands like Australia, America and South Africa.[34]

Habel learned through an Aboriginal elder, George Rosendale, to read the land theology from the perspective of the colonized. He quotes Rosendale saying:

> Little was said (by the missionaries) about the indigenous people of the land whom the Israelites conquered. No questions were asked about whether Joshua's scorched Earth policy was what God really wanted for the indigenous people. Today Joshua's mode of operation sounds to us very much like that of the British colonial conquerors. Did the British have to follow Joshua's way?[35]

Habel start his booklet with Canaan, the original land of promise, "a host country whose indigenous inhabitants welcomed immigrants such as Abraham and helped them settle peacefully."[36] Habel, unlike Brueggemann, is conscious of his context as a German settler. He acknowledges that his settler community has often "discounted the capacity of Aboriginal people"[37] who have been custodians of Australia for thousands of years, and have dismissed Aboriginal beliefs as paganism, demoting their rich spirituality. For Habel, there are two different land theologies in the Old Testament: The first theology is represented by Abraham, who understands himself as a guest in Canaan, respects the faith of the indigenous people, and enters into a peaceful treaty with them; a second one is represented by Joshua, with its militant version of the promise. This later "classical promised land ideology seems to reflect a bias based on a belief that one chosen people has a divine mandate to invade and possess a particular land and dispossess the indigenous inhabitants of that land as peoples without rights, peoples such as the Australian Aboriginal Peoples."[38]

Habel concludes his booklet by urging the church and its theologians to grasp the Kairos moment and follow the model of Abraham, thus changing their theology, attitude, and practice. He writes:

> Yes!
> IT IS TIME!
> In the light of the faith of Abraham,
> the positive relationships between Abraham
> and the indigenous custodians of Canaan,
> including worship of El, the Creator Spirit of Canaan,
> a covenant with the same Canaanite God,
> a treaty in which this God, Abraham, the Canaanites
> and the land of Canaan are partners,
> AND

In the light of how Australian settlers, influenced by a promised land ideology,
Dispossessed the indigenous custodians,
Discounted their creation spirituality
And violated the land they held sacred.
IT IS TIME
For Christian Churches
And the descendances of Christian settlers
To follow the precedent of Abraham,
To make a public acknowledgment,
A colonial confession,
AND
To promote a treaty process
That guarantees and respects the identity, rights,
Sovereignty, country and spirituality
Of the Aboriginal Peoples.[39]

Habel's approach here differs fundamentally from that of Brueggemann. Both are using the Bible and both write land theology, but they arrive at different conclusions. The Bible contains several conflicting stories, stories like that of Abraham and that of Joshua. What we find thus says not so much about the Bible, but more about us. Brueggemann's "Land" interpretation may say more about his political convictions than about biblical theology, and the same is true for Habel. The Bible has both: texts of liberation and texts of colonization. What are our minds occupied with? What is our hermeneutical key? The Holocaust or colonialism? This key determines to a great extent how we read the Bible. What is occupying our minds determines our interpretations.

We cannot separate Israeli colonial policies in Palestine from modern European colonial history. In his comparative analysis of Native American and Palestinian literary production, Steven Salaita comes to the following conclusion:

> The results of ethnic cleansing have been heartbreaking in the New World and Holy Land. It is important—perhaps even imperative—to use "New World" and "Holy Land" together with "ethnic cleansing" whenever we discuss either region. One can argue convincingly that were it not for the destruction of Native nations in North America, there would have been no destruction of Palestine. The same is true of other colonial incursions: the British settlement of Australia, the French takeover of Algeria, the European scramble for Africa. Zionism, as a European phenomenon on philosophy and execution, was produced in a culture that conceptualized foreign settlement and population transfer as viable political solutions, especially where so-called "inferior" peoples were concerned. David Ben Gurion and other prominent Zionist leaders looked to the Euro-American conquest of Native lands as a source of inspiration.[40]

No credible theologian today would accept a land theology that served the interests of the Whites in South Africa, or North America, or Australia. Why would they accept it when it serves the interests of the modern state of Israel? Why is Israel's colonization of Palestine seen as unique, biblical, and different from all others? We can't be theologically naïve to talk about "the land" meaning Palestine without reflecting on the current usage of land ideology by Jewish colonial settlers. *No one* should be allowed—not Jewish settlers, nor Israeli politicians, nor naïve Christian theologians—to use "biblical rights" to violate "human rights." We should not allow for accusations of anti-Semitism and Western guilt over the Holocaust to avert our eyes from Israel's colonial policies.

It might be that the missionaries to the Americas in the 16th century were innocent, and it might be that Brueggemann in the late 1970s was naïve, but it is high time to end this theological innocence. We ought to confess that Christian theologians have been playing, consciously or subconsciously, a major role in aiding the ongoing colonization of Palestinian land and people. The land theology was one of the theological tools used for Palestinian dispossession and oppression. Christian theologians failed to see that the promised land is but the confiscated land. The occupation of the minds of too many Christian theologians with the Bible, their fear of being called anti-Semitic, and their guilty feelings about the Holocaust have covered up the continuous colonization of Palestine. In that sense, the liberation of the Palestinian people and the liberation of Christian theological minds are bound closely together.

NOTES

1. George E. Tinker, *Mission Conquest: The Gospel and Native American Cultural Genocide*. Minneapolis: Augsburg Fortress, 1993.
2. Tinker, 120.
3. Ibid., 15.
4. Bieberstein, Klaus, and Max Kuchler. "Jerusalem: Ein Handbuch Und Studienreisefuhrer Zur Heiligen Stadt." 2 edition. Göttingen: Vandenhoeck & Ruprecht, 2013, 149–51.
5. www.templemountfaithful.org
6. David S. New, *Holy War: The Rise of Militant Christian, Jewish, and Islamic Fundamentalism* (Jefferson, NC: McFarland & Co, 2002), 154.
7. New, 155.
8. Ibid.
9. Ibid.
10. Ibid., 160.

11. https://www.nytimes.com/2000/09/29/world/sharon-touches-a-nerve-and-jerusalem-explodes.html

12. Walter Brueggemann, *The Land*, Overtures to Biblical Theology (Philadelphia: Fortress Press, 1977), 1.

13. Ibid., 3.

14. Ibid., 2.

15. Ibid., xi.

16. Ibid., xiii–ix.

17. Walter Brueggemann, *Chosen?: Reading the Bible amid the Israeli-Palestinian Conflict*, First edition. (Louisville, KY: Westminster John Knox Press, 2015).

18. Ibid., ix–x.

19. Ibid., xiv.

20. Ibid., xiv.

21. For more on this confusion, see Philip R. Davies, *In Search of "Ancient Israel": A Study in Biblical Origins*, second edition (New York: T&T Clark, 2015). Ingrid Hjelm et al., eds., *A New Critical Approach to the History of Palestine: Palestine History and Heritage Project 1*, first edition (London; New York: Routledge, 2019). Andrew Mein and Claudia V. Camp, *History, Politics and the Bible from the Iron Age to the Media Age*, ed. James G. Crossley and Jim West, Reprint edition (T&T Clark, 2018).

22. Brueggemann, *Chosen?*, xvi.

23. Ibid., 37–38.

24. Ibid., x.

25. Ibid., 7.

26. Ibid., 28.

27. Ibid., 32.

28. https://www.jpost.com/Arab-Israeli-Conflict/Israel-defends-right-to-West-Bank-settlements-at-UNSC-watch-live-588178

29. Brueggemann, *Chosen?*, 8, 12.

30. See, for example, W. D. Davies, *The Territorial Dimension of Judaism*, 1st Fortress Press edition. (Minneapolis, MN: Fortress Press, 1991).

31. Stephen R. Haynes, "Christian Holocaust Theology: A Critical Reassessment," *Journal of the American Academy of Religion* 62, no. 2 (1994): 562.

32. Norman C. Habel, *The Land Is Mine: Six Biblical Land Ideologies*, Overtures to Biblical Theology. (Minneapolis, MN: Fortress Press, 1995), 10.

33. Norman C. Habel, *Acknowledgement of the Land and Faith of Aboriginal Custodians After Following the Abraham Trail* (Australia: Wipf and Stock, 2018).

34. Ibid., 7–8.

35. Ibid., 12.

36. Ibid., 14.

37. Ibid., 67.

38. Ibid., 42.

39. Ibid., 74.

40. Steven Salaita, *Holy Land in Transit: Colonialism and the Quest for Canaan* (Syracuse, NY: Syracuse University Press, 2006), 179.

BIBLIOGRAPHY

Brueggemann, Walter. *Chosen?: Reading the Bible amid the Israeli-Palestinian Conflict*. First edition. Louisville, KY: Westminster John Knox Press, 2015.

———. *The Land: Overtures to Biblical Theology*. Philadelphia, PA: Fortress Press, 1977.

———. *The Land: Place as Gift, Promise, and Challenge in Biblical Faith*. second edition. Minneapolis, MN: Fortress Press, 2002.

Davies, Philip R. *In Search of "Ancient Israel": A Study in Biblical Origins*. second edition. New York: T&T Clark, 2015.

Davies, W. D. *The Territorial Dimension of Judaism*. first Fortress Press edition. Minneapolis, MN: Fortress Press, 1991.

Habel, Norman C. *Acknowledgement of the Land and Faith of Aboriginal Custodians After Following the Abraham Trail*. Australia: Wipf and Stock, 2018.

———. *The Land Is Mine: Six Biblical Land Ideologies*. Overtures to Biblical Theology. Minneapolis, MN: Fortress Press, 1995.

Haynes, Stephen R. "Christian Holocaust Theology: A Critical Reassessment." *Journal of the American Academy of Religion* 62, no. 2 (1994): 553–85.

Küchler, Max. *Jerusalem: Ein Handbuch und Studienreiseführer zur Heiligen Stadt*. 2., vollständig überarbeitete Auflage. Göttingen: Vandenhoeck & Ruprecht, 2014.

New, David S. *Holy War: The Rise of Militant Christian, Jewish, and Islamic Fundamentalism*. Jefferson, NC: McFarland & Co, 2002.

Raheb, Mitri. *Faith in the Face of Empire: The Bible through Palestinian Eyes*. Maryknoll, NY: Orbis Books, 2014.

———. *The Biblical Text in the Context of Occupation: Towards a New Hermeneutics of Liberation*. Bethlehem: CreateSpace Independent Publishing Platform, 2012.

———. *The Invention of History: A Century of Interplay between Theology and Politics in Palestine*. Bethlehem: CreateSpace Independent Publishing Platform, 2011.

Salaita, Steven. *The Holy Land in Transit: Colonialism and the Quest for Canaan*. first edition. Middle East Studies beyond Dominant Paradigms. Syracuse, NY: Syracuse University Press, 2006.

Tinker, George E. *Missionary Conquest: The Gospel and Native American Cultural Genocide*. Minneapolis, MN: Fortress Press, 1993.

Part II
OCCUPYING BODIES

Chapter Six

The Construction of Religious Hybrid Identities

Resulting from Colonial Occupation

Wanda Deifelt

The focus of this chapter is religious pluralism in Latin America and the Caribbean.[1] The enslavement of indigenous and African peoples was carried out through colonialism, often using theological reasoning to justify occupation through a Christendom model. While Roman Catholicism remained the predominant—and in many cases still the official—religion in the continent, religious identities are much more plural and diverse. Religious practices stemming from indigenous communities and the African diaspora in Latin America and the Caribbean served as forms of resistance and means for survival to European colonialism and occupation. These religious practices are often subsumed under broader categories of cultural expression (as folklore) or obfuscated by dogmatic or doctrinal views which restrict the concept of religion to institutional manifestations. In doing so, the hybrid religious identities that result from the negotiation between dominant religion (in this case, Christianity) and indigenous and African matrices are ignored or reduced to a bi-product of the colonial enterprise. Their potential as resistance to occupation and critical voice to Christianity itself is lost if religious pluralism, interfaith dialogue, and the legitimacy of the religions stemming from indigenous and African matrices are not acknowledged.

THE REALITY OF COLONIALISM AND OCCUPATION

Colonialism is the practice and policy of exercising political, economic, and cultural control over other countries, expanding a nation's territory by occupying it with settlers, or extending a nation's domain over other peoples and lands. Colonialism is a relationship of domination of an indigenous majority by a minority of foreign occupiers in which the latter rule in pursuit of their interests.[2,3] Occupation is one modality of colonialism. Although the expansion of colonialism has been justified through trade opportunities, the reality of colonialism is the occupation of lands, people's bodies, and minds. Colonized people and lands are prevented from self-determination and autonomy. Some theorists claim that colonialism is/was the entry way to modernity (because of the exposure of indigenous populations to European culture), the reality is that colonialism imposes a way of life and thought that is foreign: It imposes religion, family and community structures, economics, medical practices, etc.

Because of its complexity, the definition of colonialism as historically situated (restricted) is often an oversimplification. It is widely accepted that once foreign occupation ceased, nations moved into a postcolonial stage. It can be argued that in postcolonialism, the political conquest and control of people's lands are restricted—albeit not completely overcome—but economic dependence, cultural imposition, and eventually an introjection of colonial mentality as one's own still remain. This complex reality has been named coloniality. Coloniality refers to the logic at the basis of historical colonialisms, related to the colonial matrix of power, or coloniality of power.[4] It could also be named *metacolonialism*, as suggested by Hussein A. Bulhan.[5]

Aníbal Quijano's work on decoloniality points out that, in Latin America, claims of religious and racial superiority served as justification for material exploitation, cultural domination, and European self-aggrandizement. At the basis of decoloniality is a critique of Eurocentrism, that is, that the history of human civilization culminates in Europe and that European superiority is due to biological differences between races, that is, as natural phenomena not related to histories of power.[6] As Quijano aptly observes, the colonial matrix of power produced and perpetuated multi-layered forms of discrimination (racial, ethnic, anthropological, or national).

> This process implied a violent concentration of the world's resources under the control and for the benefit of a small European minority—and above all, of its ruling classes. Although occasionally moderated when faced with the revolt of the dominated, this process has continued ever since. But, now during the current crisis, such concentration is being realized with a new impetus, in a way perhaps even more violent and on a much larger, global scale.[7]

Colonialism and coloniality come with violence. The occupation of land, people, and minds requires both physical force and ideological maneuvering in order to keep the colonized in check and prevent them from breaking away. Claiming natural superiority, colonizers asserted their power though conquest and warfare, but also by manipulating and preying on local/regional/intra-ethnic conflicts. Colonizing practices were enforced and reinforced theologically through notions such as "chosen people," "expansion of the Holy Roman Empire," "advancement of Christendom," or more recently "manifest destiny."

Hussein A. Bulham argues that colonialism engendered three cataclysmic assaults by use of maximum violence (including genocide):

> The first assault was on *the world of things*, particularly the land of conquered non-European peoples to exploit gold, silver, and other commodities. The second assault was on *the world of people* for obtaining free labor and carrying out sexual exploitation. The third assault was *the world of meaning* by changing indigenous religions, knowledge, and identities.[8]

The Transatlantic slave trade is an example of how the assault on the world of things, the world of people, and the world of meaning are interlocked. The violence of colonialism impinges on lands, peoples, and their psyche. The Transatlantic slave trade is the largest documented and systematic transplantation of people in history.[9] In the African context, the slave trade impoverished and depopulated the continent by stealing young and productive members of local communities. It is estimated that between 10 million and 13 million enslaved Africans were transported across the Atlantic Ocean to the Americas from the 16th to the 19th century.[10]

The enslavement of African peoples derailed the continent's economic development and dwarfed its political history. Economic incentives for tribes to engage in the slave trade promoted further violence. Depopulation and the fear of captivity affected agricultural development. It solidified the dominant-dominated relations between Europeans and indigenous populations (whether in the Americas or in Africa), based on a notion of natural superiority that feeds into racism. In this colonial arrangement, the Europeans were the ones who benefitted the most: slaves were shipped from Africa to the Americas, sugar and coffee from the Americas to Europe, and arms, textiles, and wine from Europe to Africa. The Portuguese were among the first to capitalize on this practice but were not the only ones.[11]

The Portuguese slave trade took advantage of a slave system that already existed in West Africa. John Thorton writes: "slavery was widespread and indigenous in African society, as was, naturally enough, a commerce in slaves."[12] His argument is that the slave trade should not be seen as external imposition, (an "impact") brought from the outside. It grew out of and was rationalized by the African societies who participated in it and had complete control over it until the slaves were loaded onto European ships for transfer to Atlantic societies.[13] The Portuguese position was that they trafficked people already in bondage, making the slave trade legal and justifiable within the accepted norms of the age. Thorton's observation, however, overlooks the reaction that the increased demand for slaves in the New World created. Yanking shackles in the Americas meant that more Africans were pulled into the chains of slavery in the African continent.

Colonizers differed in their modes of interaction with populations in colonized nations. While British colonialism did not allow for easy social or sexual contact with local peoples, the Portuguese and Spanish settled down in the lands they colonized, often adopted local manners and inter-married in a way the English derided. Ania Loomba notes that inter-marriages and concubinage eventually blurred racial distinctions and gave place to a population that acted as a base for colonial rule. While some commentators see the practice of inter-marriage as a "lack of racial feeling" by the Portuguese and Spanish, Loomba points out that "colour and race consciousness marked even the policy of co-habitation, and racial distinctions continued to inform the subsequent 'mixed' social order."[14] This is the trifecta of the transatlantic slave trade: the greed for material possession and consumption, an ideology of racial superiority vis-à-vis indigenous populations, and the sense of entitlement that furthering the borders of Christendom gave to the colonizers.

THEOLOGICAL ARGUMENTS FOR AND AGAINST ENSLAVEMENT

The debate at Valladolid (1550–1551) is described as the first ethical and theological debate, by colonizers, on the treatments of colonized people. At the core of the debate is the justification for the relation between Europeans and indigenous peoples—misnamed "Indians." Bartolomé de las Casas (a Dominican friar and bishop of Chiapas) argued that, in the natural order of creation, despite the practice of human sacrifice, the natives were free and deserving the same rights as the colonizers. Juan Ginés de Sepulveda (a Spanish Renaissance humanist, theologian, and philosopher) argued that cannibalism and the sacrifice of innocent people were crimes against nature and should be suppressed by any means possible, including war. The theme seems to be academic, but in reality, the debate was about the ways in which indigenous people were to be part of colonial life, their rights and obligations, and their conversion to Catholicism.[15]

Although both sides claim to have won, Las Casas entered history as a defender of the "Indians," even if there were others who did so before him.[16] Ironically, however, the indigenous population did not benefit in any tangible way from the debate.[17] Yes, Las Casas managed to keep the plight of the indigenous people at the center of attention, but the system of *encomienda* was not eradicated. Through the *encomienda,* indigenous workers were allocated to Spanish settlers on the understanding that they would be instructed in the Christian faith in return for their labor. In reality, however, *encomenderos* treated the indigenous as property and behaved as if they were slaves.

In its intellectual debate on the right to just war and conquest, Valladolid represents the use of European reasoning to decide the fate of indigenous peoples.[18] Natural law was used to justify slavery. As noted by Sepulveda,[19] "being slaves by nature, [the Indians], uncivilized, barbarian and inhuman, refuse to accept the rule of those civilized [the Spaniards] and with much more power than them."[20] The concept of natural superiority enabled colonial powers to wage war and enslave those deemed inferior and in need of intervention. Sepulveda's argument was largely based on Aristotle. He argued that, given their natural condition, the indigenous people were unable to govern themselves and the Spaniards had a duty to act as masters. Similarly, the Spaniards had the responsibility to prevent cannibalism and human sacrifice as crimes against nature. Above all, it was necessary to convert the natives to Christianity.[21]

Las Casas objected Sepulveda's argument that the barbaric nature of the indigenous people justified waging war against them. He argued that Aristotle's definition of barbarism and "natural slave"[22] did not apply to the natives in the Americas because they were capable of reason.[23] They should be brought to Christianity without force or coercion. At a meeting of the two disputants at Valladolid, in 1550, Las Casas defended that the indigenous kingdoms in Mesoamerica had many characteristics of the ideal state outlined by Aristotle. Hence, they were not barbarous or naturally servile but rational beings whose polities deserved to be compared with the great states of antiquity.[24]

Earlier, in 1516, Las Casas had suggested importing slaves from Africa in order to preserve the rapidly declining Taino population in the island of Hispaniola. His view was neither original nor isolated. It combined a defense of the indigenous people with a juridical and religious oversight that regarded the subjection of infidels to slavery as legitimate. He eventually regretted this position. In his *History of the Indies*, he included an apology for advocating African slavery by stating that he "repented and judged himself guilty of ignorance," coming to "realize that black slavery was as unjust as Indian slavery and was no remedy at all."[25] He pondered whether his ignorance and good faith would excuse him in the eyes of God.

The Iberian Peninsula had a long history of slavery, and African slaves were predominantly Berbers and Arabs from the North African coast, known as Moors to the Iberian. By the time Las Casas reached the Americas for the first time (in 1502), the Portuguese had been importing African slaves into Iberia for half a century. At first, they were typically enslaved during wars and conquests between Christian and Islamic kingdoms (during the

Reconquista), but in 1455 Pope Nicholas V had given Portugal the rights to expand their trade along the whole west coast of Africa, under the provision that they convert all people they enslaved. The juridical and religious argument for slavery was that the subjection of heathens was legitimate because the slaves would benefit from the guardianship of Christian lords.

Because slavery was commonplace in the Iberian peninsula and enslaved people were rarely used in agriculture or plantations (but fit into society as the Moorish slaves and, through conversion, absorbed into local society), some scholars paint a rather irenic picture of slavery in Portugal and Spain.[26] One author claims: "African slaves readily adopted the culture, language, and religion of their masters."[27] But in reality, slavery was never devoid of cruelty and violence.

The Atlantic slave trade disrupted African societies, families, and kin groups. Along the path, men, women, and children were imprisoned, separated, raped, and killed by war, famine, and disease. Enslaved bodies were treated as chattel, and that gave their masters the right over their sexuality and offsprings. The objectification of bodies, particularly that of indigenous and African women and girls, was ubiquitous also in the Iberian Peninsula. Already in 1563, at the Council of Trent, the Catholic church noted and critiqued widespread immorality, but this had little effect in the New World. This might explain the common Portuguese saying *"Não existe pecado do lado de baixo do Equador"* (there is no sin south of the Equator), which justified a rape culture in the past and continues to be downplayed by modern scholars as well:

> We must not forget that black and Indian women were greatly prized as objects of sexual desire. The children of such mixed-race unions were visible throughout Portugal, particularly in the south and in the Empire. As a result, in 1563, at the Council of Trent, the church strongly criticized widespread immorality. There was little change in attitudes, and little inclination from lonely young white males in Africa, Asia, and Brazil to resist Nature. In the Empire even the clergymen behaved badly and did not respect their sacred vows. How could they resist temptation with so many alluring primitive Eves about? Most men accused of fornication by the Jesuits had not one but many women.[28]

More than a religious endeavor, slavery was a commercial enterprise carried out under the veneer of furthering Christendom. Infante Dom Henrique of Portugal (also known as Prince Henry the Navigator) held the monopoly on all expeditions to Africa until his death in 1460. Afterward, any ship sailing for Africa required authorization from the crown. All slaves and goods brought back to Portugal were subject to duties and tariffs. As noted earlier, slavery was a common practice in the Iberian peninsula and beyond due to a shortage of laborers.[29] Even if it was more expensive to purchase a slave than it was to employ a freeman, the sparse population and the lack of free labor made the purchase of a slave a favorable capital investment.

Slaves were baptized before shipment and the condition for enslavement was their conversion. Magalhães argues that black slaves were in higher demand than Moorish slaves because they were easier to convert to Christianity (as opposed to the Muslim *conversos*, called *moriscos*) and less likely to escape. Black African slaves were expected to be more compliant. The Moors, even if Christianized, were always considered dangerous and potentially treacherous. Black African slaves, one the other hand, in spite of being deeply traumatized by the violence of their capture and removal to another completely different society, were described as presenting no particular difficulties in their integration.

> The increased trade began when the Portuguese first arrived in the black-populated lands to the south of the Sahara. In 1444 Prince Henry (known as the Navigator) introduced the sale of black Africans in Lagos (Algarve). His chronicler, Gomes Eanes de Zurara, described the cruelty of this market in a vivid chapter: families separated, children torn from their mothers, men parted from their women. But their suffering was depicted as nothing compared to the joy at their conversion to Christianity, because their souls were on the way to Salvation. As Joao de Barros wrote some decades later, Africa offered *"almas criadas na jnnocencia de seus primeiros padres, que cõ mansidã e obediencia metem o pescoço per fe e baptismo, de baxo do jugo Evangelico."* Obviously, to his mind, it was easier to convert animist peoples than Muslims.[30]

This idealistic description of slavery—where human beings meekly bow down to accept the yoke of Christianity and become model slaves—has been rightfully discredited in light of the numerous accounts of escapes and revolts. Christianity was not always unanimously accepted by indigenous peoples, and its imposition also resulted in movements of cultural and religious resistance and resilience (more about this in the portion about hybrid religious constructions). Nevertheless, it is necessary to acknowledge the lingering presence of this rhetoric also in academic settings in order to deconstruct it and to point out the fallacy of historical records written from the perspective of the colonizers.

HYBRID RELIGIOUS CONSTRUCTIONS

The type of Christianity brought to the Americas was far from uniform. John Lynch notes that the conquerors were familiar with a religion based on "vows, shrines, and miracles centered on local communities, and Catholic devotions of this kind were easily transplanted to America.[31] Similarly, the encounter between different systems of belief, tradition, and rituals was not uniform: "Spaniards preserved their religion without surrendering to cultural relativism, and Indians clung to reserves of their own culture without challenging Christian beliefs."[32] This diversity is particularly evident in popular religiosity but also in the religious expressions that found their unique voices in Latin America and the Caribbean.

From the beginning of colonialism, there was clearly a distinction between the practice of religion and the official discourse (dogmas and doctrines) of Catholicism. When Pedro Cortés y Larraz, the newly appointed archbishop of Guatemala, arrived in 1770, he recorded that the Catholicism practiced by the indigenous people had no resemblance to that familiar to him in Europe. He concluded that Christianity among the native population was an exterior display and lacked any foundation except love of music, fireworks, and ornament. He blamed the early missionaries for baptizing converts before properly instructing them and criticized clergy for being overindulgent. He wrote: "Even though some are persuaded that the Christian religion is well established among the Indians because of what they spend on churches and ornaments, this argument is very mistaken, since they use them for their own idolatry."[33] In his remark, the archbishop reveals the transformation Catholicism suffered in the New World.

The association between old and new gave religion a Latin American and Caribbean identity—and a diversity—not easily classified and not immediately recognizable. What results did these encounters entail? Is it fusion, acculturation, or syncretism? There are many words to express the effects of colonialism and occupation: *mestizage*, hybridity, creolization, in-betweenness, liminality, cross-over, diaspora, etc. Those whose land, bodies, and minds were occupied by colonizers juxtaposed the ideas and practices established by the colonizer with indigenous ideas and practices, reading them through their own interpretative lenses, and using what they had been taught to assert their own cultural identities.[34] Although colonial powers premised their efforts upon cultural and religious purity, the result was often hybridity.[35]

Sylvia R. Frey notes that the history of African Atlantic religions is "an epic story of continuous creation" because it is multilayered and moves through multiple transformations.[36] Several religions developed as a result of the transatlantic slave trade in Latin America, the Caribbean, and the United States. In Brazil, the most notable are Candomblé, Umbanda, Quimbanda, and Tambor de Mina. Santería, Cuban Vodú, and Palo (also known as Reglas de Congo), and Abakuá are well-known in Cuba. There is Dominican Vudú (Dominican Republic) and Haitian Vodou. Suriname has Winti and Guyana has Comfa. In Jamaica, there is Kumina and Obeah. Spiritual Baptist and Trinidad Orisha appear in Trinidad and Tobago. And the list goes on.

The main concern of the Catholic church was the salvation of souls. Slaves, therefore, were baptized immediately before transportation. There was no concern for their physical wellbeing. Only once, in 1562, did the high clergy complain about the conditions of slavery.[37] But despite the institutionalization of baptism, not all slaves converted. Many practiced Christianity outwardly but continued to draw from their own religious traditions through ritual, dances, prayers, honoring ancestors, or worshipping African deities. There were also similarities between Bantu religious practices and that of native peoples (particularly the use of herbs and plants). In Brazil, for instance, adherents of African based religions saw similarities between Catholic saints and *orishas* (a spiritual manifestation of Yoruba deities) in their own religion, and observance of Catholic practices enabled traditional systems to survive. Sacred symbols persisted though the figures of Catholic saints. African religious traditions such as national kingships or tribal chiefdoms—such as the *congada* (the symbolic coronation of the King of Congo)—were incorporated in the yearly festival of Our Lady of the Rosary, who became the patron saint of the African slaves.

Thorton argues that African and Christian beliefs had many important factors in common. Among them was a cosmology in which another world that cannot be seen requires revelations to make this otherworldliness intelligible and known. He defines the mixture of the African and Christian beliefs as "a form of Christianity in that its followers accepted as genuine a series of revelations in which various otherworldly beings, primarily saints that were recognized by Catholic Christians through their own tradition of revelations, now revealed themselves and were thus accorded status and worship by Africans."[38] Thorton also claims that this practice was not new in the Americas but happened already in Africa, as Christianity found its way in the continent. Acceptance of parts of Catholicism followed the practice of incorporating new elements into Central African religions, and they often began with a revelation (a dream or vision by a religious leader or ruler).

One of the most important institutions to propagate Christianity were lay groups called *irmandades*. Similar to the Portuguese, enslaved and formerly enslaved folk organized themselves into brotherhoods, confraternities, or mutual aid societies (known as *irmandades*). These voluntary associations of lay men and women were attached to churches, convents, and monasteries. In her research, Patricia A. Mulvey argues that 18th century urban slave confraternities were the only lay religious associations open to all people regardless of class, race, sex, or ethnic background—even if they met separately.[39] In colonial Brazil, there were separate lay associations for different races, although these racially suggested societies might parade together during religious festivals and share side altars in a common church. In was common that Afro-Brazilian brotherhoods congregated at the side altars of parish and other churches while the main seats were reserved for white Portuguese descendants. White confraternities also discriminated toward and excluded the poorer non-white population, so free blacks, mulattoes and slaves joined separate religious associations. These Catholic fraternities were an opportunity for enslaved and formerly enslaved people to meet.

The success of Catholicism seems to be confirmed by the creation of black fraternities and the edification of churches of their own. Joining a brotherhood, however, was not simply an accommodation to Catholicism. Among these brotherhoods, some tended to differentiate themselves according to tribal distinctions, language, social condition, and the extent of assimilation in Brazilian society. Such differentiation enabled the practice of African religions, including drumming, dances, and holding feasts on special religious days. Meeting in these fraternities was also a chance to plan rebellions and escapes.

> The brotherhoods of the rosary created a social space which the Africans utilized according to their own understanding of society. They used the brotherhoods as to move from marginality to incorporation into their new society, both vertically horizontally. They rearticulated the African community by creatively molding cultural icons into symbols familiar to them—again according to their own understanding of the world.[40]

This is the case with the Church of the Third Order of Our Lady of the Rosary of the Black People in the Pelourinho (in Salvador da Bahia, Brazil), an 18th century Roman Catholic church created by the brotherhood known as the *Irmandade de Nossa Senhora do Rósario dos Homens Pretos de Pelourinho*. Our Lady of the Rosary of Salvador was chartered in 1685, following similar orders established in Olinda (mid-sixteenth century), Rio de Janeiro (mid-seventeenth century), Recife (1654), and Belém do Pará (1682). Our Lady of the Rosary was the subject of particular devotion to slaves and freed people of African descent in colonial Brazil. The Church of the Third Order of Our Lady of the Rosary of the Black People started to be built in 1704, when the brotherhood had raised sufficient funds, but the construction was a slow process and continued for one hundred years.

CANDOMBLÉ AS EXAMPLE OF HYBRID RELIGION

In the diaspora, enslaved and formerly enslaved Africans refashioned their customs and religion as mode of survival. They asserted their culture as a contesting space that could offer refuge from the brutalities of enslavement. The religious expressions that resulted from the displacement caused by slavery provided support, healing, and protection. Religion served as a form of resistance against enslavement. Rachel E. Harding defines Candomblé this way:

> Candomblé is a rich and complex portico of ritual actions, cosmology, and meaning with deep and obvious roots in several religious traditions of West and West Central Africa—especially Yoruba, Aja-Fon, and Bantu. It is a (re)-creation of these traditions, and others, from within the matrix of slavery, colonialism, and mercantilism which characterized Brazil and other new societies of the western hemisphere from the sixteenth through the nineteenth centuries.[41]

One of the characteristics of Candomblé is the overlap between Roman Catholic saints and African *orishas*. It is an amalgamation of the religious ideas of the various West and Central African ethnic groups that arrived in Brazil and Roman Catholic practices. Given the fact that the Catholic church had feast days and celebrations for particular saints, these were also opportunities to honor African deities. Thus, for instance, Saint Barbara is associated with *Iansã*, from the Yoruba tradition, as the warrior who commands winds, storms, and lightning. She also controls the mysteries that surround the dead. The warrior *Ogum* is linked to Saint George, and *Iemanjá*, the sea goddess, is sometimes associated to the Virgin Mary. Millions of Brazilians flock to the seashore to bring offerings (such as flowers or champagne) every New Year's Eve, to appease *Iemanjá's* vanity and gain her favors.

Candomblé is headed by *mães/pais de santo*, priestesses and priests who are able to contact the *orixás*, the ancestral spirits. The *orishas* are usually identified with natural forces such as thunder, water, and the sea, and, during the ritual, participants present their offering depending on the domain of each *orisha* (such offerings include animals, plants, and minerals). *Olodumaré* is one all-powerful deity (similar to God, the creator) and is served by the other deities. One of the leading *orishas* is Oxalá, who is often identified with Jesus. In Salvador da Bahia, the church of *Bonfim* (*Nosso Senhor do Bonfim*) offers evidence of the overlap between Jesus and Oxalá. Worship occurs in the *terreiro* (temple and adjacent space and buildings) and includes drumming, singing, dancing, and spirit possession (when the *orishas* descend upon the initiated).

Candomblé was condemned by the Roman Catholic church and was violently persecuted. Nevertheless, "the drum ceremonies of the Nagôs, the Jejes, and to a lesser extent, the Hausas and various Angolan peoples, were the means by which the Afro-Brazilian identity was maintained amid the horrors of a slave society."[42] Only recently has Candomblé—and other religions stemming from indigenous and African matrices—been recognized. For many followers, Candomblé is not only a matter of religious belief, but also of reclaiming African culture, heritage, and history. Although the separate tribal identities have been obscured by peoples being mixed in communities during and after slavery, Candomblé has claimed the Yoruba tradition as its main root. In this sense, also the historical identity of ethnic Africans might be hybrid.

From its inception, colonialism had economic, political, cultural, psychological, and religious underpinnings. If its economic and political effects have been more obvious, it is perhaps the cultural, psychological, and religious aspects that present a counter narrative of resistance and resilience. While the transatlantic slave trade resulted in the movement of peoples and goods, it also created tastes, images, and ideas that challenged the colonial enterprise and its mentality of occupation. The legacy of enslavement is still tangible in racial and cultural stratification—and often in outright examples of racism. But the religious expressions stemming from African and indigenous matrices also present a counter-narrative, one of reliance and resistance. It is this ongoing adaptation, transformation, and reinvention of religious identities that makes them at once so fascinating and dynamic.

NOTES

1. Research for this chapter was carried out at the Stellenbosch Institute for Advanced Studies (STIAS) with the financial support of the Wallenberg Research Centre at Stellenbosch University, South Africa, in the first semester of 2019.

2. Lorenzo Veracini, *Settler Colonialism: A Theoretical Overview* (New York, NY: Palgrave Macmillan, 2010), 5.

3. See also the works of Edward Said, Gayatri Spivak, and Homi Bhabha.

4. Water Mignolo, *The Darker Side of Western Modernity: Global Futures, Decolonial Options* (Durham, NC: Duke University Press, 2011), 2.

5. "Metacolonialism revives an old system of colonial exploitation and oppression that masquerades in the more savory euphemism of globalization" (Bulhan 2015:244).

6. Aníbal Quijano and Michael Ennis, "Coloniality of Power, Eurocentrism, and Latin America." *Nepantla: Views from South* Vol. 1 No. 3 (2000), 542.

7. Aníbal Quijano, "Coloniality and Modernity/Rationality" in *Cultural Studies* Vol. 21, No. 2–3 (March/May 2007), 168.

8. Hussein A. Bulhan, "Stages of Colonialism in Africa: From Occupation of Land to Occupation of Being" in *Journal of Social and Political Psychology* Vol. 3, No. 1 (2015), 242.

9. I use the category of documented slavery to call attention to modern forms of slavery, which are largely not documented because they are illegal. According to research compiled by the International Labor Organization (ILO), more people are enslaved today than any other time in history: One in 200 people is enslaved. While there were around 13 million people captured and sold in the transatlantic slave

trade, today an estimated 40.3 million people are living under some form of slavery. See https://www.theguardian.com/news/2019/feb/25/modern-slavery-trafficking-persons-one-in-200?utm_term=RWRpdG9yaWFsX1VTTW9ybmluZ0JyaWVmaW5nLTE5MDIyNQ%3D%3D&utm_source=esp&utm_medium=Email&utm_campaign=USMorningBriefing&CMP=usbriefing_email.

10. https://www.britannica.com/topic/transatlantic-slave-trade

11. "By the 1480s, Portuguese ships were already transporting Africans for use as slaves on the sugar plantations in the Cape Verde and Madeira islands in the eastern Atlantic. Spanish conquistadors took African slaves to the Caribbean after 1502, but Portuguese merchants continued to dominate the transatlantic slave trade for another century and a half, operating from their bases in the Congo-Angola area along the west coast of Africa. The Dutch became the foremost slave traders during parts of the 1600s, and in the following century English and French merchants controlled about half of the transatlantic slave trade, taking a large percentage of their human cargo from the region of West Africa between the Sénégal and Niger rivers." See https://www.britannica.com/topic/transatlantic-slave-trade.

12. John Thornton, *Africa and Africans in the Making of the Atlantic World*, 2nd ed. (Cambridge: Cambridge University Press, 1998), 73.

13. Ibid, 94–96.

14. Ania Loomba, *Colonialism/Postcolonialism* (London/New York: Routledge, 1998), 110.

15. Lewis Hanke, *All Mankind is One: A study of the Disputation Between Bartolomé de Las Casas and Juan Ginés de Sepúlveda in 1550 on the Intellectual and Religious Capacity of the American Indian* (DeKalb, IL: Northern Illinois University Press, 1974), 67.

16. See, for instance, the words of Antonio de Montesinos (one of the first Dominicans to arrive in the island of Hispaniola) spoken in 1511: "I am the voice crying in the wilderness . . . the voice of Christ in the desert of this island . . . [saying that] you are all in mortal sin . . . on account of the cruelty and tyranny with which you use these innocent people. Are these not men? Have they not rational souls? Must not you love them as you love yourselves?" (Bakewell, 1997:83).

17. See the summary presented by John Lynch: "The arrival in Spain of Indian slaves brought by Columbus in 1495 caused moral confusion at court but eventually right reason prevailed and they were returned to their homeland in 1500. From then on royal policy insisted that the natives of the Indies, as vassals of the crown, could not be enslaved. But there were three exceptions. The Caribs were regarded as cannibals and propitious for slavery. Indian prisoners taken in a just war also qualified for slavery. And Indians already slaves of Indians and now bought or 'rescued' by Spaniards, *indios de rescate* as they were called, were also lawfully enslaved. Arguments among churchmen raged over the subject and although they attacked abuses and most of the exceptions in general they accepted the policy. Finally the Dominicans went to Rome for judgement and Paul III declared in the bull *Sublimis Deus* (2 June 1537) that Indians were human and could not be deprived of liberty or reduced to slavery, even if they were not Christians. In 1542 the Spanish crown prohibited slavery and ordered the liberation of those who had been enslaved. But realistically this was not the end

of the matter, for *encomenderos* treated their Indians as their property and behaved as though they were slaves" (2012:32).

18. The prolonged dispute at Valladolid shows how seriously the Spanish crown took its moral responsibilities in the Americas, but also how difficult it was to enforce the imperial will on colonists thousands of miles away.

19. Juan Ginés de Sepúlveda, *Tratado sobre las Justas Causas de la Guerra contra los Indios,* (Mexico DF: Fondo de Cultura Económica, 1941), 153.

20. The original is titled *Democrates alter sive de justi belli causis.*

21. For a detailed account of the use of Aristotle's philosophy in Sepulveda's argument, see Hanke, *Aristotle and the American Indians* (1959).

22. Aristotle argues in his *Politics* (Book I, section II, paragraph 7) that "one who is a human being belonging by nature not himself but to another is by nature a slave, and a person is a human being belonging to another if being a man he is an article of property, and an article of property is an instrument for action separate from its owner."

23. Hanke, *All Mankind is One*, 67.

24. G. L. Huxley, "Aristotle, Las Casas and the American Indians" in *Proceedings of the Royal Irish Academy. Section C: Archaeology, Celtic Studies, History, Linguistics, Literature* (80C 1980), 57–68.

25. Bartolomé de Las Casas, *History of the Indies* (New York, NY: Harper & Row, 1971), 257.

26. Here is a depiction of slavery in the Iberian peninsula: "How conscious was the boy Las Casas of African slaves in his hometown of Seville as he grew to manhood at the end of the 15th century? They may have numbered at least 10% of the population by the early 16th century. Notarial records from 1501 to 1525 indicate 5,271 slaves in Seville, and of these almost 4,000 were listed as blacks or mulattoes. They were certainly visible and accepted as a part of the local scene, working in urban industries, going to Church, forming part of the general population, not particularly deprived, oppressed, or stripped of much of their humanity as would occur in the plantations of the Americas by the 18th century. They were well acculturated into early modern Hispanic society and there was even a small but significant element of free blacks in the population, manumitted by either owners or having bought their way to freedom through Spain's slave codes. Numbers of Africans and their descendants in southern Spain worked in the maritime industries as well, some as sailors in the Atlantic commerce. It was this form of slavery that Las Casas was acquainted with when he suggested importing more slaves to the islands of the Caribbean in 1516." (Clayton 2009:1527).

27. Herbert Klien, *The Atlantic Slave Trade* (Cambridge, GB: Cambridge University Press, 1998) 13.

28. Joaquim Romero Magalhães, "Africans, Indians, and Slavery in Portugal" in *Portuguese Studies* 13 (1997), 149

29. Slavery was not new to Portugal or other Mediterranean societies at this time. The enslavement of Moors by Christians, or Christians by Moors, was common practice on both shores of the Mediterranean (Magalhães 1997:143–51).

30. The translation of the Portuguese poem: "souls created in the innocence of their first priests, who with meekness and obedience bow down their necks for faith and baptism, under the yoke of the Gospel."

31. John Lynch, *New Worlds: A Religious History of Latin America* (New Haven, CT: Yale University Press, 2012), 161–62.

32. Ibid, 162.

33. Ibid.

34. Ania Loomba, *Colonialism/Postcolonialism*, 174.

35. An example is the encounter between Christianity and Nahua tradition: "Louise Burkhart has studied the conceptual change from Nahua morals to Christian morals as an intense 'dialogue' on sin, purity, and pollution, virginity, incest, and other forms of behavior. Some of these concepts were more easily adaptable to Nahua (and by extension other indigenous) thought than others. Burkhart suggests that in the end, Christianity was 'Nahuatlized.' Because the friars appropriated the moral authority of the elders and took the upper hand in the definition of proper sexual behavior, the colonial indigenous moral world remained a slippery one. On the other hand, the persistence of pagan practices and their implicit moral meaning tainted the adoption of Christianity. In fact, through these underground practices some members of the group-maintained positions of power in their communities. However, by adopting Christian practices they could also gain power while transforming their understanding of gender, albeit not always in tandem with normative Christianity" (Lavrin 2011:132).

36. Sylvia R Frey, "Remembered Pasts: African Atlantic Religions" in *The Routledge History of Slavery*. Ed. by Gad Heuman and Trevor Burnard. (Abingdon: Routledge, 2011), 153.

37. Magalhães, "Africans, Indians, and Slavery in Portugal," 149

38. Thornton, *Africa and Africans*, 254.

39. Patricia A. Mulvey, "Slave Confraternities in Brazil: Their Role in Colonial Society" in *The Americas* Vol. 39, No. 1 (1982), 39–68.

40. Elizabeth W. Kiddy "Congados, Calunga, Candomblé: Our Lady of the Rosary in Minas Gerais, Brazil" in *Luso-Brazilian Review* Vol. 37, No. 1 (2000), 47–61.

41. Rachel E. Harding, *A Refuge in Thunder. Candomblé and Alternative Spaces of Blackness* (Bloomington, IN: Indiana University Press, 2000), xiii.

42. Joseph M. Murphy, *Working the Spirit: Ceremonies of the African Diaspora* (Boston: Beacon Press, 1994), 47.

BIBLIOGRAPHY

Aristotle. *Politics*. Cambridge, MA: Harvard University Press, 1944.

Bakewell, Peter. *A History of Latin America. Empires and Sequels 1450–1930*. Malden, MA: Blackwell Publishers Inc., 1997.

Bulhan, Hussein A. "Stages of Colonialism in Africa: From Occupation of Land to Occupation of Being." *Journal of Social and Political Psychology* Vol. 3, No. 1 (2015):239–56.

Clayton, Lawrence. "Bartolomé de Las Casas and the African Slave Trade." *History Compass* Vol 7, No. 6 (2009):1526–41.

de Sepúlveda, Juan Ginés. *Tratado sobre las Justas Causas de la Guerra contra los Indios*. Trans. by Marcelino Menendez y Pelayo and Manuel Garcia-Pelayo. Mexico DF: Fondo de Cultura Económica, 1941.

Frey, Sylvia R. "Remembered Pasts: African Atlantic Religions." *The Routledge History of Slavery*. Ed. by Gad Heuman and Trevor Burnard. Abingdon: Routledge, 2011.

Hanke, Lewis. *All Mankind is One: A study of the Disputation Between Bartolomé de Las Casas and Juan Ginés de Sepúlveda in 1550 on the Intellectual and Religious Capacity of the American Indian*. DeKalb, IL: Northern Illinois University Press, 1974.

———. *Aristotle and the American Indians; a Study in Race Prejudice in the Modern World*. London, GB: Hollis & Carter, 1959.

Harding, Rachel E. *A Refuge in Thunder. Candomblé and Alternative Spaces of Blackness*. Bloomington, IN: Indiana University Press, 2000.

Huxley, G. L. "Aristotle, Las Casas and the American Indians." *Proceedings of the Royal Irish Academy. Section C: Archaeology, Celtic Studies, History, Linguistics, Literature* 80C (1980):57–68.

Kiddy, Elizabeth W. "Congados, Calunga, Candomblé: Our Lady of the Rosary in Minas Gerais, Brazil." *Luso-Brazilian Review* Vol. 37, No. 1 (2000):47–61.

Klein, Herbert. *The Atlantic Slave Trade*. Cambridge, GB: Cambridge University Press, 1998.

Las Casas, Bartolomé de. *History of the Indies*. Trans. by Andrée Collard. New York, NY: Harper & Row, 1971.

Lavrin, Asunción. "Sexuality in Colonial Spanish America." *The Oxford Handbook of Latin American History*. New York, NY: Oxford University Press, 2011.

Loomba, Ania. *Colonialism/Postcolonialism*. London/New York: Routledge, 1998.

Lynch, John. *New Worlds: A Religious History of Latin America*. New Haven, CT: Yale University Press, 2012.

Magalhães, Joaquim Romero "Africans, Indians, and Slavery in Portugal," *Portuguese Studies* 13 (1997): 149.

Mignolo, Water. *The Darker Side of Western Modernity: Global Futures, Decolonial Options*. Durham, NC: Duke University Press, 2011.

Mulvey, Patricia A. "Slave Confraternities in Brazil: Their Role in Colonial Society." *The Americas* Vol. 39, No. 1 (1982):39–68.

Murphy, Joseph M. *Working the Spirit: Ceremonies of the African Diaspora*. Boston: Beacon Press, 1994.

Quijano, Aníbal. "Coloniality and Modernity/Rationality." *Cultural Studies* Vol. 21, No. 2–3 (March/May 2007):168–78.

Quijano, Anibal, and Michael Ennis. "Coloniality of Power, Eurocentrism, and Latin America." *Nepantla: Views from South* Vol. 1 No. 3, (2000):533–80.

Thornton, John. *Africa and Africans in the Making of the Atlantic World, 2nd ed.* Cambridge, GB: Cambridge University Press, 1998.

Veracini, Lorenzo. *Settler Colonialism: A Theoretical Overview*. New York, NY: Palgrave Macmillan, 2010.

Chapter Seven

The Boys in the Mirror

Luciano Kovacs

The clang of the metal structure erected on the imaginary line is deafening. The clamor in the surrounding area is provoking the military dogs into barking ferociously at the people shaking the barrier in their attempts to tear it down. Their aim is to pass through the border which has imprisoned them for the last fifteen months. Such a long time has elapsed between their arrival in the refugee camp and this day they had marked for action to bring about freedom. Dying in a flurry of bullets would be better, they had come to believe, than rotting in wet, dirty, and anonymous tents. This was the mantra that had circulated among the leaders of the planned operation.

Ahmed is looking toward the horizon, searching for the signal the older men had promised he would need to start running. They cautioned him not to expose himself to the attacks they might be subjected to by the police. The military had been patrolling the boundary religiously since the caravan had arrived in this God-forsaken no-man's land. No, he thinks, as soon as the phrase hits his brain; he should not use that word. God does not abandon any land. God is trapped in those barriers together with us, he keeps telling himself, while taking a swig from the bottle of water he has been able to grab from the infirmary where he was taken care of for a serious case of dysentery.

The rebellion had been brewing for a few weeks in the camp. He had caught wind of it on an evening when he stopped by the tent in which his friend Abdullah was staying with his family and had overheard a group of men and women talking by a fire. There was a sense of longing by the people who were temporarily living in this in-between place; it was a longing for a different destiny. To grab the bull by the horns and change the course of history for good or for bad.

The camp had been in a stew since the word had been going around that the governments on both sides of the border had come to an agreement to raid the camp, dismantle the tents, and detain all the people who had been in this limbo since the UN had set up this arrangement. The government. What a strange concept, thought Ahmed, as he imagined a few nondescript people (although he had pictured them all as short, chunky, bald men) waking up in the morning at the same time, having breakfast at the same time, taking a dump at the same time, driving through traffic at the same time, to reach a sumptuous palace where, at the same time, they would all make decisions that would impede him from crossing an imaginary line. One that birds fly over freely, lizards crawl under swiftly, and bullets pass through uncontrolled.

Ahmed was not his real name. That's what people called him in the camp. His real name was Leo. His father had insisted to his wife that they should name their first child after the Italian genius Leonardo Da Vinci. He had devoted his whole life studying Da Vinci as part of his scholarship at the university where he taught art history. That university is now rubble, as is the city his family had been living in for centuries. Leo's father was killed in an air raid, or was collateral damage, as the superpowers like to call it when locals fall victim to so-called liberating strikes.

They have "liberated" me from my family, Leo thinks sarcastically, as he crouches and hides behind a mound of dirt, waiting for the crowd to finish crushing the barbed-wire fence. The men in uniform have launched tear gas canisters to try and hold back what they see as a threatening attack. This land belongs to them, after all. Leo shoots a wicked glance to the soldiers. They must be just a little bit older than me, he thinks, as he imagines them in their pajamas at home, ruffled hair, their moms cooking their breakfast. He imagines them holding their coffee cups in the same hands they are now shooting people with, as they flee.

Why are we being met with fire instead of flowers? Leo asks himself as the scalding sun burns his skin and helicopters hover above his head. We should be welcomed into people's homes, put up in residential halls, treated like brothers and sisters who happened to be born in the underbelly of the planet! Instead, just thwack; rage kicks in, hatred suddenly creeps up, humans become ferocious beasts gone mad. Because if there are soldiers on the other side of the fence, young men ready to kill unknown people, steely glances frozen in the echo of stern orders, there must also be an underlying sense of ownership of what's considered sacred territory ruled from on high.

Those are Amira's words, uttered to him last night as they sipped hot tea by the fire. Amira was a student of Leo's father. One evening, at dinner, he had told his family about this student who had written an outstanding paper on the influence of Islamic art and culture on Venetian merchants. He wanted to have her over for dinner so that she could meet them, but the bombing had shattered that plan. As it had also shattered the future of the many students who had perished at the hands of the liberators. The same hands now throwing explosive devices to prevent them from entering a swath of land that does not differ that much from the area where Leo was born. Well, I don't know if these people are the same as us, he thinks, but certainly they are human like me. We tread the same Earth, we breathe the same air, we digest and evacuate food the same, and we look at the same Moon shining over any piece of land that God created. This makes Leo melancholy. Layers of feelings stack onto each other. He must not yield to his poetic inclination, he thinks, but steel himself to run as soon as the signal comes in to storm the fence.

Amira had not died in the raid because she had to go back to her village to bury her grandmother. Her grandma's death had prevented hers. But many of her fellow students did perish. Dreams ravaged by fire, futures annihilated by weapons that are worth mansions, bodies, minds, and relationships, interrupted by . . . by what? Leo is paralyzed by terrifying thoughts. What am I going to do once I cross that line? Who is going to be my family now that all of them are either a heap of ashes or skeletons being feasted upon by worms? What is in store for my future? The air is becoming thick with fumes. I don't want to panic, Leo thinks, as his eyes are burning and his heart pounding. His eyes are desperately darting around, looking for Amira. She is the only link left to his past. Will she be a vital piece of his uncertain future?

Leo starts thinking of boys and girls his age being pampered by their parents on the opposite side of that damn arbitrary line, ensconced in their classrooms as they stare with boredom into thin air. On a bus on which they commute to go to school. Walking leisurely in the streets without fear of shrapnel wounding their lily-white bodies. A pang of envy grabs Leo by the throat and makes him gasp for air. Air contaminated by the poison the soldiers are throwing at harmless, unarmed, terrified people fleeing for their lives. Then he shoos away his thoughts and removes from his satchel the object for which he would give his own life. His flute.

Leo remembers a video his mom took when he performed for the first time in front of an audience. He was six years old. His school had organized a concert for musically-talented kids and some of his classmates dabbled with a variety of instruments and ran through the notes they had learned by heart. They sounded good with what they had memorized. But Leo did not dabble. He bordered on being a flute genius, a musical prodigy.

In that video he was arrested in time, without fear. His mouth agape with wide eyes fixed on an imaginary spot behind the audience, he displayed sensitivity. Then, without seeming to take a breath, he started playing graciously, bringing a hush into the room. His virtuosity brought Beethoven back to life, incarnated in the sound filling the theater hall. Everyone was mesmerized by the divine perfection reverberating through the hall, feeding each person sitting there with the illusion that life would be as sweet as that sound. The pleasure his parents had derived from their son's performance had quelled their unstated but certainly shared fears that Leo would suffer in life. They took refuge in the vision that one day sweet Leo would be bringing down the music halls of the major capitals and be a world-famous flautist.

That vision now fades into the streaks of smoke polluting the camp. The gesture he had made when he finished his performance, by gently bringing down his arms after lifting his flute to the heavens, blends with the trembling of his hands firmly holding the instrument now as if it was an amulet for safe passage. In the heat of the moment, a desire comes over him to lie down, close his eyes, and abandon himself to any fate that could befall him. He would have liked to fall asleep and awaken in his bedroom, with his sheets tucked in by his mother and the voices of his family seeping through under the door. If he could do it through sheer will, he would be back on that truck where his brother had been dragged by the traffickers . . . for no reason: possibly because a word, an expression, a wink of his eye, had rubbed them the wrong way, and caused them to shoot to kill. If he could go back, he would defend his brother, clubbing those human traffickers with the flute if need be. He would be a butterfly up high and with the sound of his wings convince those who were about to drop a bomb on his father's school to stop. He would divert those who were making wrong-headed decisions in the halls of power, causing them to leave the room and grab a coffee instead, or make love to their spouses, or go get ice cream with their children. He would stop those who over the centuries had occupied his land, even let the refugees return to their crops and live under the gaze of the Sun, the Moon, and the whole firmament above.

A sudden sound of a drum shakes him from these dreams. The screams of a panicked rush startle him out of the numbness into which he had fallen. The deafening sound of firearms explodes in the air, making him realize that there is no turning back. He puts his flute back into his satchel, he runs his fingers through his hair as though he were readying himself for a normal day ahead, he taps his thighs to bless his legs for the feat ahead, and he lunges towards the unknown.

* * *

The bus has ground to a halt. Frederick gets off together with the rest of his fellow travelers. Most of them are senior high school students. Others have taken a break from their university courses. There are a few activists from organizations involved in advocacy work for migrant justice, a few freelance journalists, and a couple of faith-based organizers, including an operative from Mediterranean Hope, the Italian Waldensian Church's agency working with refugees and migrants.

Frederick's backpack is heavy on his shoulders. Although he can live for many days in a row without a change of clothes, he cannot stay away from his books and his guitar, which he has strapped onto his back. His mother had tried to dissuade him from taking this long journey. Exams are fast approaching and she was worried he would flunk them. Don't worry, I have no real desire to miss out on a school year, he had told her, in a muddle of hurried thoughts, before kissing her goodbye and closing the door behind him. But justice cannot wait either, he said with a hint of a smile as he rushed down the stairs of their house.

Frederick does not know if she heard him utter those last words. For many years, she had found herself divided between loyalty to her husband, a bigshot for a weapons manufacturer, and her precocious activist son who had repudiated his father at an early age for his role in killing innocent people around the world. His mother eventually divorced her husband, not so much for political convictions, but for the love of her son, which eventually superseded her marriage. The acrid atmosphere they lived in for many years of fierce battles between father and son did not allow for their survival as a family.

Fredrick's group is headed to the area where a few thousand people are relegated to a UN refugee tent camp in a no-man's land between two countries which politicians on both sides of the border want to get rid of for electoral gains. People escaping war and poverty have become a ball and chain for politicians who want to hold on to power. Profits over people is a long-held habit in politics, one that is shaking the continent to its core, thinks Frederick as he stares worriedly into space. His thoughts are immersed in the contradictions he has always felt over his citizenship. He firmly believes in the federation project of the EU as an antidote to fascism and xenophobic nationalism, but he is also aware that his privilege as a European stems from the history of pillage and exploitation the EU countries sit on. Besides, he knows that part of his upbringing and the privilege he enjoyed was entangled with the bloody hands of his weapons-exec father. Frederick knew that his father was inconsolable when he realized his child did not want to have anything to do with him anymore, but he saw this distress as nothing more than crocodile tears. To Frederick, the hours he spent rebuking his father for how he made a living were his way of escaping that reality. His arguments with his father were the result of an uneasy struggle to shake off the whole belief system he had been raised in so he could embark on a new path to make his life worth living.

At school he had his arguments with some of his classmates whose anti-immigrant rhetoric was a mirror of the wide-spread sentiments that were furiously engulfing the social discourse, the streets of small towns and in the cafes where young people cut their teeth in becoming involved citizens.

Now, Frederick's group is following a local member of a militant group that has taken great risks in feeding and helping migrants to cross the border. New laws have made it much more difficult for people to apply for asylum, and even the activists are often at a loss as to how to help people who want to start their lives anew. Frederick walks stealthily, as though it is he who must avoid the authorities in a confused search for a way out of a limbo status. Lisa, a friend from school, is strutting arrogantly beside him. She'd been ranting the whole bus ride about the lack of focus on the root causes of forced migration.

"It is almost like people believe the displacement of migrants is a rightful punishment, and not because they have had to flee situations that our society is partly responsible for," Lisa says reproachfully, as she quickens her pace and wipes her forehead sweating from the scorching sun.

"I know, Lisa," Frederick responds. "This was the theme of my speech at the student assembly the other day. The one interrupted by the neo-Nazi group who barged into the study room where we were holding our meeting." Frederick waves his hands as though they were unconsciously sliding upwards to impart a lesson to the heavens. For a moment, a large cloud gives a reprieve from the hot sun to the group, now moving slowly through the bushes dotting the hilly region in which the border rises out of history.

Some of the taller trees looming from afar announce the beginning of a forest, frowning from a distance over the fence aspiring to be a deciding factor on how animals and humans should roam about the land. Fredrick has recently read that parts of the wall already separating Mexico and the United States are not only illegitimately occupying a natural preserve that belongs to the whole planet Earth, as opposed to a specific nation-state, they are also creating an ecological crisis. Wilderness animals that freely wandered the desert on the border—as did Native American tribes, before there was an arbitrary line set by white people dividing countries—have their routes diverted by a scandalous metal wall, dropped into the middle of the desert by insane human design.

Fredrick peers over, raising his eyebrows as though his gaze could clamber over the walls that have been built all over the world to exclude other human beings from the astonishing bounties that nature intends freely for the whole world. His look flies high as an eagle ready to strike, anger an all-devouring desire. However, unlike the rapacious bird, once he's passed the pinnacle of the tallest fence, a sense of common destiny makes his swooning gentler. Fangs are smoothed into caressing tools. Talons into welcoming hands. Pointed beaks into smiles that tell a new story yet to be told.

Suddenly, the soldiers he sees from a distance are transformed. They assume his father's demeanor, his gloomy face, his accomplices' voices. The money they disbursed left and right seems to rise up and up and up, color the fences with an ominous, shining, golden, deceiving glow. Frederick's glance climbs up to see over the heights that these weapons people have constructed. Stray bullets pierce the sky, a deafening rumble fills up a bombed-out land, fumes engulf the surrounding forest, birds meet his stare while an inscrutable cloud of legs, feet, dirty shoes, bandaged limbs, emaciated looks, and hollowed eyes, rushes through the fence, now a pile of ashes, an illusion of the fateful, unnecessary, brutal instinct to protect what is deadly.

"Run, Lisa, run," says Fredrick with a flutter of excitement and fear. They seem to have arrived at a pivotal moment. The border flares up in flames; people are going to die. Here are those deemed by our fellow Europeans as the new invaders, thinks Frederick, as everything around him becomes blurry. Part of the effect the stampede has on him is a clear sense of being enveloped by impenetrable dark. A sooty cloud hangs over him. The crime these people were detained for was their victimhood. The legal charges that activists were handed down was their solidarity.

Here we are. Children of children of children of those who were occupied and were occupiers. We must pull through this darkness, thinks Fredrick, as he tries to disentangle himself from the imaginary metal net that has immobilized him. The invaders are the children of those whose lands were occupied by the fathers of those who feel invaded. Everything makes sense now. In this bloody field, beyond his books, his theories, his student assemblies.

A boy with a flute in his hands is running toward him. He is the only human figure he can make out in the indistinguishable mass of humanity. The boy stops. Fredrick looks at him. Both are struck by the resemblance they see in each other. It is like each is holding up a mirror for the other to see himself. Leo's eyebrows start twitching, then his thumping heartbeat slows down, only to start racing again, but this time not because of fear. Or because of the corpses he has leapt over, or the kilometers he has accumulated in his tired limbs. For the first time since he locked the door behind him that he might never open again, Leo can sit down and breathe.

The air is pure again. God assumes the gait of Leo's mother. The chains are broken. She can now walk free. Toward the lights she had no longer seen when her heart had stopped.

Leo takes out his flute and starts playing. The melody summons a rainbow, which suddenly arches over where the fence once stood. The memories of his parents and his brother now populate the land, no longer a battlefield, but a soft grass meadow where his family can lie down and rest.

His reflection with the guitar strapped on his back now starts singing, as though the tune coming from Leo's flute was also emanating from his own deepest core.

It is an ancient, mythical, universal tune.

> A redemptive song.
> For a new Eden.
> Full of color.
> Free of the clang of imaginary lines.

Part III

OCCUPYING SPIRIT

Chapter Eight

The Devil that Occupies US

Social Sin and Sacred Silence in a Trumped Era

Stacey M. Floyd-Thomas

To be sure, as my colleague Miguel A. De La Torre states, "Occupation of our minds is more insidious than the occupation of our lands." It occupies our bodies as well. When one considers the spate of unarmed shootings of innocent Black bodies in the United States within recent years, including the Charleston 9, along with the history of chattel slavery that has loomed large and manifested itself in lynchings, racial segregation, racial profiling, police brutality, the prison industrial complex, forced sterilization, and sex trafficking, it has been made poignantly clear, in the public square, that Black lives do not matter. Thus, we must seriously revisit William R. Jones's seminal question encapsulated in the title of his 1973 text, *Is God A White Racist?* Simply put, does occupation take up not only the power of this land, but divine power as well? This chapter, however, maintains that it is not God who is a white racist; in turn, it is white racists who posit themselves as God and their authority as both absolute and divine in nature. Therefore, the question of the 21st century is whether white supremacy has become God. This phenomenon of conflating white patriarchal supremacy with God and the divine is what I identify as "American eminence," another way of saying that white supremacy is the implicit, inherent and institutional occupation of the U.S., such that it exerts the power of God and the rule of law in a way that imperialism claims sovereignty that occupies not only the land, but also colonizes as its territory the blackened bodies that inhabit it.

"American eminence" is the exaltation of white domination materialized as divine authority through the conjoined power of law and civil religion. The force of white supremacy—in both its universal power and ubiquitous quality—lends itself to one singular categorical imperative, namely the control of the black body, be it as enslaved labor, menial low-wage workers, societal obsolescence, fodder for the prison industrial complex, or a repository for white supremacist sexual perversion. Beyond chronicling the genealogy and historiography of white supremacy, it is imperative that liberationist scholar-activists propose a pragmatic epistemology in keeping with human flourishing both as a statement and as a practice, thus reclaiming God and divine purpose and transcending white racist idolatry. Further, it is necessary to explore how to develop social interventions that disrupt these normative patterns of discrimination *and* facilitate the elimination of racially-based, gender biased societal structures and practices in order to facilitate critical pedagogy, moral leadership, legal practice, and social movement organizing.

The truth is that white supremacy has become a god in the United States, and acquiescing to this state of affairs has become our religion. To those who are religious among us, this sounds blasphemous, and to those who are secularists, this may sound ludicrous. Nevertheless, it is the functional definition of religion in contemporary American society and culture that I advance in this essay.

As I have stated in my previous work, *The Altars Where We Worship: The Religious Significance of Popular Culture*, "Though we claim to serve those things we deem sacred, in actuality things become sacred that serve us."[1] Racism, classism, and sexism are the veritable cornerstones of American success and given their essential role in our first world power, white supremacy is sacred in American culture and can be examined critically under the rubric of American eminence. This definition suggests that day-to-day realities dictate how we ultimately express and embrace our most primal commitments, regardless of our professed religious identification. As such, the ritual practices, sacred imagery and rhetoric, belief systems and moral framework help constitute many of the core commitments that inhabit our lives because they serve to express how we define meaning and the value of human life. Meanwhile, these essential commitments involving our deepest loyalties and most profound ideas about what is most highly valued and meaningful is in and of itself *religious* in nature.

Central to this functional definition of religion is a discussion of sacred commitments in an increasingly secular world in which the reality and meaningfulness of such commitments finally can be determined, expressed, and actualized only by the individuals and institutions that make them. Within the scholarly realm of religious studies and theology, our definition of "religion" takes into consideration perspectives of the religious believers and non-believers alike insofar as all people grapple with religion in terms of it being their "ultimate concern." Drawing insights from some of the most renowned thinkers and scholars of religion and culture such as Mircea Eliade, Paul Tillich, Sigmund Freud, Peter Berger, Karl Marx, and Michel Foucault we are reminded in various disciplinary contexts (history, theology, psychology, sociology, economics, and postmodern philosophy respectively), that this notion of the sacred is not defined concretely by religious commitments associated with mainline religious traditions, but rather by how those things akin to this form of sacrality operate in our daily mundane lives in discernibly "religious" ways. By this token, religion is no longer about the normative sacred rhetoric we attach to communities of faith and their related institutions, nor how we purportedly derive meaning from them. Rather, it is about "meaning-making," those things that actually end up providing the resources from which people gain meaningful understanding about themselves, others, and the world in which they live. Consequently, Americans often derive more meaning from altars found in the supposedly "secular" arena rather than those in traditionally sacred locations.

In the 1960s, religious scholar Ninian Smart examined the interaction between religion and human experience and concluded that all religion contains at least seven dimensions that make it "religious."[2] Smart's seven dimensions of religion (myth, doctrine, ritual, experience, institutions, ethics, and materiality), therefore, are not limited to religious traditions. Instead, they are pervasively characteristic of much that passes for what Robert Bellah calls "civil religion,"[3] or what I envision as popular culture *qua* religion.

More than traditional faith communities, major world religions, civil religion, and popular culture, to the extent that religious communities have engaged in significant ways with the myriad contemporary issues that shape social formation and transformation, no religion has been more impactful than white supremacy. Yet, the religious aspects of white supremacy that drive law and culture have hardly ever been given explicit consideration. My efforts are to examine the dimensions of religion as operative in American eminence, as it has had the most indelible impression upon social transformation, and our meting out of justice in order to provide a counternarrative of inclusive human flourishing.

It is vital that we expose connections between civil religion and legal practices, particularly in the service of white supremacy. In the name of justice, the founding fathers of Western philosophy have seized the epistemology of the philosopher-kings (i.e., Plato, Aristole) and the church fathers (i.e., Thomas Aquinas and Saint Augustine) in order to pervert notions of the good life and godly living for the purposes of imposing their will on both the text and texture of Black bodies and white souls. This grafting takes the form of racial dehumanization, sexual exploitation, and class stratification. Toward this end, white supremacy, through civil religion and law, have formed, sustained, and perpetuated the American social order as seamless and natural. This obfuscation of justice not only produces, but also reproduces the ways in which the original framers and thinkers transformed religious sentiments into policing policies that give patriotism and prosecution political weight and sacred meaning. Law and civil religion create the conditions under which religious fervor shrouds oppression.

The works from critical race theory, social ethics, liberation theology, and feminist/womanist thought help us to critically reflect on the religious, legal, and intellectual mileau out of which white supremacy saturate our understanding of normativity and patriotism. Such an intersectional analysis maps and critically examines the multiple trajectories along which the moral authority of the state is engendered by the convergence of racism, sexism, and classism under the guise of normality, social order, common good, and divine will. Further, they develop interventions that disrupt these normative patterns of discrimination and facilitate the elimination of racially-based, gender biased structures and practices in order to facilitate critical discourse, pedagogy, moral leadership, legal practice, and social movement organizing that lend themselves to a revisionist project of human flourishing.

A womanist ethical reading of literature from criminology, critical race theory, liberation ethics, and Black feminist/womanist thought exposes the religious, legal, and intellectual context out of which white supremacy, hypermasculinity, and economic exploitation pervade our understanding of normativity. It particularly maps and critically examines the multiple trajectories along which the moral authority of the state is engendered by the convergence of racism, sexism, and classism under the guise of normality, social order, common good, and the will of God.

There are four operations of the American eminence: *white immanence*, the domination of the black body for purposes of free labor and property; *eminent domain*, the reduction of the Black body to cheap labor; *imminent threat*, the recognition of the Black body as obsolete and fodder for the prison industrial complex; and *sexual imminence*, the utilization of the black body for purposes of sexual exploitation and the desires of white supremacy. After surveying these phenomena, we offer as the conclusion an epilogue that maps the necessary stages for immanent transcendence of white supremacy and an epistemological lexicon—presented as a glossary of theories employed throughout the text—that are both necessary for unpacking American eminence and embracing immanent transcendence.

THE PRE-OCCUPATION: AMERICAN EMINENCE

The first landmark of American eminence is the development of "the ontology of whiteness" and the blackness that it creates as the primary marker of the Western world. Thus, we need a framework for understanding the complex series of psychological and ideological mechanisms that reinforce white supremacy. This conceptual approach entails examining the blackness that whiteness created by bearing witness to: (1) the permanent role of white supremacy in defining how whiteness not only creates blackness, but also creates a perpetual cycle of power with the joined forces of civil religion and law; (2) the normalization and pervasiveness of race as a marker for classifying citizens along a continuum of honorary whiteness or dishonorable blackness; (3) the invisibility of whiteness as privilege and hypervisibility of white victimization; and (4) the relationship between epistemologies of oppression and the oppressed.

ACT 1: WHITE IMMANENCE

This first region of American eminence is white immanence, which is the way in which philosophical and metaphysical theories endow white supremacist social order with a divine presence, giving the white body the power to own and the black body the plight of being owned. Merging the central argument of critical race theorist Cheryl Harris's groundbreaking essay "Whiteness as Property"[4] and philosopher Pierre Bourdieu's notion of "cultural capital,"[5] it is critical to focus on how the enslavement and disenfranchisement of Blacks, upholds Blacks themselves as a form of American capital used at the dispensation of white profit.

Highlighting two seminal cases, *Dred Scott v. Sandford*[6] and *United States v. Amy*,[7] we may note three simultaneous functions: First, the courts mark enslaved Blacks as the property of their masters for purposes of exploitation. The courts do not recognize Blacks as persons, they have no agency, and they have no access to the courts for purposes of protection or vindication. Second, when enslaved Blacks, however, are viewed as engaging in crime, they do have agency inasmuch as they are viewed as accountable for their crimes for purposes of punishment, leaving their masters free from responsibility. Their masters are not culpable and Blacks' agency is fully theirs for purposes of criminalization. Third, although the courts can recognize Black persons for purposes of criminalization and can exercise jurisdiction over them for that purpose, Blacks have no claim to a vindication, and/or redress in the courts. Given these functions, blackness remains a capital and whiteness is concretized by the right to own property and the entire schema operates as a social relation that the law cements. Consequently, Blacks were pervasively owned as property and criminalized as persons. This particular social formation of cultural capital serves as the perennial social relation within a system of exchange that insists that the accumulation of property, the cultural knowledge, and legal fitness to uphold it, confers power and status to whites who alone are citizens, leaving Blacks with one alternative masquerading as two: to be property or to be criminal, the latter functioning to make Black people property again.

ACT 2: EMINENT DOMAIN

In a strict legal sense, eminent domain is the critical act of occupation by force—the very taking of private property for public use. However, I use the term eminent domain as a metaphor for explaining how American eminence not only has the power of immanence, the right to possess bodies, and pass judgment, but also eminent domain or the ability to usurp space. If whiteness is a kind of property or asset (i.e., real property, money), that has a monetary worth, then one of the ways of protecting that property or asset is to keep people of color in their place, in their own neighborhoods, to segregate them, and exclude them. Therefore, where whites can no longer own the black body through enslavement, white supremacy turns its emphasis on marking the boundaries of space as the exclusive domain of whites. Thus, white supremacy retains its power through exclusionary authority.

American eminence gives whiteness not only the power and freedom of social mobility, but also the power to claim openness, infinity, and unrestricted space as exclusively its own. Space is marked off and defended against anyone outside the realm of whiteness. As geographer Yi-Fu Tuan makes clear, "spaces" become "places" wherein the people who inhabit them are valued and are empowered because these designated spaces are where their biological needs, social desires, and political authority are satisfied, while they have simultaneously have the authority to exclude all others, making it their place and theirs alone (1977:3). The inhabitants of these raced, classed, engendered, and sexed demarcated places have exclusive privileges to access them and impose boundaries to exclude all others. What begins as space becomes place as white supremacy endows it with its value and solidifies its borders as exclusive. The ability to make a place out of space is essential to American eminence because it becomes both the expectation and experience of American existence. This is so clear that it becomes the popular ontology of children's rhymes: "*If you're white you're right, If you're brown, stick around, if you're yellow, you're mellow, but if you're black, get back!*"[8]

This act of eminent domain marks both space and place as a way to reify white superiority and sovereignty. White supremacy becomes the organizing principle that literally structures and orders its entire universe such that those who do not affirm its demarcations are considered bodies out of place. Philosopher and cultural critic Cornel West's notion of the "normative gaze" (1982), and historian and sociologist W. E. B. Du Bois' concept of "double-consciousness,"[9] illustrate how the critical cultural approach to the white production of place is key to the project of American eminence. Black bodies are subjected to a set of discourses among white philosophers that define the supposed nature of Blacks as irredeemably deficient, inferior, and animalistic. Inasmuch as Blacks were liberated from the mark of slavery of their bodies, whites continued to control their liberty, freedom, and mobility by confining them to highly specific places—literally drawing lines around their space and ensuring that those places were deficient, inferior, and animalistic. *Plessy v. Ferguson* paradigmatically exemplifies this process of eminent domain by literally drawing lines of what is black and what is white space while maintaining that this Jim Crow tactic was nevertheless "separate but equal." While *Brown v. Board of Education* was an attempt to take down the lines of separation and dismantle the power of eminent domain, it nonetheless kept separation in tact by allowing the line to open long enough to allow the honorary entry of a few although it was still understood as entitled white space. *Bakke v. California* drove this point home as white protest mounted across the country in claiming that Black admission into what was predominately white institutions was viewed as reverse racism by whites who claimed that deficient Blacks took the place to which they were entitled. Thus, in spaces where Black bodies entered into what was regarded as a white place, Blackness was held in contempt and considered trespassing, overruling remedial Affirmative Action efforts of desegregation.

ACT 3: IMMINENT THREAT

The third act of American eminence insists that not only are Blacks inferior and deficient, but that Black bodies themselves epitomize the symbol of danger and suspicion. As a result of this ingrained prejudice, they must be controlled no longer through chattel slavery, Jim/Jane Crow segregation, but now it is the school-to-prison pipeline. Concretely, the existence of the Black body in any space poses an imminent threat of harm to the security and safety of white citizens. This logic ensues that where Black bodies are present, dangerous, and deleterious behavior lurks. Legal scholar Ian Haney Lopez notes that liberal and conservative politicians have often cherry picked provocative stereotypical cases that profile Black people as posing imminent threat in what he terms "racial demagoguery" (2014: 35). Highlighting these individual incidents as an accurate understanding of all Black people as muggers, murderers, ghetto rioters, rapists, and welfare queens without using explicit racial language serves as a dog whistle appeal that births and nurtures in the minds of white Americans an enduring relationship of Blacks with crime, lawlessness, and danger. What is used in electoral politics is carried over into daily social life wherein, for the Black individuals their lives are in danger because of the racial demagoguery that has been attached to their very existence. Daily activities become criminal acts: Driving becomes drug smuggling or carjacking; walking becomes trespassing or loitering (Trayvon Martin); playing loud music becomes disturbing the peace (Jordan Davis); talking to the nation from the well of Congress during the annual State of the Union address becomes lying (President Barack Obama); grocery shopping becomes shoplifting (Forrest Whitaker); entering your own home becomes burglary (Henry Louis Gates); gathering and assembling becomes a group of people who must be dealt with (Charleston 9); and reaching for a driver's license, after being ordered to do so by a police officer, becomes reaching for a weapon (Levar Jones).

The prevailing demonization of Blacks which depicts them as posing imminent threats provides the impetus for Americans of all backgrounds to racially profile, police to use excessive force, schools to target at risk youth for imprisonment, and courts to sentence, imprison, and, at times, mete out the death penalty to Black defendants accused of taking or violating white life. Thus, imminent threat operates as the divine authority that can discern the evil, coerce confession, prophesy imprisonment and render the final judgment of life or death over black bodies. In turn, Black people become endangered in that human flourishing is annihilated and their agency is arrested such that they are often forced to make what we call "death-dealings," by accepting this lot as their penultimate condition which often results in: confessing to crimes they did not commit (*Central Park Exonerated 5*); becoming entangled in a cycle of incarceration without adequate substantive and procedural protections via the school-to-prison pipeline (*B.H. et al. v. City of New York et al.*); being victimized in interracial crimes where law enforcement sees no humans involved (NHI); or being disproportionately sentenced where there is a white victim (*McClesky v. Kemp*).

In light of these examples, we can understand the various ways in which imminent threat politics bleed over into policing and the criminal justice system generally, as evidenced in *Tennessee v. Garner, Mississippi v. Brown,* and *McClesky v. Kemp*. Taken together, this phenomenon of American eminence can be viewed as legal precedent that provides for an unspoken, yet shared assumption, about the racial demagoguery of Blacks as the permanence of racism that has death-dealing consequences for Blacks interracially, intracommunally, and introspectively.

ACT 4: SEXUAL DESIRE IMMANENCE

As the fourth and final act of American eminence, the occupation of whiteness maps the boundless accessibility of Black bodies for the imminent sexual desire of white supremacy. The cumulative effects of slavery, segregation, and demagoguery stereotypes of Black people are most poignant in the state sanctioned sexual violence and subsequent social denial of Black people's bodily autonomy. During enslavement, Black bodies were owned so the slave master's commonplace sexual assault on enslaved Black women (often in with the knowledge of or in the presence of their "husbands") was not considered rape. This practice carried over into the era of segregation wherein a white man could rape a Black woman with little fear of legal or social recourse, because of the fact that Black women were still considered unrapable. Nevertheless, a Black man often could and would be lynched if he allegedly spoke to a white woman in a manner that was deemed sexually suggestive (Emmet Till). In like fashion, Black men were often killed for the projected sexually deviant thoughts of white people. Moreover, attached to the state sanctioned rape of Black women was also the persistent state of apprehension and violation of Black men who were often fondled, stripped searched, and/or penetrated as racially profiled policing (Abner Louima). This collusion of sexual assault, racism, and state-sanctioned violence exposes the sexually imminent desires of American eminence and the ways in which it intimately affected Black women's lives, due to the combined forces of racial, misogynist and economic disparities.

This final act culminates in the intersectional axis of divinely sanctioned male aggression and Black denigration, as black bodies are the perpetual and unprotected repository for violent male sexual performance. In a very real sense, sex trafficking, gang rape, and bodily disposal of Black women are the hypermasculine gender performances of male bonding and commonplace fraternization in which men violate and often exchange Black women in order to forge alliances among themselves and to prove their manliness. Even further, the triple jeopardy of racism, classism, and sexism leave Black women particularly vulnerable for several reasons. First, they are viewed as unrapable because they do not reflect the feminine ideal of virtue (exclusively the domain of white women). Secondly, they are considered lewd and licentious in their own right and thereby soliciting risky sexual activity (typically considered the disposition of Black people). Lastly, they often are relegated to making profit through the only goods they have to trade on the open market (the generalization of the poor who have to "work" their bodies to make money). Here, imminent sexual desire demonstrates how American eminence empowers men as superior in a social system that grants them both a material and psychic sense of mastery over Black women as well as an immediate apprehension of their power and release of their masculine angst.

Here we can deconstruct how law and religion collude to make the Black female body the canvass for and prone to male performance, which inherently demands violence. As demonstrated in *New York v. Strauss Kahn*, the very locale where Black women should seek protection and vindication, the court system, becomes the legal process by which Black female victims are tried as perpetrators and trespassers against white male innocence. The sum total relegates Black women to a constant state of being prone and vulnerable to white male dominance, exploitation, and aggression without recourse legally or politically.

SALVIFIC ACT: IMMANENT TRANSCENDENCE

As a counternarrative to American eminence, I offer a closing argument for human flourishing and the resurrection of justice not only for Black people, but for all whose development has been arrested and distorted due to the illusory trappings of the social construction and spiritual sanctioning of white supremacy. Herein, it is necessary to make real an alleged intention toward equality in both the practice and reality of human flourishing. Rather than engaging in a Hammurabian code of justice or reverse discrimination and, thereby, exacting a role reversal where the oppressed becomes privileged and the privileged becomes oppressed or merely dismantling the "master's house with the master's tools," we are engaged in the construction of new foundations grounded in the human flourishing as an expansionist enterprise to achieve a great awakening of justice.

This epilogue illustrates that the power of law and religion and the promise of American equality is not merely corrupt, but has transformative power when divine justice is linked to social justice. Thus, our interdisciplinary work must see difference as an asset, not a deficiency or grounds for hierarchical degradation. We must understand that deconstruction necessitates reconstruction and that the two go hand in hand. Justice is a sacred right of everyone and thus, it cannot stand outside the law. When justice lies only in the hands of a few, its power is limited. Our work must be restorative and rehabilitative, and resurrect God who is the good in all of us and dictates that we must face and defy the devil within US in order to deliver us from evil.

NOTES

1. Juan Floyd-Thomas, Stacey Floyd-Thomas and Mark Toulouse, *The Altars Where We Worship: The Religious Significance of American Culture* (Louisville, KY: Presbyterian Publishers, 2016), 2.

2. Ninian Smart, *The Religious Experience of Mankind, 2nd Edition* (New York: Scribner's, 1976).

3. Robert Bellah, "Civil Religion in America" in *Journal of the American Academy of Arts and Sciences* Vol. 96, No. 1 (Winter 1967) 1–21.
4. Cheryl Harris, "Whiteness as Property," *Harvard Law Review* Vol. 106, No. 8 (June 1993): 1707–91.
5. Pierre Bourdieu, "The Forms of Capital" in *Handbook of Theory and Research for the Sociology of Education.* Ed. by J.G. Richardson (New York: Greenwood Press, 1986).
6. While the name of the Supreme Court case is *Scott v. Sandford*, the respondent's surname was actually "Sanford." A clerk misspelled the name, and the court never corrected the error (Vishneski 1988:373–90).
7. United States v. Amy. https://law.resource.org/pub/us/case/reporter/F.Cas/0024.f . . . /0024.f.cas.0792.2.pdf
8. Lyrics originally appeared in Big Bill Broonzy, "Black, Brown and White" recorded in Paris, September 20, 1951; published and released on February 22, 2000 by Smithsonian Folkway on the album: *Trouble in Mind.*
9. W. E. B. DuBois, *Souls of Black Folk* (New York: Vintage Books, 1903), 8–9.

BIBLIOGRAPHY

Bellah, Robert. "Civil Religion in America." *Journal of the American Academy of Arts and Sciences* Vol. 96, No. 1 (Winter 1967): 1–21.

Bourdieu, Pierre. "The Forms of Capital." *Handbook of Theory and Research for the Sociology of Education.* Ed. by J.G. Richardson. New York: Greenwood Press, 1986.

DuBois, W. E. B. *Souls of Black Folk.* New York: Vintage Books, 1903.

Floyd-Thomas, Juan, Stacey Floyd-Thomas, and Mark Toulouse. *The Altars Where We Worship: The Religious Significance of American Culture.* Louisville, KY: Presbyterian Publishers, 2016.

Haney Lopez, Ian. "How Coded Racial Appeals Reinvented Racism and Wrecked the Middle Class." New York: Oxford Press, 2014.

Harris, Cheryl. "Whiteness as Property." *Harvard Law Review* Vol. 106, No. 8 (June 1993): 1707–91.

Jones, William R. *Is God A White Racist?: A Preamble to Black Theology.* Garden City, NY: Anchor Press, 1973.

Smart, Ninian. *The Religious Experience of Mankind,* 2nd Edition. New York: Scribner's, 1976.

Vishneski, John. "What the Court Decided in Dred Scott v. Sandford." *The American Journal of Legal History.* Vol. 32, No. 4 (1988): 73–390.

West, Cornel. *Prophesy Deliverance!: An Afro-American Revolutionary Christianity.* Louisville, KY: Westminster John Knox Press, 1982.

Yi-Fu Tuan. "Space and Place. The Perspective of Experience. Minneapolis: University of Minnesota Press, 2001 [1977].

Chapter Nine

The Motherly Spirit

A Geotheological Power of Life in Papua

Toar Hutagalung

INTRODUCTION

The Motherly Spirit should be our theological concern in understanding our presence in the midst of the living and the non-living on earth.[1] To pursue this direction, I strive to offer a geotheology as pneumatological discernment.[2] My attention as an Indonesian is drawn to the context of Papua. The violence in Papua "territory" has been wounding not only the Papuan people and the lands, but also ourselves and the Spirit of God. To reach this conclusion, it is important to expose the occupying power in geopolitical and geological concern, which have become a sort of governmentality *à la* Foucault. I use Rifkin's analysis to expose the governmentality, which I address later as onto/geontopower as explained by Povinelli and Massumi. Then, to construct my pneumatology with this Nonlife focus, I use the idea of animacy as the act of the Spirit in animating things, as well as Papuan spirituality on land/mountain as mother. I hope the Motherly Spirit as geotheology becomes a counter-power against the violent acts toward the Life in Papua. Thus, I will begin with the occupying structures of power: colonialism, racism, and mining.

COLONIALISM

The effect of colonization in Papua can be seen in the history of treating Papua and Papuan people as objects without agency. During the pre-independence discussions, Indonesians debated whether to include Papua in their independence bid or not without any representative from Papua itself.[3] During the post-independence era, the colonizing Dutch argued that Papuans were not ready yet to speak on behalf of themselves.[4] They claimed that

Papuans were naïve and infantile, and that the Papuan children still needed their Dutch father for the process of independence. Arguments continued as the Indonesian government claimed the Dutch were trying to divide the country by creating a separate Papuan state,[5] while the Dutch argued that Papua had different ethnicities and cultures than the Indonesian majority.[6] In other words, the Papuans' agency was overlooked and suppressed in determining their own future.

Despite these suppressions, on December 1, 1961, Papuans raised their national flag, the *Bintang Kejora* (Morning Star), with "Hai Tanahku Papua" (Hi Papua My Land) sung as the national anthem. This marked their "Independence Day." After the fall of Soeharto, many Papuans gathered in Imbi Square, raised the flag and held a thanksgiving service on December 1, 2000 to celebrate the day, including Theys Eluay, one of the Papuan leaders from *Presidium Dewan Papua* (Papuan Presidium Council). In 2001, there was no more celebration, since Eluay was murdered three weeks earlier.[7] Nevertheless, the year 1961 marked a decolonization agenda that is still living in the Papuans. Singing the anthem and raising the flag has become their method of resistance.[8] In fact, when the flag was flown on December 1, 2000, an unknown person wrote on the flag: "Whoever pulls the flag down by force will be damned by God."[9]

During the 2000s, because of the proximity of the churches to the people, the Indonesian government officials tended to be suspicious about the relation of the churches to the OPM (*Organisasi Papua Merdeka*/Free Papua Movement). The military suspected that the OPM was supported by the churches that received money from the international community.[10] In 2013, the Papuans founded a Melanesian Spearhead Group as a way to reconstruct their political identity to be culturally affiliated with Melanesia instead of Indonesia. However, this led to the arrest of around 482 Papuans by the police in the year of 2015.[11] In this way, the Life of the Papuans has been withheld by the power of Indonesian government.

Transmigration, Religious and Economic Conflict, and Settler Colonialism

From 1964 to 1999, the Indonesian government facilitated so-called "official transmigrations," to move people, the majority of them Muslim, from Java island to Papua.[12] Because it was official, the government grabbed the Papuans' lands to be distributed to the transmigrants as their new place to settle. This caused tensions and violent clashes between the locals and the settlers. Furthermore, Hermawan notes that the opportunities to get into job markets and in economic areas were higher for the non-Papuan settlers.[13]

Many new migrants to Papua were Muslim, in part leading to religious conflict among the population. Soekarno himself decided to build a large mosque in predominantly "Christian" area in Biak. In other villages, many Christian Papuans became Muslims. The motive behind these conversions was questioned, because being a Muslim allegedly had some material benefits and privileges, especially from the government. A pastor from this area mentioned that many Papuan children wanted to go to schools organized by Muslim officials, because they provided funding.[14] These economic factors made a deep impact on religious tension between Christians and Muslims. According to censuses taken between 1964 and 2004, there was a dramatic jump in the number of Muslim transmigrants to Papua, especially between 1975 and 1985. Around eight percent growth happened during the time when government-sponsored transmigration was in full swing.[15] The rise of fundamentalist groups from both sides, combined with interventions from people from outside Papua in the name of "solidarity," had worsened interfaith relations.[16] This religious conflict became a bumper for the government, as they were not noticed as the ones who sponsored the transmigration while benefitting from it by extending their power through decentralization.

I am indebted to how Mark Rifkin explained the involvement of the government by designating "nature" as an indigenous territory in his analysis on *Walden* by Thoreau. In this way, Native sovereignty over their own land was *derealized* into a concept of "wilderness." In other words, to claim the sovereignty of the Natives over their own land, the US government made the land into a "territory," which meant the land was then under the definition of US territoriality. Consequently, this caused the nonnative settlers to clash with the local American Indians by grabbing the land.[17] The legitimation of living as a transmigrant in Papua was based on the claim of Papua as Indonesian territory. Consequently, the settlers felt they had the same rights as the locals to have their own land to live, because it was legitimized by the law. The arrival of new settlers became a problem for the locals ethnically, religiously, and politically, as well as "legally." Yet, this entry of the transmigrants was used politically by the Indonesian government to extend its grip of power.

RACISM

The problem of racism is deeply embedded in Papua. During Dutch colonialism, Papuans felt they were treated as primitive by the Westerners because of their black skin. They felt they had been despised and treated as savages.[18] In the US, the death of Michael Rockefeller, son of New York governor, Nelson Rockefeller, during his trip to Papua, deepened the image of "hopelessly exotic, hostile, and primitive" Papua.[19] However, the idea of Papua as primitive was also supported by Indonesia.

The Papuans were called *terasing/terbelakang* (alien/backward tribes). The Indonesian government believed that after liberating them from colonialism, "the next step was to liberate them from backwardness." Indonesia's policy, in the words of Foreign Minister Subandrio, was to "get them down out of the trees, even if we have to pull them down."[20] Many Papuans felt they were treated like a *binatang* (animal), "as being dumb and not able to speak good Malay (Indonesian) by their Indonesian teachers. Papuans who had obtained positions in the administration felt that they were kept in the lower positions by Indonesian officials, who regarded them as incapable of being anything else."[21]

Racism and discrimination also happened by forcing the Papuans to wear clothes. It was called *Operasi Busana* (Operation of Fashion). For the government, wearing clothes signified being educated and progressive.[22] The racism was also present in sport. Because they were considered *bodoh* (stupid), many Papuans were directed to invest their life mostly in sport.[23] It is as if sport only needs muscles, not intelligence. Speaking about this modernism force, I want to point out the analysis of Rifkin toward Melville's book, *Pierre*. In this analysis, Rifkin points out how metropolitan life has taken away the Native Americans' traditional way of life. In the process of assimilation, they were forced to forget about their homelands.[24] In the case of Papua, fashion and sports are two examples of the way native Papuans were uprooted from their culture and relationship to the land and were forced into a modernism driven by racism.

Racism and fear of rebellion were intertwined in the minds of Indonesian government officials. While other ethnicities could freely express their language and traditions, Papuans could not use their own language, even in song. Although there are around 250 various languages in Papua, the idea of nationalism was strongly injected into this form of expression. During Soeharto's regime, while local language was taught in other provinces in early grades, the only language allowed in Papua was *Bahasa Indonesia*. If Papuans were caught using local languages, they were considered treacherous and anti-Indonesian. The local language was considered the language of "separatism," which needed a violent repression.[25] Many people were tortured and killed for singing Papuan songs, even the national anthem.[26]

MINING: THE EXTRACTIVE ZONE

A major problem I must emphasize in this work around Papua is mining. In 1936, a Dutch geologist, Jean Jacques Dozy, discovered a mountain of ore which he called Ertsberg. In 1959, Freeport geologist Forbes Wilson heard about Dozy's report. In 1965, almost two months after the coup which toppled Soekarno, the US mining giant, Freeport McMoran, came to establish the relation between Jakarta (Soeharto) and Freeport.[27] The mining contract was then established in 1967. In 1988, Freeport announced another finding of ore (gold), this time in Grasberg, although rumors said that they already had discovered it a decade earlier.[28]

The Ertsberg mining caused many Papuans to live with significant disadvantages. People complained that they received no compensation from Freeport and the government for the land that they lost. While Freeport and the government claimed that it was state land, it was traditionally their lands.[29] It is true that in the constitution, UUD 1945, chapter 33, point 3 says, "Earth and water and natural richness consisted in it are controlled by the state and are used for the maximum wealth of the people."[30] Indonesia also has a certain policy and law on how to deal with the issue of *tanah negara* (state land) vs *tanah adat* (traditional land). Nevertheless, the result is mostly determined by the government and this result harmed the Papuan people.

Many Amungme people were forced to sell their rainforest land for timber resources, not only for the copper and gold. Especially in Soeharto's era, since 1967, many Amungme people who lived around the mines were displaced from their homes. They were promised new settlements, but many were killed in a malaria epidemic before this could happen. The workers in the mines were critically underpaid, making only 10 cents an hour. Once a revolution to sabotage the pipeline happened, but Soeharto's iron fist called Operation Annihilation, burning homes, torturing, and killing hundreds of rebels. In 1994, about 2,000 Amungme who lived near the mining were relocated by force.[31] Freeport had also been dumping hundreds of thousands of tons of mining tailings into the Ajkwa river daily. The tainted water affected the forests along the river as well as the Kamoro people who lived downstream. For them, their sago stands, hunting grounds, and forest resources were all damaged by the toxic tailings.[32]

ASSEMBLAGE OF GEONTOPOWER IN PAPUA

I have found colonialism, racism, and mining to have assembled an occupying power that is able to determine the life of Papuan people who receive the direct impact. Here, I will also argue that the idea of preemptive power as explained by Brian Massumi and the theory of geontopower/geontology by Elizabeth Povinelli are both valuable resources that can be used to look deeper into the situation in Papua.

The Preemptive Power/Ontopower

Brian Massumi asserts that there is an ontopower in ecology. Ontopower is not a power-over, but a power-to bring a formative tendency or potentiality into being. It carries this not-yet-fully-emerged into the present. This way, ecology of power works within preemption/preemptive power, which is one of Massumi's foci.[33] To explain more, he links the reality of war and weather. For former president George W. Bush, military response against "the terror of weapons of mass destruction" was more important than the natural disaster. In fact, military response should be ready for any threat of war.[34] Massumi argues that this preemptive power is a formative force on nature. In other words, humanity must take action to do something against a territory that has a nature of threat toward the living beings on the land.[35] The preemptive power becomes the environmental power. It affects the environment's conditions of emergence. It is more about how it can affect the potentiality of living, of creating life and letting die. It is seen in how Bush did not promise to bring life back to normal or to as it was, but just mentioned bringing the life itself back. It is just a way to bring that potentiality of life, without any assurance of life. It works in a prototerritory of designing the nature and it creates life as far as it is emergent, just as preemption's target is the emergence of life.[36]

Geontopower/Geontology

In similar fashion, I turn into Elizabeth A. Povinelli's work on geontopower. The difference is Povinelli highlights the presence of geontology as the main agents. By focusing on *geos*, she points to the role of Nonlife that has that preemptive power of affecting living beings. That nonliving entities indeed have power to create beings or to not let the living beings live. This becomes a matter of extinction of not only humanity, but the whole planet.[37] Through the geontological governance, as it resounds in Foucauldian governmentality, Povinelli offers the view of the Desert, the Animist, and the Virus. The Desert basically refers to the possibility of Life, similarly to Massumi's prototerritory. The idea of the Animist expounds the *affectus,* or the ability of the Nonlife, like the Desert, to affect and be affected by the living beings. Unfortunately, the Virus seeks to disrupt the movement of the Life and the Nonlife. The Virus changed not only the Life, but also the Nonlife. This is the geontopower.[38] Here, Life is determined by Nonlife, a geological concept. In Povinelli's words, "Nonlife is what holds, or should hold for us, the more radical potential . . . Life is merely a moment in the greater dynamic unfolding of Nonlife."[39]

Based on Massumi's and Povinelli's works, I want to draw our attention to how occupation does not only happen through the hard power of colonialism.

I argue, it is deeply intertwined into that geontopower that pushes the Life and the Nonlife to move from the living space into a space of void or extinction. We indeed need to see issues in Papua as *geo*political as they are related to ecological threat. But to direct this to a theological problem too, we need to relate these geopolitical and ecological threats to the Spirit.

AMUNGME'S SPIRITUALITY, ANIMISM-ECOTHEOLOGY, AND THE COSMIC SPIRIT

Here, I feel the urgency to move to animism and ecotheology to see Papua in a different perspective while keeping our minds on what Massumi and Povinelli have explained. I use Amungme's spirituality and Mark I. Wallace's concern on animism in his ecotheology.

Antonius Kelanangame, an activist from Amungme tribe, mentioned that "his people have names for all mountains and look on them as women whose breasts provide them with life."[40] The Amungmes' relationship to the mountain is indeed very close. It is noted that "among the revered snow-capped peaks near the Freeport site is the home of Jo-Mun Nerek, the Amungme's ancestral spirit. Many West Papuans are Christian, but links with the spirit world remain strong."[41] Therefore, the relation of Spirit and the mountains among Amungme is very strong. Chris Ballard asserts that,

> Amungme cosmography conceives of a landscape possessed and inhabited by female earth spirits. The most significant of these female spirits, Tu Ni Me Ni, represents the ultimate locus of fertility in the Amungme cosmos, the source both of nourishment and of retribution . . . She is often described as embodying the landscape, with her head in the mountains, her breasts and womb in the valleys, and her legs stretched out toward the distant coast.[42]

This feminist perspective is also present in how they view the land/the mountain as their mother. For Amungme people, "[Freeport] is digging out [their] mother's brain. That is why [they] are resisting."[43] That same call persisted in 2017, when Odizeus Beanal, one of the Amungme leaders, criticized Freeport, saying "Don't make a hole in our mother (land). We are not talking about the owners of the shares. But the destruction of the environment and the cultural symbolic order that has been destructed must be restored for a just dignity."[44] For Papuans who live in the Meeuwodide area, a real Papuan respects a land as her/his real mother who gives birth, raises, and nurtures. The land is significantly the Life of the people.[45]

Mark Wallace offers his theology to express that the Spirit and Earth are bound together. God in and through the Spirit exists together with the nature. To see the incarnation is not only to see Christ as fully divine and fully human. Wallace says, "God is carnal, God is earthen, God is flesh." The earth can be seen as the body of the Spirit too.[46] Likewise, speaking about the earth and the Spirit, each thing of the Earth "[shares] in the Spirit's very nature as the Spirit is continually enfleshed and embodied through natural landscapes and biological populations . . . The spirit is an earthen reality."[47] It also means that if we hurt the Earth, the Spirit also suffers when She endures the loss of natural resources that can lead to extinction.[48] My point is, the life-giving energy of the Spirit indeed exists not only in Life but also in Nonlife beings. By relating the land to the Spirit, we also see now how we are also called to care for God, who is caring and nurturing us through nature. In animistic terms, Wallace argues that the Spirit is "alive in every rock, tree, animal, and body of water [human beings] encountered."[49] To offer a Christian animism, Wallace tries to simply say that the Earth is God's natural home.[50] It is not a surprise if God, as the Spirit, talks through a rock, because the rock has a consciousness as given by the Spirit, as mentioned by "Tink" Tinker.[51] But, how can a non-sentient object experience pain and loss? Wallace answers this question by referring to the rocks in his wall as vital structural elements that support his whole family's existence in his home.[52] We survive because of them. We are the integral member of the whole cosmic body that resides and flourishes in the love of the Spirit on Earth.[53]

THE MOTHERLY SPIRIT AS GEOTHEOLOGY

I am convinced that we all agree that the Holy Spirit is present within all creation. We have our root in the Spirit. Without the Spirit, we cannot have our existence, our Life. She has shared her presence with us. We as Christians affirm that the energy of the Spirit is infused within creation. The Spirit dynamically interconnects all of us. The relational bonds, social, economic, and ecological, are fused together in a convivial love of the Spirit. We become interdependent beings through the series of our vital connections. As Timothy Eberhart says, we are "interconnected with the whole multitude of living and nonliving entities that inhabit the biosphere . . . 'We are connected through air, water, and soil; we are animated by the same source in the sky above. We are quite literally air, water, soil, energy and other living creatures.'"[54] Therefore, our penumatological calling is to live as a collective of economic and ecological Life as well.[55] Our Life cannot continue without the interconnections of all the living and the non-living components, such as plants, animals, human beings, infrastructures, water and land, soil, and climates.[56]

In the case of Papua, the mountains, the rivers, the trees, and even the coppers, the silvers, and the golds should not be exploited. Damaging the land of Papua is damaging the Spirit who nurtures our Life together. We see how creations are dying and groaning under the sentence of death through the flow of time. The colonialism, racism, and mining lead to a violent occupation of creation, of Earth. It is happening through technologies and neoliberalism that poison the possibility of the living altogether with the nonliving. If Jürgen Moltmann says that the weakest member of the community of creation will die first, such as the plants and animals, I will say that most vulnerable creation is the land, the mountains that are filled with copper, silver, and gold. They will die first as the drilling continues widening the holes on Earth.[57]

In the Bible, a personal image of the Holy Spirit is shown as a mother in whom we should be born again. The Holy Spirit is *the Mother* who gives birth to all created beings. She is also *the Well of Life* that nourishes, protects, and consoles the creation.[58] The Spirit then can be seen in term of the nonliving as well. Both figures show how the Spirit carries a vitalizing and dynamic energy.[59] The Spirit moves and gives the breath of Life. She (or It) animates.[60] Therefore, when the Spirit is breathed out to creation when God speaks and creates, the Spirit is already present in all parts of creation, animating them. This animation happened through the Pentecostal event, when the Spirit was poured out again on creation.

We have discussed the idea of preemptive power and geontology/geontopower as power similar to biopower that tries to govern the livability of human beings. The occupations of Papua by the colonial Dutch and Indonesia have proven that colonialism and racism are significant factors, but not the only ones that shaped the Life of Papuans. Mining by Freeport and political connections to Jakarta, and even the United States, have created a situation where the locals are suffering from ecocide, not to mention other human rights violations by armed forces. This ecocide does not only refer to the damaging of trees and animals, nor is it only about the human rights violations from relocation, low wages, and murders. This ecocide is a geocide itself.

Saying this is a geocide is perhaps not even acceptable for some people who might think I am sanitizing the situation in Papua. I have never been to Papua and grew up in Jakarta within a middle-class family, although I was born in a small province and moved often as a child. However, my concern is to emphasize that this geocide affects all of us, Living and Non-living. In fact, this is one possible way we can feel the deep connection between land and the people. That is the importance of focusing on geontopower. It works through the preemptive actions of the rulers that created the situation in Papua as it is in the current moment. All things have been done to make sure that "Life" seems present in the land of Papua, while the destruction of the Earth is still happening, and all things that try to obstruct the mining have been suppressed under various ways. Nevertheless, we also see how resistances keep taking place. Although I realize how complex the issue is and how many parties are involved in Papua, I think we cannot not be resistant to the destruction of the *geos*. The Life and Nonlife beings are all worth it. In our theological journey, to believe in the Holy Spirit as our source of Life means to act to defend our Life as well. This is then my geotheological offer.

CONCLUSION

For many Papuans, land is very close to their Life. The mountains as well as the lands are their mothers who gave them Life. They also believe that the mother is closely linked to the Spirit. Papuans (not limited to the Amungme tribe) already practice the meaning of the Holy Spirit as Mother, as source of Life. Therefore, we should be able to construct our counter-power to the geontopower or any preemptive power that tries to determine our livability. We should construct our pneumatological understanding of a geotheology where the *geos* is our source of Life, the Spirit itself, that is present with us to resist the infliction of pain toward God, nature (the Life and Nonlife), and ourselves. We should re-assert that the Motherly Spirit is the Spirit that animates the living and the non-living beings, not a sort of power that benefits the neoliberalists. Therefore, when we think about Papua, we should think on how the land carries the animating energy of the Spirit. We are not able to live without the health of the Earth.

NOTES

1. This chapter was first prepared for the Discernment and Radical Engagement Conference in Taipei, Taiwan, June 19–22, 2019.

2. Geotheology here is to give a significant emphasis on the geos, or Earth, as a spatial reality that conveys not only the living beings but also non-sentient or non-living beings, such as dirt, land, minerals, waters, air, etc.

3. Richard Chauvel, "Papua and Indonesia: Where Contending Nationalisms Meet," in *Autonomy and Disintegration in Indonesia*, ed. Damien Kingsbury and Harry Aveling (New York: RoutledgeCurzon, 2003), 118.

4. Budi Hermawan, "Papua and Bandung: A Contest between Decolonial and Postcolonial Questions," in *Meanings of Bandung*, ed. Quỳnh N. Phạm and Robbie Shilliam (London: Rowman & Littlefield International, 2016), 179.

5. David Webster, "Race, Identity, and Diplomacy in the Papua Decolonization Struggle, 1949–1962," in *Race, Ethnicity and the Cold War: A Global Perspective*, ed. Philip E. Muehlenbeck (Nashville, TN: Vanderbilt University Press, 2012), 99–101.

6. Chauvel, "Papua and Indonesia," 117.
7. Ibid., 116–17.
8. David Webster, "'Already Sovereign as a People': A Foundational Moment in West Papuan Nationalism," *Pacific Affairs* 74, no. 4 (Winter, 2001–2002): 508.
9. Chauvel, "Papua and Indonesia," 122.
10. Richard Chauvel, "Papua Nationalism: Christianity and Ethnicity," in *The Politics of the Periphery in Indonesia: Social and Geographical Perspectives*, ed. Minako Sakai, Glenn Banks, and J. H. Walker (Singapore: NUS Press, 2009), 211.
11. Hermawan, "Papua and Bandung," 180–81.
12. "Program Transmigrasi Di Papua," Pemerintah Provinsi Papua, accessed December 17, 2019, https://www.papua.go.id/view-detail-berita-1308/program-transmigrasi-di-papua.html.
13. Hermawan, "Papua and Bandung," 182–83.
14. Chauvel, "Papua Nationalism," 213–14.
15. "Indonesia: Communal Tensions in Papua," *International Crisis Group* (June 16, 2008), 12.
16. See chapter 7: "New Muslim and Christian Religious Groups," in International Crisis Group, *Indonesia*.
17. Mark Rifkin, *Settler Common Sense: Queerness and Everyday Colonialism in the American Renaissance* (Minneapolis: University of Minnesota Press, 2014), 116–17.
18. Webster, "Race, Identity, and Diplomacy," 93–94.
19. Ibid., 102–103.
20. Webster, "'Already Sovereign as a People,'" 516.
21. Chauvel, "Papuan Nationalism," 203.
22. Webster, "'Already Sovereign as a People,'" 517.
23. Ibid., 523.
24. For the depth of his work, I recommend seeing the whole chapter four of his book, "Dreaming of Urban Dispersion," in Rifkin, *Settler Common Sense*, 141ff.
25. Bilveer Singh, *Papua: Geopolitics and the Quest for Nationhood* (New Brunswick, NJ: Transaction, 2008), 99.
26. Jacques Bertrand, "Language Policy and the Promotion of National Identity in Indonesia," in *Fighting Words: Language Policy and Ethnic Relations in Asia*, ed. Michael E. Brown and Šumit Ganguly (Cambridge, MA: MIT Press, 2003), 286.
27. Freeport had a strong relation with Washington at that time. Denise Leith, *The Politics of Power: Freeport in Suharto's Indonesia* (Honolulu: University of Hawai'i Press, 2003), 1–2.
28. Ibid., 64.
29. John McBeth, "Indonesia, The Lost Mountain: Plunged into the 20th Century, Tribes Struggle to Cope," *Far Eastern Economic Review*, March 24, 1994, 31. The current President, Joko Widodo, indeed has been able to take over the 51% shares from Freeport to Indonesia, although it is still administered by Freeport. See CNN Indonesia, "Freeport Tetap Pengelola Meski Mayoritas Saham Dimiliki RI," *CNN Indonesia*, 22 Desember 2018, https://www.cnnindonesia.com/ekonomi/20181222110549-85-355695/freeport-tetap-pengelola-meski-mayoritas

-saham-dimiliki-ri. But, this impact is debatable whether the Papuans will get any benefit or not. At least, being reelected as the next president, many Indonesian people also hope that he will pay real attention for the sake of Papuans people.

30. The word "controlled" can be equated to "possessed" or "mastered." My translation.

31. Julia D. Fox, "Leasing The Ivory Tower at a Social Justice University: Freeport McMoran, Loyola University New Orleans, and Corporate Greenwashing," *Organization & Environment* 10, no. 3 (September 1997): 264–66.

32. Ibid., 267.

33. Brian Massumi, *Ontopower: War, Powers, and the State of Perception* (Durham, NC: Duke University Press, 2015), vii–viii.

34. Ibid., 27–28.

35. Ibid., 34–36.

36. Ibid., 40–41.

37. Elizabeth A. Povinelli, *Geontologies: A Requiem to Late Liberalism* (Durham, NC: Duke University Press, 2016), 4–8.

38. Ibid., 16–19.

39. Ibid., 175–76.

40. McBeth, "Indonesia, The Lost Mountain," 31.

41. Aidan Rankin, "Mind Who You Call Primitive; The West Papuans Holding a Group of Europeans are Fighting Against Extermination, Says Aidan Rankin," *The Independent (London)*, January 17, 1996, 15.

42. Chris Ballard, "The Signature of Terror: Violence, Memory, and Landscape at Freeport," in *Inscribed Landscapes: Marking and Making Place*, ed. Bruno David and Meredith Wilson (Honolulu: University of Hawai'i Press, 2002), 18.

43. Rankin, "Mind Who You Call Primitive," 15.

44. Muhammad Razi Rahman, "DPR: Perundingan Pemerintah-Freeport Indonesia Perlu Dipercepat," *Antaranews*, 8 Maret 2017, https://www.antaranews.com/berita/616860/dpr-perundingan-pemerintah-freeport-indonesia-perlu-dipercepat. My translation.

45. Ernest Pugiye, "Filosofi Tanah sebagai Mama," accessed July 9, 2019, http://www.papuaposnabire.com/News/Read/6198-filosofi-tanah-sebagai-mama.

46. Mark I. Wallace, *Finding God in the Singing River: Christianity, Spirit, Nature* (Minneapolis, MN: Augsburg Fortress, 2005), 22–24.

47. Mark I. Wallace, "Sacred-Land Theology: Green Spirit, Deconstruction, and the Question of Idolatry in Contemporary Earthen Christianity," in *Ecospirit: Religion, Philosophy, and the Earth*, ed. Laurel Kearns and Catherine Keller (New York: Fordham University Press, 2007), 296.

48. Ibid., 301.

49. Ibid., 313.

50. Mark I. Wallace, *When God Was a Bird: Christianity, Animism, and the Re-Enchantment of the World* (New York: Fordham University Press, 2019), 4.

51. Ibid., 9.

52. Ibid., 146.

53. Ibid., 151–52.

54. Timothy Reinhold Eberhart, *Rooted and Grounded in Love: Holy Communion for the Whole Creation*, Distinguished Dissertations in Christian Theology 14 (Eugene, OR: Pickwick, 2017), 90–91.
55. Ibid.
56. Ibid., 93.
57. Jürgen Moltmann, *The Source of Life: The Holy Spirit and the Theology of Life* (Minneapolis, MN: Fortress, 1997), 113.
58. Jürgen Moltmann, *The Spirit of Life: A Universal Affirmation* (Minneapolis, MN: Fortress, 2001), 157–59.
59. Ibid., 195.
60. Etymologically, "animate" has the root of "ane-," which is "to breath." From "Animus," Online Etymology Dictionary, accessed April 25, 2019, https://www.etymonline.com/word/animus#etymonline_v_13459.

BIBLIOGRAPHY

Ballard, Chris. "The Signature of Terror: Violence, Memory, and Landscape at Freeport." In *Inscribed Landscapes: Marking and Making Place*, edited by Bruno David and Meredith Wilson, 13–26. Honolulu: University of Hawai'i Press, 2002.

Bertrand, Jacques. "Language Policy and the Promotion of National Identity in Indonesia." In *Fighting Words: Language Policy and Ethnic Relations in Asia*, edited by Michael E. Brown and Šumit Ganguly, 263–90. Cambridge, MA: MIT Press, 2003.

Chauvel, Richard. "Papua and Indonesia: Where Contending Nationalisms Meet." In *Autonomy and Disintegration in Indonesia*, edited by Damien Kingsbury and Harry Aveling, 115–27. New York: RoutledgeCurzon, 2003.

———. "Papua Nationalism: Christianity and Ethnicity." In *The Politics of the Periphery in Indonesia: Social and Geographical Perspectives*, edited by Minako Sakai, Glenn Banks, and J. H. Walker, 200–18. Singapore: NUS Press, 2009.

CNN Indonesia. "Freeport Tetap Pengelola Meski Mayoritas Saham Dimiliki RI." *CNN Indonesia*, 22 Desember 2018. https://www.cnnindonesia.com/ekonomi/20181222110549-85-355695/freeport-tetap-pengelola-meski-mayoritas-saham-dimiliki-ri.

Eberhart, Timothy Reinhold. *Rooted and Grounded in Love: Holy Communion for the Whole Creation*. Distinguished Dissertations in Christian Theology 14. Eugene, OR: Pickwick, 2017.

Fox, Julia D. "Leasing The Ivory Tower at a Social Justice University: Freeport McMoran, Loyola University New Orleans, and Corporate Greenwashing." *Organization & Environment* 10, no. 3 (September 1997): 259–77.

Hermawan, Budi. "Papua and Bandung: A Contest between Decolonial and Postcolonial Questions." In *Meanings of Bandung*, edited by Quỳnh N. Phạm and Robbie Shilliam, 175–84. London: Rowman & Littlefield International, 2016.

"Indonesia Communal Tensions in Papua, New Guinea," *International Crisis Group* (June 16, 2008).

Leith, Denise. *The Politics of Power: Freeport in Suharto's Indonesia*. Honolulu: University of Hawai'i Press, 2003.
Massumi, Brian. *Ontopower: War, Powers, and the State of Perception*. Durham, NC: Duke University Press, 2015.
McBeth, John. "Indonesia, The Lost Mountain: Plunged into the 20th Century, Tribes Struggle to Cope." *Far Eastern Economic Review*, March 24, 1994.
Moltmann, Jürgen. *The Source of Life: The Holy Spirit and the Theology of Life*. Minneapolis, MN: Fortress, 1997.
———. *The Spirit of Life: A Universal Affirmation*. Minneapolis, MN: Fortress, 2001.
Online Etymology Dictionary. "Animus." Accessed April 25, 2019. https://www.etymonline.com/word/animus#etymonline_v_13459.
Pemerintah Provinsi Papua. "Program Transmigrasi Di Papua." Accessed December 17, 2019. https://www.papua.go.id/view-detail-berita-1308/program-transmigrasi-di-papua.html.
Povinelli, Elizabeth A. *Geontologies: A Requiem to Late Liberalism*. Durham, NC: Duke University Press, 2016.
Pugiye, Ernest. "Filosofi Tanah sebagai Mama." Accessed July 17, 2019. http://www.papuaposnabire.com/News/Read/6198-filosofi-tanah-sebagai-mama.
Rahman, Muhammad Razi. "DPR: Perundingan Pemerintah-Freeport Indonesia Perlu Dipercepat." *Antaranews*, 8 Maret 2017. https://www.antaranews.com/berita/616860/dpr-perundingan-pemerintah-freeport-indonesia-perlu-dipercepat.
Rankin, Aidan. "Mind Who You Call Primitive; The West Papuans Holding a Group of Europeans are Fighting Against Extermination, Says Aidan Rankin." *The Independent (London)*, January 17, 1996.
Rifkin, Mark. *Settler Common Sense: Queerness and Everyday Colonialism in the American Renaissance*. Minneapolis: University of Minnesota Press, 2014.
Singh, Bilveer. *Papua: Geopolitics and the Quest for Nationhood*. New Brunswick, NJ: Transaction, 2008.
Wallace, Mark I. *Finding God in the Singing River: Christianity, Spirit, Nature*. Minneapolis, MN: Augsburg Fortress, 2005.
———. "Sacred-Land Theology: Green Spirit, Deconstruction, and the Question of Idolatry in Contemporary Earthen Christianity." In *Ecospirit: Religion, Philosophy, and the Earth*, edited by Laurel Kearns and Catherine Keller, 291–314. New York: Fordham University Press, 2007.
———. *When God Was a Bird: Christianity, Animism, and the Re-Enchantment of the World*. New York: Fordham University Press, 2019.
Webster, David. "'Already Sovereign as a People': A Foundational Moment in West Papuan Nationalism." *Pacific Affairs* 74, no. 4 (Winter, 2001–2002): 507–28.
———. "Race, Identity, and Diplomacy in the Papua Decolonization Struggle, 1949–1962." In *Race, Ethnicity and the Cold War: A Global Perspective*, edited by Philip E. Muehlenbeck, 91–117. Nashville, TN: Vanderbilt University Press, 2012.

Chapter Ten

Resistance and Reconciliation through the Arts

Volker Küster

This chapter focuses on the arts as a non-verbal discursive instrument to resist occupation, overcome trauma in post-conflict situations, and negotiate reconciliation. Case studies from South Korea, South Africa, West-Papua and NagaLand in India explore intersections of class, race, ethnic identity, gender, religion, culture, militarism, globalization, and empire. How did the progressive art scenes in Korea and South Africa respond to the societal changes? From resistance against a military dictatorship or apartheid to healing and resilience in societies that have been torn apart. Papuans and Nagan's struggle for self-determination and independence against central governments that have been democratically elected. How does art manage to communicate their stories to the outside world? How does it empower people? The choice of cases and artists is informed by a typology of occupation. The case studies are followed by a theological reflection on story, self-reconciliation and restorative justice focusing on the South African case, where a reconciliation process is under way.

TOWARD A TYPOLOGY OF OCCUPATION

Even after the era of decolonization of Africa and Asia in the second half of the 20th-century there remain occupied territories around the world.[1] At the same time the socio-economic and political consequences, cultural alienations, and distortions, as well as collective and individual traumas prevail long after independence. Further, new dependencies and structures of exploitation developed in the new world order after World War II structured by the coordinate system of the East-West and the North-South conflict. Proxy wars on foreign territories in the global South were the battle grounds of the Cold

War, the Korean War, the Vietnam War or the Angolan Civil War, to name just a few. Also the Arab-Israeli conflict up to the current civil war in Syria have to be mentioned here.

Occupation occurs in different forms and for varied purposes. In what follows I distinguish three historic types of the 20th and 21st century: Colonialism has been followed by prevailing external forms of neo-colonialism and empire as well as internal postcolonial nationalisms. Both offspring of colonialism are interrelated.

Colonialism

While Latin America has already been decolonized in the 18th and 19th century, Africa and Asia had to wait until the second half of the 20th century. The Western colonial project knew two forms of occupation for different purposes:

- Trade posts were established in the coastal regions to extract goods from the colony. The colonizers were cooperating with local elites as trading partners. Sometimes they would secure or even develop local infrastructure to transport the goods from the interior.
- Another form of colonialism was territorial occupation that eventually led to settler states, sometimes as a second step to the trade posts. Prominent examples of settler states are the Americas, Australia, New Zealand, and South Africa.[2]

Neo-colonialism and Empire

After decolonization, new occupations occurred in the form of neo-colonialism under empire. These may have strategic or ideological reasons.

- The geo-political location of South Korea, Japan, and the Philippines led to the establishment of American military bases on foreign territory in Seoul, Manila, Okinawa and other parts of these countries.
- Besides the US military bases in Central America, there has been a kind of virtual occupation for ideological reasons by the presence of the CIA and mercenaries in the so-called Banana-Republics of the cold war era.

Post-colonial Nationalism

Next to new foreign or global forms of occupation, there also occurred glocal forms of post-colonial nationalism triggered by economic or political reasons.

- West-Papua is a prime example of glocal occupation for economic reasons. The natural resources are exploited by American multi-nationals like Freeport with the consent of the Indonesian government.
- Nagaland in India is occupied by the Indian military for political reasons to avoid a separation from the Indian nation-state.

Common strategies in these three forms of occupation include military intervention, torture, rape, racism, and economic exploitation. In what follows I look into four different cases of occupation illustrating the suggested typology: South Korea, South Africa, West-Papua, and Nagaland. After a short introduction of the prevailing conflict I go into dialogue with an artist from that particular context, who deals with it from an aesthetic point of view and negotiates issues of resistance and reconciliation.

ARTISTS AS AGENTS OF RESISTANCE AND RECONCILIATION

In the identity wars of the 20th and 21st century culture and religion have proven to be strongholds of resistance against oppression and globalization of neo-liberal consumer capitalism. Yet they have also been used for propaganda and manipulation. There is certainly a dark side to them too, fluidity and ambiguity are part and parcel.[3] I nevertheless focus here on the positive, constructive aspects. Artists respond very sensitive to the signs of the times and create their own aesthetic language beyond the spoken or written word. This makes their interventions often more complex and multilayered. They give food for thought. The artists' portraits show how they have changed in their artistic production when the political tides changed. During the struggle they were agents of protest, propaganda, and resistance and later dealt also with issues of trauma, healing, and reconciliation, which often involved self-reconciliation through their art works.

Hong Song Dam (*1955), South Korea

Korea has been under consecutive but different forms of occupation by China, Japan (1910–1945), and the US (in the South since 1945). The centuries-long tributary relationship with the Chinese Empire left Korea overall in relative freedom and found its main expression for a long time in a yearly tribute legation to the Chinese court that usually returned with rich gifts for the Korean court. Japan, to the contrary, annexed Korea in 1905 after it defeated its rivals in the Japanese-Chinese (1894–1895) and Russian-Japanese

(1904–1905) wars and made it into a Japanese colony in 1910. The Japanese tried to erase Korean identity by forcing the Japanese language as well as Shinto worship on the population, and even demanding the Koreans to bear Japanese names. The Japanese military forced Koreans into labor in the weapons industry, and Korean women into sex slavery. Up until today, there was neither excuse nor reparation. The Treaty on Basic Relations between Japan and the Republic of Korea (1965) negotiated by the military dictator Park Chung-Hee (1917–1979; in office 1963–1979) was treason against the victims of Japanese colonialism.

After the end of World War II in the Pacific the Koreans were hoping for national independence. Instead, the country was divided along the 38th parallel, between the emerging power-blocks of the East-West conflict. A border that has been tighter than the iron curtain in Europe. A short intermezzo under the sunshine policy of President Kim Dae-Jung (1924–2009; in office 1998–2003) was the only exception. On the Korean peninsula the cold war in fact never ended. American military bases in the South are a new form of occupation that is welcomed by the conservative majority of the South Korean population and has been criticized repeatedly by the democratization and civic movements.[4] Meanwhile, the North Korean regime was under strong Russian and Chinese influence.

Hong Song-Dam is a son of the rebellious Cholla-Province. Born on the small island Haui, his youth was overshadowed by poverty and illness. Yet after his artistic talent was discovered he was supported and given an art education. Hong was an eye-witness of the Kwangju-massacre of 1980 when the government sent in troops to crush down on the civil citizens of Kwangju who were rallying for Democracy. The soldiers were said to be drugged, it came to rape and murder. Official sources admitted 200 civilian casualties, human rights organizations spoke of at least 2,000. Today the victims are remembered in a national memorial. Still the massacre remains a collective trauma of the citizens of Kwangju.

To overcome his personal trauma as well as the communal trauma, Hong produced a series of woodcuts that visualize the cruelties. This *Kwangju-Cycle* only contains very little Christian motives. The most prolific may well be regarded as the icon of Minjung Theology (figure 10.1).[5] It shows Jesus Christ at the bottom of the picture. His hands and feet are beyond the margins of the print. Above the crucifix there is a lorry with three bodies hurled down on the platform. They bear the marks of the cross on their hands and feet. The dead and heavenly wounded victims of the Kwangju massacre have been carried away on such lorries and buried secretly in the mountains that are sketched out with a few lines on the horizon of the picture. "In the suffering

Figure 10.1. Hong Song-Dam, *Kwangju*, 1980s, courtesy of the artist.

minjung we met the suffering Christ" as Ahn Byung-Mu, one of the fathers of Minjung Theology once put it (1982:295).

Hong Song-Dam was imprisoned and tortured in 1991, years after the official end of the military dictatorship, because of alleged violations of the anti-communist laws that were still valid. He had sent slides of a mural that he produced together with other artists via the United States to the 13th World Festival of Youth and Students (WFYS) that was held from 1–8 July 1989 in Pyongyang, where this painting was reconstructed by North Korean artists.

Again Hong turned to art to overcome his personal trauma. Having grown up on an island he always had a very positive attitude toward water until he was subject to water torture. In the first painting of the series *20 Days in Water* the artist portrays himself tied to a chair drowning head down under water (figure 10.2). Fish are swimming around his head, a rice bowl is drifting on

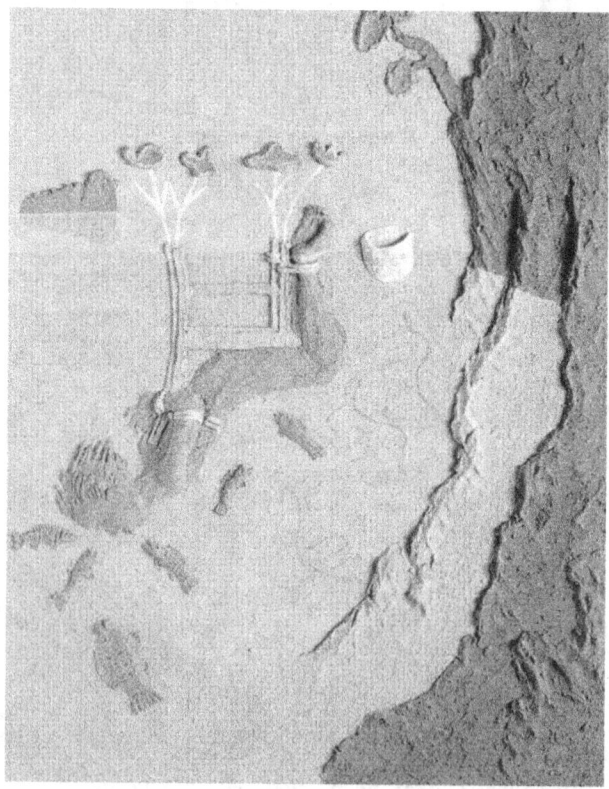

Figure 10.2. Hong Song-Dam, *The Twenty Days in Water* 1, 1999, courtesy of the artist.

the water, and in the background one can see his island. Flowers are growing from the feet of the chair. Hong shares the story that as a child he was running to the seaside in the morning and flowers like these seemed to be floating on the water, what in reality was morning dust. The picture series shows not only allusions to the water torture but also how the artist slowly turns into a fish (figure 10.3). The classical form of the mandala shows him swimming with a fish in a circle. The last two pictures show a rice bowl in

Figure 10.3. Hong Song-Dam, *The Twenty Days in Water* 4, 1999, courtesy of the artist.

138 Volker Küster

the center changing its color from yellowish in the second to last to white in the last. Hong problematizes the famous catch phrase of his friend, the then catholic poet Kim Chi-Ha "Rice is heaven." "Before they torture you they will feed you with rice because otherwise you pass out too soon."[6] The glimmering light of the rice bowl in the last painting, however, is symbolizing self-reconciliation. The artist has transformed completely into a fish. The one who has been tortured by water has become the one who cannot live without water (figure 10.4).

Hong Song-Dam remained a critical spirit throughout. When Park Geun-Hye (born 1952; in office 2013–2017) the daughter of the former dictator, Park Chung-Hee, was elected president of South Korea he published a number of critical cartoons like *Golden Time*, 2011, or *Bariquand 1*, 2011, for

Figure 10.4. Hong Song-Dam, *The Twenty Days in Water* 8, 1999, courtesy of the artist.

which he was heavily critiqued. Yet history proved him right. The Sewol ferry incident, when 250 schoolchildren drowned on a ferry and President Park did not show in the public in what was later coined the "seven hour mystery," was a classical minjung event. Greed, corruption, administrative chaos and political incompetence were the ingredients of this disaster. A lingering question is: What would have happened if this would have been children of the rich attending one of the elite schools instead of common people's kids? Again Hong responded with a large scale painting, *Sewol Owol*, 2014. Park was finally impeached and is serving a prison term, which is a late triumph of the young Korean democracy.

Paul Stopforth (*1945), South Africa

The original inhabitants of the land were overrun by Bantu migration around the 3rd century. First contact with the Western colonial project were the Portuguese who were establishing trade posts along the African coastline while looking for a passage to India. The Dutch and the British consecutively brought in settlers to occupy the land. After independence from the British Empire, apartheid was established as the new order, which had its foundation already in the British pass law. With the election of Nelson Mandela as the first Black president of South Africa colonization of the African continent formally came to an end. The Truth and Reconciliation Commission (TRC) was an attempt to find a third way between a tribunal like Nurnberg and general amnesty. Amnesty would be granted instead to those who confessed in front of the TRC. In reality, it was more victims who shared their stories of torture and rape than perpetrators showing repentance for their deeds. The South African writer Antje Kroog is ashamed of the little interest of her white folks. At the same time, she relates that the victims were already relieved that there was a space for them to share their stories.[7]

With *The Interrogators* (1979), Paul Stopforth[8] created a kind of vertical triptych that portrays the torturers of his friend Steve Biko,[9] who died in police detention of a brain hemorrhage in 1977 (figure 10.5). The *Biko Series*, 1980 realized by making use of autopsy photographs shows the dead body of Biko on a mortuary table (figure 10.6) and his hands and feet reminiscent of the extremities of the crucified Christ (figures 10.7 and 10.8). *Freedom Dancer* (1996) displayed in the permanent collection of the South African Constitutional Court, breathes the enthusiasm of the New South Africa. A young break dancer jumps up high (figure 10.9). Even though the artist lives today in US, American exile paintings like *African Spice* (2014) seem to reconcile him with his South African homeland (figure 10.10).

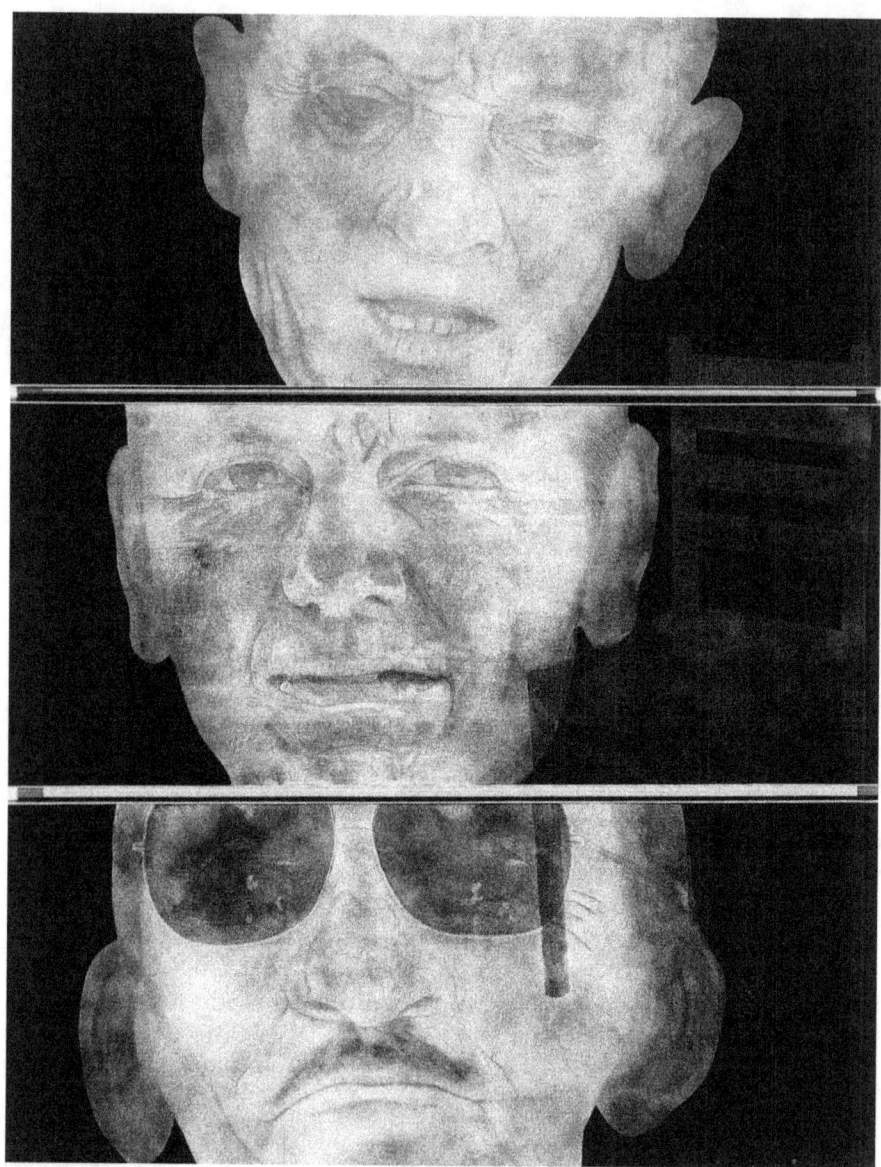

Figure 10.5. Paul Stopforth, *The Interrogators*, 1979, courtesy of the artist.

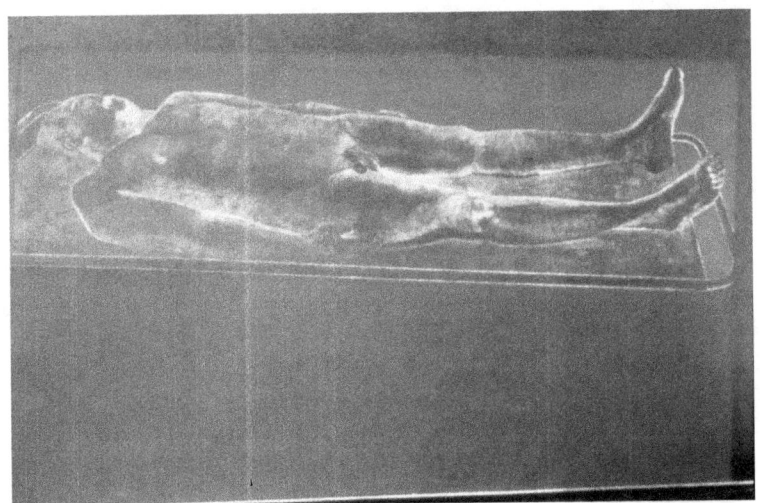

Figure 10.6. Paul Stopforth, *Biko Series*, 1980, courtesy of the artist.

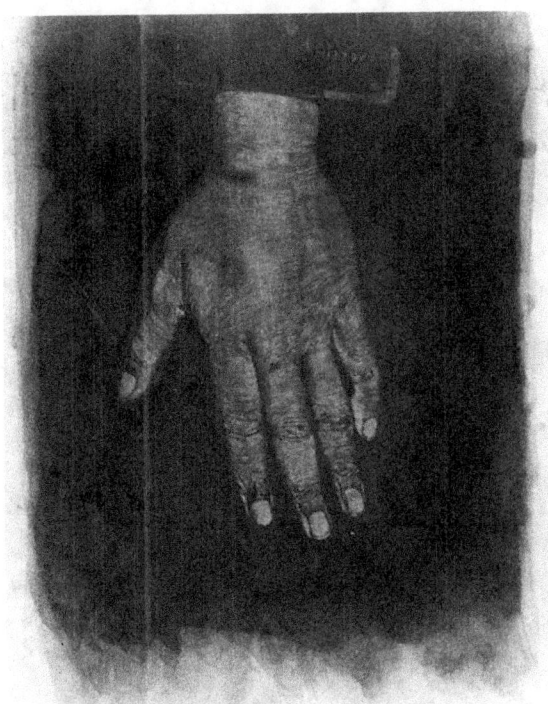

Figure 10.7. Paul Stopforth, *Biko Series*, 1980, courtesy of the artist.

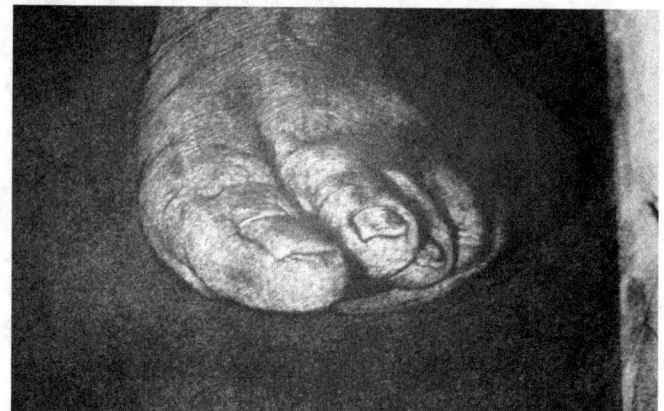

Figure 10.8. Paul Stopforth, *Biko Series*, 1980, courtesy of the artist.

Figure 10.9. Paul Stopforth, *Freedom Dancer*, 1993, courtesy of the artist.

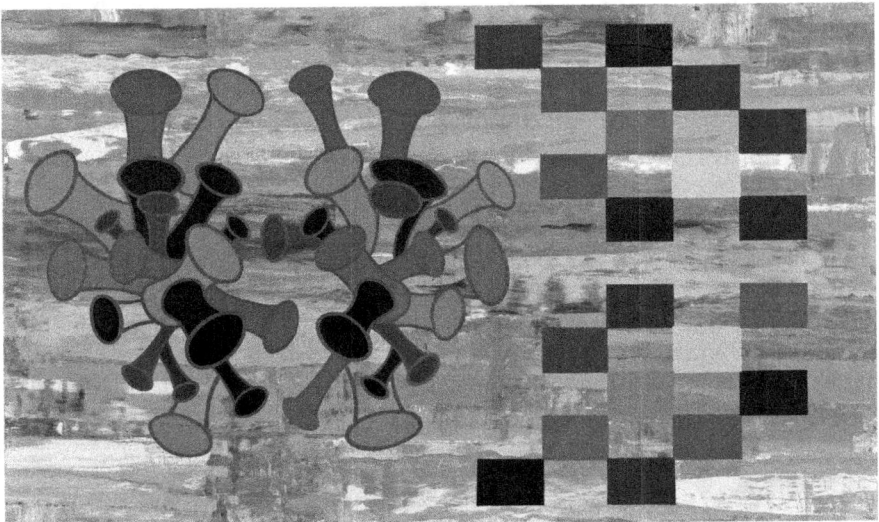

Figure 10.10. Paul Stopforth, *African Spice*, 2014, courtesy of the artist.

Donatus Moyen (1947–2018?), Papua

Already the Sultan of Ternate claimed hegemony over New Guinea in the 16th century. The Dutch after finally accepting the independence of Indonesia still argued that Papua had never been a part of the archipelago and wanted to keep it as their colony. When the Papuans declared independence in 1961–1962 the Indonesian army invaded Papua. It came to military clashes with the Dutch army. American diplomatic intervention in favor of the Indonesians was driven by their own economic interests in the region.[10]

The transmigration program, which was originally intended to regulate the heavy overpopulation of Java and Bali and to overcome poverty by giving land to the resettled families, was clearly used for political ends. More than 50% of transmigrants among the Papuan population will not allow for a renewed attempt of voting out for independence. At the same time, this is also an interreligious power play bringing Muslim transmigrants into an overwhelmingly Christianized Papua. Already, Sukarno, the founder of the nation, was afraid that the predominantly Christian outer islands like Papua or Timor would break away from the young nation if he would allow for an Islamic state. He therefore invented Pancasila, which granted religious freedom to all religions that believe in a supreme being.

Christian art in Papua is close to graffiti and street art. Pop culture is an important form of resistance. Postcolonial minded visitors may consider Donatus Moyen's murals in the Catholic Cathedral of Jayapura as mere orientalism.[11] Yet for Moyen the insight that Jesus and the other biblical figures were not white like the Dutch colonizers was decisive (figure 10.11). In the design of the cathedral only the angels are Papuan with Papuan instruments (figure 10.12). Quite different is his design for a chapel on the grounds of a Catholic hospital where the artist had his studio. On the two concrete shields to the left and right of the entrance door everything is Papuan (figure 10.13). Like story boards the four sides are covered with illustrations of biblical stories and Papuan symbols. Jesus is depicted as a Papuan tribesman (figure 10.14). The church is about the only public institution that eventually sided with the Papuans against the Indonesian occupation. Yet even the clergy is predominantly non Papuan. Therefore, Moyen is giving expression to Papuan pride and self-esteem by portraying Jesus as one of their kind, which can be also considered a form of self-reconciliation.

Figure 10.11. Donatus Moyen, detail of murals, Cathedral of Jayapura, photo by the author, by permission of the artist.

Figure 10.12. Donatus Moyen, detail of murals, Cathedral of Jayapura, by permission of the artist.

Figure 10.13. Donatus Moyen, mural, Hawaii-Chapel, photo by the author, by permission of the artist.

Figure 10.14. Donatus Moyen, details mural, Hawaii-Chapel, photo by the author, by permission of the artist

Amar Kanwar (*1964), Nagaland

Already under British colonial rule which started in 1881 in the Naga Hills, the Naga tribes maintained a certain sovereignty. After independence they joined India, claiming that the Naga Hills District and Naga Tribal Area should be formed into a Naga state with extensive autonomy. The Indian government negotiated a Nine Point Agreement (1947) with the Naga National Council, the successor of the Naga Club which represented Naga interests against the British. Yet there were also forces that were rallying for Naga independence and a Naga state that included Naga territories in the neighboring Northern states Assam, Manipur, and Arunachal Pradesh as well as in Myanmar. Already in 1947, one day before the declaration of independence of India it came to a declaration of independence of Nagaland. In 1952 the Indian government sent in troops. As a consequence it came to murder and rape among the Naga by the Indian army. In 1963 Nagaland became a federal state under the State of Nagaland Act of 1962. Yet the conflict between rivaling guerilla forces for Naga independence, the largest and most influential of which is the National Socialist Council of Nagaland—Isak-Minvals (NSCN-IM), and the Indian Army never really ceased. Nagaland is the state with the largest percentage of Christians (80%) among its population of roughly two million. In times when Hindutva, Hindu-Nationalism is gaining strength and even ruling the country through the Bharatya Janata Party (BJP), this adds to the ethnic conflict a religious dimension. There are ongoing negotiations about a "virtual state" which would grant the Naga rights to maintain their cultural identity and traditional land transfer practices without any territorial changes and end the Armed Forces (Special Powers) Act.[12] The stalemate in these negotiations hampers the "Act East" policy of the Indian government that is supposed to bring economic development to the region.

In *The Lighting Testimonies* (2007) (a digital video installation involving eight synchronized projectors, color, black and white, and sound; 32 minutes and 31 seconds, loop) Indian documentary film maker and video artist Amar Kanwar traces stories of sexual violence against women in independent India. The project according to the artist is about "How to remember. What remains, and what gets submerged."[13] Each projection deals with a particular story of rape as a means to execute state and military power. One episode tells the story of the mother of a Naga girl who has been raped and killed by an Indian soldier in Yangkeli Village Nagaland. It shows her weaving the memory into traditional Naga textile to memorize and overcome her trauma.[14] Similar to West-Papua Naga traditional and popular culture have proven to be strong media of resistance against Indian hegemony.

The case studies on occupation from South Korea, South Africa, West Papua and Nagaland in India have demonstrated intersections of class, race, ethnic identity, gender, religion, culture, militarism, globalization, and empire. Hong Song-Dam and Paul Stopforth produced a broad oeuvre that allows us to trace an artistic development over a longer period of time and through the political changes of their countries. The contributions by Donatus Moyen and Amar Kanwar are much more singular but still nourish resistance and reconciliation with a strong reference to tribal and popular culture. The narrative character is the common denominator of all the works discussed. In sharing stories of resistance and reconciliation they simultaneously become agents of these processes.

STORY, SELF-RECONCILIATION, AND RESTORATIVE JUSTICE

Human beings live by stories. According to German philosopher Wilhelm Schapp they are even enmeshed in stories.[15] Depending on the particular situation, people tell the story of their life differently. If they are Christian they may also relate it to their faith experience. "We are the text, and the Bible and tradition of the Christian church are the context of our theology" says Korean theologian Chung Hyun-Kyung.[16] Text and context are related in a hermeneutical circle.[17] Out of pain and shame, stories of gross human right violations, torture and rape are not told. People are silenced by brutalizing experiences. "Can the subaltern speak?" is the famous question raised by Gayatri Chakravorty Spivak.[18] It kicked of a whole discussion who is speaking on behalf of whom. Intercultural theology creates a third space to allow stories of suffering and joy alike to be told and shared.

I am taking here the case of post-occupational South Africa as an example of how reconciliation is negotiated in post-conflict situations. The memory of the names of the victims and their suffering has to be preserved in order for the survivors to live on and create a better future. Johann Baptist Metz speaks about a "soteriological circle," implying that there is a kind of theological orientation that makes it easier for churches and individual Christians to forgive the perpetrators than to heal the wounds of the victims.[19] In a similar mode, Alan Boesak comes down harsh on the South African Truth and Reconciliation Commission for allegedly putting pressure on the victims to forgive the perpetrators. Boesak talks about "an almost calculated form of emotional blackmail."

> If you did not forgive your torturer, you were made to feel as if there was something wrong with you. [...] There is a place for rightful anger. [...] So far

only forgiveness by the victims has been truly realized. All the other elements without which reconciliation cannot be genuine—restitution, reparation, restoration, justice—are left to languish on the ash heap of the stories, told, listened to, not acted upon, and forgotten.[20]

Desmond Tutu, the chair of the TRC, takes a different stance: "If the victim could forgive only when the culprit confessed, then the victim would be locked into the culprit's whim, locked into victimhood, whatever her own attitude or intention."[21]

These considerations have affirmed me in my concept of self-reconciliation. Frantz Fanon, one of the fathers of Postcolonial criticism, relying himself on Sigmund Freud, has inspired the famous dictum that 'you should not internalize the perspective of the oppressors. Likewise you should not wait until the oppressors are willing to repent. Putting it theologically, if God is present in Jesus Christ in the suffering of the people then the victims are already reconciled through the presence of Jesus Christ in God. The human dignity of the victims is granted by God, not by the perpetrators.

Still the perpetrators will have to repent and seek reconciliation in order to restore their own dignity. The sphere of their deeds is resting upon them ("schicksalswirkende Tatsphere").[22] If evil is enclosed in God's creation too, then there must be an unreconciled space too and eternal damnation is a valid option. It is God who grants reconciliation, it is not at the disposal of human beings. Speaking in legal terms different from punitive, respectively retributive justice or rehabilitative justice, the concept of restorative justice implies that the perpetrator is brought into dialogue with the victims and their families and friends as well as the community at large about the deed and its consequences as well as exploring possibilities of restitution.

The ritual feet washing performed by former South African minister for Law and Order Adriaan Vlok on Frank Chikane, whom he once had tried to kill with poisoned underwear smuggled into his suitcase, was a symbolic act to show repentance and ask for forgiveness. Yet this can only be a first step in healing social relations restitution respectively reparations are inevitable to restore justice. This includes a class aspect as well, Chikane is part of the black elite. As a member of the new ruling class, he is not depending on reparations in order to resume his life. The failure in providing reparations for the victims was a major critique on the work of the TRC. The fact that Vlok is doing charity work in a township and has opened his house to the needy shows that he at least has learned his lesson.

Theologically, this is a twofold good news to those who are suffering from occupation and its consequences. God is not only present in their suffering in Jesus Christ and empowers them in their struggle for survival, but God is also the one who shares in their traumas and enhances self-reconciliation. The soteriological circle is thereby deconstructed. The perpetrators, on the other hand, not only need to be liberated from their role as oppressors as first generation liberation theologians claimed, they also have to repent in order to restore their dignity and actively seek reconciliation with their victims in front of God and the human community. It is perpetrator and victim alike who have the potential to work on themselves to overcome guilt and trauma in these processes of self-reconciliation and restorative justice.

NOTES

1. Cf. https://decolonialatlas.wordpress.com/about/.

2. The decolonial atlas also includes Taiwan and Israel. See the contributions of Sui-Chi Lin and Mitri Raheb in this volume.

3. Cf. Volker Küster, *Gott—Terror. Ein Diptychon*, Stuttgart: Kohlhammer 2019.

4. See the contribution of Junghyung Kim in this volume.

5. Cf. Volker Küster, *A Protestant Theology of Passion. Korean Minjung Theology Revisited*, Leiden: Brill 2010.

6. Hong Song-Dam during a conversation in his studio in May 2008.

7. Antje Krog, *Country of my Skull*, London: Vintage 1999. Cf. South African artist Sue Williamson (*1941) deals with the work of the Truth and Reconciliation Commission in the picture series *Truth Games* (1998). In *There is something I must tell you* (2013) she documents processes of memory and reconciliation. Cf. https://www.sue-williamson.com/; Sue Williamson, *Resistance Art in South Africa* (1989 [2010]). Cf. Küster, *Gott/Terror*, 82–87.

8. http://paulstopforth.com/.

9. Steve Biko is the founder of the Black Conciousness Movement. Cf. Steve Biko. *I write what I like*, Johannesburg: Picador Africa 2004.

10. See the contribution of Toar Hutagalung in this volume. Cf. Volker Küster, *Zwischen Pancasila und Fundamentalismus. Christliche Kunst in Indonesien*, Leipzig: Evangelische Verlagsanstalt, 2016.

11. The building has in the meantime been torn down and replaced.

12. Bendangjungshi, *Confessing Christ in the Naga Context. Towards a Liberating Ecclesiology*, Münster: LIT, 2011.

13. https://www.tate.org.uk/art/artworks/kanwar-the-lightning-testimonies-t15031.

14. https://www.youtube.com/watch?v=KZtZYuKSxMU.

15. Wilhelm Schapp, *In Geschichten verstrickt*, Hamburg: Richard Meiner, 1953; id., *Philosophie der Geschichten*, Leer/Ostfriesland: Gerhard Rautenberg, 1959.

16. Chung Hyun-Kyung, *Struggle to be the Sun again. Introducing Asian Women's Theology*, Maryknoll, NY: Orbis Books 1990, 111.

17. Cf. Volker Küster, *A Protestant Theology of Passion*.

18. Gayatri Chakravorty Spivak, "Can the Subaltern Speak?" *Marxism and the Interpretation of Culture*, ed. Cary Nelson and Lawrence Grossberg, Urbana: University of Illinois Press 1988, 271–313.

19. Johann Baptist Metz, *Memoria Passionis. Ein provozierendes Gedächtnis in pluralistischer Gesellschaft*, Freiburg im Breisgau etc.: Herder 2006, 10 and 57.

20. Allan A. Boesak, *The Tenderness of Conscience. African Renaissance and the Spirituality of Politics*, Stellenbosch: Sun Press 2005, 195–98.

21. Desmond Tutu, *No future without Forgiveness*, London etc.: Rider, 1999, 220.

22. Cf. Klaus Koch, Gibt es ein Vergeltungsdogma im Alten Testament?, in: *Zeitschrift für Theologie und Kirche* 52, 1955, 1–42.

BIBLIOGRAPHY

Ahn Byung-Mu, "Was ist die Minjung Theologie?" in "Junge Kirche 43 (1982): 290–96.

Bendangjungshi, *Confessing Christ in the Naga Context. Towards a Liberating Ecclesiology*, Münster etc.: LIT, 2011.

Biko, Steve. *I Write What I Like*, Johannesburg: Picador Africa 2004.

Boesak, Allan A. *The Tenderness of Conscience. African Renaissance and the Spirituality of Politics*, Stellenbosch: Sun Press, 2005, 195–98.

Grossberg: *Marxism and the Interpretation of Culture*, Urbana: University of Illinois Press 1988, 271–313.

Hyun-Kyung, Chung. *Struggle to be the Sun again. Introducing Asian Women's Theology*, Maryknoll, NY: Orbis, 1990.

Koch, Klaus. Gibt es ein Vergeltungsdogma im Alten Testament?, in: *Zeitschrift für Theologie und Kirche* 52, 1955, 1–42.

Krog, Antje. *Country of my Skull*, London: Vintage 1999.

Küster, Volker. *A Protestant Theology of Passion. Korean Minjung Theology Revisited*, Leiden: Brill 2010.

Küster, Volker. *Zwischen Pancasila und Fundamentalismus. Christliche Kunst in Indonesien*, Leipzig: Evangelische Verlagsanstalt 2016.

———. *Gott—Terror. Ein Diptychon*, Stuttgart: Kohlhammer 2019.

Metz, Johann Baptist. *Memoria Passionis. Ein provozierendes Gedächtnis in pluralistischer Gesellschaft*, Freiburg im Breisgau: Herder, 2006.

Schapp, Wilhelm. *In Geschichten verstrickt*, Hamburg: Richard Meiner, 1953

Schapp, Wilhelm. *Philosophie der Geschichten*, Leer/Ostfriesland: Gerhard Rautenberg, 1959.

Spivak, Gayatri Chakravorty. "Can the Subaltern Speak?" Marxism and the Interpretation of Culture, Urbana: University of Illinois Press, 1988.

Tutu, Desmond. *No Future without Forgiveness*, London: Rider 1999.

Williamson, Sue. *Resistance Art in South Africa*, 1989 [2010].

Chapter Eleven

Beauty in the Rubble?

Genuine Encounter, Self-Transformation, and Transnational Community in Activism for Palestine

Marthie Momberg

INTRODUCTION

Transnational activists who campaign for an end to Israel's oppression of the Palestinians constantly navigate a paradoxical reality. They are frustrated by insufficient progress and by having no guaranteed outcomes. They risk disappointment, harassment, social isolation, imprisonment, and are often called "liars," "terror-loving, Hamas-supporting, anti-Semites," "traitors," "outcasts," and "self-hating Jews." Why do they continue with their advocacy against Zionism in the face of these and many other obstacles?

Zionism is commonly used as an umbrella term for Israel's injustices against the Palestinians. In our era, Zionism is generally understood as Israel's political or state project that values exclusivism and exceptionalism, and aims to establish socio-economic and political control over all of current Israel and Palestine without granting the Palestinians full human rights and citizenship. The continued alienation of the Palestinian population, the ongoing confiscation of their land and resources, and the erasure of their identity over a period of more than seven decades can be regarded as one of the most protracted and entrenched situations of human rights violations of our time.

Dehumanized and relegated to the status of an unwanted and exploited population, Palestinians have been made to pay the price for Europe's persecution of the Jews over two millennia and five centuries of Western colonialism that culminated in the Holocaust. The state of Israel is often viewed as an underdog, created through heroism and bravery against hostile Arab forces. In reality, Israel is a military superpower with a nuclear reactor. Since World War II, the United States has been contributing more funding to Israel than it has contributed to any other country. Israel receives the money under conditions not available to other beneficiaries of the US, especially regarding military purposes while Israel pursues some of its military programs jointly with the United States.[1] Over the years the US has protected Israel's expansionist interests at the cost of Palestinians' land, resources and livelihood by vetoing most of the United Nations' resolutions that hold Israel accountable for its human rights abuses. More recently, the Trump administration, in alliance with neo-conservative Zionist Christians, openly supported Israel's ongoing illegal confiscation of Palestinian land.

Christian Zionism transfers the identity of the ancient Israelites directly to all Jewish people and regards all of current Israel and the occupied Palestinian territory as the rightful homeland of Jews. Many Christians who do not specifically declare themselves as Zionists or support an apocalyptic theology[2] also accept an ideology of exceptionalism with respect to the Jews. Uncritical or *de facto* support for Israel's oppression of the Palestinians on the part of many Christians is informed by mainstream myths, nostalgia for a biblical Israel, and guilt about the persecution of Jews before and during World War II. To such Christians, to support the cause of Palestinian rights is to abandon support for the Jewish state as a vehicle of repentance and to betray the postwar program of reconciliation with the Jewish people. Even progressive Christians steer away from criticizing Israel. The Palestinians' 2005 civil call for non-violent boycott, divestment, and sanctions (BDS) as a means to put pressure on Israel to end its occupation of Palestinian land, to grant Arab citizens equal rights, and to recognize the right of return of Palestinian refugees as allowed for under international law is deemed particularly problematic. International supporters of BDS, including conscientious Jews, are harassed, blacklisted, and detained by Israel. In 2019, the German Parliament formally condemned the BDS campaign as anti-Semitic.

The tension between Israel and the Palestinians is more than a national or a regional matter. The thin strip of land called Palestine and Israel has become a testing ground for international law, theological understandings, and the very notion of what it means to be human in this world. Thus, to speak of Zionism today is to go beyond the issue of Jewish aspirations, beliefs, and history, the supposed fulfillment of a divine promise or covenant, or colonialism. Religious Zionism, political Zionism, Holocaust Theology, and the many myths and distortions that accompany mainstream attitudes and beliefs about Israel cannot be separated from one another. Rather, the dominant, mainstream form of Zionism must be seen as the embrace and expression of a spectrum of interrelated ideologies that partake of empire, quid pro quo business deals, settler-colonialism, militarism, patriarchism, fundamentalism, apartheid, double standards, ethnic nationalism, and an "us vs. them" worldview that is in violation of international human rights laws, universal compassion, and human dignity. To speak of occupation in the context of Palestine today calls forth the need to discern within a matrix of imperialist agendas which aims to to control strategic land, decision making bodies, and resources at the cost of human lives.

When global institutions are unable to implement resolutions, there is an increased responsibility on members of the public to step forward as leaders and drivers of social and moral change. The role of activism in the Palestinian struggle—particularly the kind that may contribute to sustainable, just peace through non-violent means—is important. It is urgent, and it may have bearing on the occupation of realities, religions, mindsets, and moralities far beyond the geographical areas of Israel and Palestine.

In this chapter, I reflect on whether or not a group of 21 transnational activists in the Palestinian struggle derive existential meaning, belonging, or worthwhileness from their advocacy and if, in the midst of upheaval and tragedy, such encounters motivate their activism. I start the discussion by declaring my own biasedness and with the reasons why the views of South Africans and Jewish Israelis are of interest. This is followed by an overview of the research design of the case study in empirical ethics that I refer to in this chapter before turning to the research respondents' impressions. The chapter concludes with brief thoughts about how these results can help energize a global community of shared struggle.

FROM PASSIVE OPPRESSOR TO ACTIVIST-SCHOLAR

In 2010, I attended an evening of lectures on Palestine and Israel at my university. I realized that evening when listening to a Jewish scholar that my naïve perceptions on Israel had unwittingly been informed by a Zionist narrative. Less than a year later I arrived in the West Bank to monitor human rights violations in Palestine and Israel with other ecumenical accompaniers in the World Council of Churches' EAPPI programme. As my colleagues and I logged daily reports on Israel's systemic human rights abuses it dawned on me that as a white South African who did nothing to end apartheid in my own country, I could not repeat my previous mistake of hiding behind silence and apathy about a crime against humanity. Since my return back home, I have met and advocated with highly dedicated individuals. They include Muslims, Jews, Christians, and others from Israel, South Africa, Palestine, and elsewhere. These people, almost always at their own financial and personal expense, and in the face of great social resistance as a result of exclusivist Zionism or common myths, steadfastly advocate for the Palestinians' rights through non-violent means. I began to ask myself: Why are some people publicly involved in the plight of an oppressed other when it implies facing so many obstacles? Are they motivated by a sense of solidarity, religious reasons, morals, law, a desire for inclusive, pluralistic societies, a consciousness of interconnectedness, or perhaps something else?

When I reflect on my own involvement, it is not primarily based on empathy, morality, biblically based convictions, or even a desire to adhere to applicable international laws—even though all these factors are clearly important and relevant. They contextualize my actions, but they are not the primary reasons motivating me. As I witnessed what is happening in Palestine, I became involved, and increasingly experienced an intertwined relationship between the lives of others, my own existence, and the enveloping dynamics of our mutual journeys. My life path and my exposure connected me to the plight of the people from Israel and Palestine just as much as I am connected to the plight of the people of my own country. In turn, I am shaped by all these contexts. In short, my desire to understand what drives transnational citizens to provide viable alternatives to a narrative that promotes the oppression of Palestinians is therefore personal too. That said, I cannot conclude that my self-assumed national responsibility, my sense of interconnectedness, and my quest for human dignity are shared, or play a role, in the motivation of those who advocate for a just peace on behalf of the Palestinians.

There were many publications, films, and other media in support of transnational activism in the Palestinian struggle, but only a few studies focused on Jewish Israeli activism. None investigated *why* the actors were activists. I found no empirical research specifically on South African activists and none on both South Africans and Jewish Israelis. This appeared to be a conspicuous oversight given that links of systemic racial discrimination between South Africa, Israel and the Palestinian struggle have been pointed out explicitly by several authors.[3] This gap and my personal desire to understand what drives transnational activists to advocate for an end to the decades of spiralling violence and destruction led to my research with 21 South African and Jewish Israeli citizens to understand their perspectives on what motivates their advocacy for Palestinian rights.[4]

A CASE STUDY WITH 21 ACTIVISTS

I used a case study method with in-depth personal interviews, followed by qualitative, inductive thematic analysis in an exploratory design in the field of empirical ethics. The respondents were a mix of personal contacts, people who were introduced through mutual contacts, and people whose work I encountered and to whom I wrote without any prior introduction. Half of them were South African and half were Jewish Israelis.[5] Their experiences as activists in the Palestinian struggle ranged between 18 months and over 30 years and they were from different religious orientations, generations, and genders. Nearly two thirds had been involved in the Palestinian struggle for ten years or more and almost a quarter had been activists for over 30 years. Most (16 participants) became activists before the age of 30. The qualifying age of 20 created space for conscientious objectors in Israel. The aim was to investigate the *is* relations (nonnormative) of their ethics and not what *ought* to be or what *should be*. Therefore, the interviews were guided by a general paradigm of inquiry.

The inductive analysis was applied on a contextualist level which is located between the two poles of essentialism and constructionism to examine how individuals find and make meaning in and of their experiences in a broader social context. Similarities and differences were treated as part of the same continuum, since exceptions, contradictions, and silences in information are as important and as relevant as clear-cut patterns. The interpretation was a systematic, continuous, recursive, non-linear process of asking questions,[6] and of comparing information from a descriptive level to interpretations at a conceptual level. The result was a network of multiple interrelated links in a hermeneutic platform from which I filtered and grouped overlaps, silences, and differences.

One of the most important critical skills required to investigate the views of others is the ability to hear their voices on their own terms. The exploratory nature of the research, which acknowledges that one does not know what one does not know, called for a receptive open-mindedness in service of the respondents' views as told from their perspectives. Yet such openness is not a blank sheet. I was interested in the self-perceived views of activists who campaign through non-violent means for a just peace in line with international human rights laws. As such, I am not neutral and I declared my preference for an advocacy agenda of inclusive human rights as opposed to an agenda that ignores the systemic injustice. Still, I was aware of the possibility to influence the study in inappropriate ways by stringing together lines from the transcript into an argument that projects my own views, albeit unconsciously, or even with the very best of intentions. The study also did not espouse a naïve realist view by simply staging the voices of participants. I did the analysis being mindful that the act of grouping arguments and sub-themes into themes and the consequent highlighting of issues in an attempt to answer the research question implies normative and conceptual reasoning. I acknowledge the deductive element of my grouping of the information into overarching themes. Nevertheless, I tried my best to portray the contents, the tone, and the manner of the respondents in plausible, verifiable, nuanced arguments.

Perhaps the biggest and also the most hidden risk was not my politics, but a projection of my own (inevitably partial) perspective of life. Having a preference for the notion of different, changing, and emerging realities is no guarantee that I was open enough to hear plural perspectives on the respondents' own terms. It was possible, for example, to project my own paradigm onto another, or be closed to the views of someone with a positivist ontology and its assumption of an independent world "out there." Even with the best of intentions to investigate the views of others, a researcher can fall short of that aim, because of a personal (and deeply embedded) sense of reality. It was my task to distinguish consciously between my perceived felt sense of reality and convictions and those of others. I tried to remain aware of the need to test my understanding as much as possible during the interviews and to be sensitive to any discrepancies between what I thought and what the respondents were saying. On the subtler level of symbolic perceptions, I had to distinguish between my own feelings and those of others in a systematic, logical manner. I was well aware of this risk and took it into account as best I could.

EXPERIENCES OF CONNECTEDNESS IN A DIVISIVE CONTEXT

No one spoke out on their own about any personal risks and costs. Upon my probing it turned out that for them activism is not a burden. If there is a cost, they bear it without complaint. Likewise, the aspect of meaning and worthwhileness as a motivating factor was generally not raised by the respondents of their own accord except for some unsolicited comments on aesthetic experiences. Only upon asking did they speak of unexpected transformative encounters with existential implications in the midst of tragedy as described below.

Many warn strongly against the idea of utopia, nirvana, or some flawless, final solution. All accept that they simply cannot do it all and they are accountable only for their own actions, not the outcomes. Thus, parallel to a dedicated drive for real, tangible results in a seemingly daunting task, activism in the case study was characterized by widely shared experiences of insufficient progress. Within this tension and paradox, they nevertheless "struggle toward"—guided by their values and the desire for congruency.

A QUEST FOR INTEGRITY

The respondents expressed a strong desire for synergy between their values, identities, and life views, and their behaviour in respect of the Palestinians.

They feel disjointed, and experience discontent, a sense of complicity, disenchantment, and a lack of existential integration if they remain silent about the treatment of the Palestinians. The responsibility of applying one's values in respect of all parties is seen as inextricably bound to the ability to face oneself and the consistent application of inclusive values vis-à-vis the Palestinians, all other parties, and themselves as indicative of integrity. The more they experience themselves as embodying values such as altruistic love, compassion, equality, justice, and honesty in all relations, the easier it is to face themselves.

This desire for authenticity and congruency in the applications of their values is both a personal quest in their own relations and a yearning for a communal shift from selfishness, dualism, and alienation to inclusive, life-enhancing relations. Especially the Jewish respondents recall feelings of guilt, outrage, shame, and horror upon realising the reality of the Palestinians' suffering and that they have been living a lie. "Too many people are living—whether they know it or not—in a dishonest reality. And we deserve better. We deserve to live truth."[7] Another felt despairing and miserable before turning to activism because his commanders, his teachers, his parents, and everyone else in his society misled him. "I felt that they turned all of this generation into murderers,"[8] he exclaimed. Speaking up and acting bring a sense of relief since facing the reality squarely, working with the oppressed and acting in the interests of the other make them feel more integrated within themselves.

South African respondents assumed responsibility because of the intersections with their local anti-apartheid and other societal struggles. They noted obvious and graphic similarities: struggling against colonialism, land dispossession enforced by militarization, systemic discrimination justified by manipulation of the Bible, the Torah and/or social Darwinism in the service of political power, the imprisonment and exile of people, and the portrayal of the oppressed as nameless "tickers" in the media. Their deep responsibility toward the Palestinian people stems also from the fact that Palestinians stood with South Africans in their struggle against apartheid. The shared issue is that of being oppressed and not some other affinity. Hence some noted that if the Palestinians, after their liberation, were to oppress the Jewish Israelis, they would still be in solidarity with the oppressed and advocate for no oppression of Jews.

From this follows that the respondents do not see themselves and others as people with mono-identities in opposition to one another. They reject the idea of unilinear relations which limit or reduce a person to someone with a state and a flag, a religious identity, a culture and an ethnicity, for example. They do not feel that they are "owned" by the state and other institutional powers, but locate themselves in relational, contextual identities, and act from internal loci of control. They live "from the inside out" to effect changes to the varied components that give rise to the oppression of the Palestinians. Their drive to campaign for Palestinian rights centred around this expressed desire for moral consistency in their experiences of an interconnectedness that goes deeper and further than the specific struggle itself. The crux for them remains their inclusive, consistent embodiment of values in all relations as opposed to a select application of worthy values or a special affinity for one group over another.

FULFILMENT AND HAPPINESS VERSUS WHOLENESS AND BEING A WITNESS

What does it mean in light of the activists' desire for integrity and their crossing over to the other in a context broader than the particular struggle when a Muslim South African talks of her "tremendous sense of fulfilment" after Palestinian farmers thanked her for a social media campaign during the War on Gaza in 2014? Or when a Jewish Israeli speaks of "satisfaction" after challenging her community on what is good and what is right? It would be naive to argue that impressions of meaning and worthwhileness in the case study boil down to unidirectional, self-centred experiences of "getting" or "receiving," or a victorious assuredness. In fact, some respondents expressly warn against simplified understandings of terms such as "fulfilment," "happiness," "satisfaction," and "doing good."

It is more accurate to say that the two women's comments point to experiences of meaningful connection with Palestinians and a hopeful possibility that alternatives and improvements are possible. In other words, the perceived meaning exists in interaction with the responses of others, and hence, as mutual interactions that effect some change in both the respondents' own and in other lives. An atheist Jewish South African spoke of a shift towards "wholeness" that happens through improved understanding in critical engagement with fellow activists and with those who differ from him. The process of being consistent and living with coherence in one's values brings relief and healing, he explained. He qualified his sense of meaning as not quite satisfaction, fulfilment, or doing good:

It's not that type of comfort. It's the opposite, It's very uncomfortable very often. But it has moments of great—I don't know what the word is—satisfaction or fulfilment where . . . you get closure, where you feel like you understand things a lot better now.[9]

A Muslim respondent actually refused to use the word "fulfilled" since it implies "some sense of contentment." He regards himself as troubled, restless, and agitated in the sense of being unable to keep quiet when he sees injustice:

I act because I have to live with myself. So I speak, because I have to live with myself. So in this there is a sense of self-righteousness, there is a sense of presumptuousness, there is a kind of moral indignation which assumes that you have the moral high ground. But I'm happy to assume all of those things . . . future generations may expose me as inadequate, as shallow, as inconsistent, as hypocritical, hopefully only inconsistent, but I think in some phases of my life also hypocritical.[10]

This man's activism is encapsulated in the word *zaria*, which means being a means of God working in the world. He perceives a relational dimension in his accountability to God as a witness bearer in the question of justice and a responsibility to co-participate with others in the quest for a safer world.

The notion of "happiness" too was viewed as a dangerous or a slippery term, since "it smells like a privileged White person happy to be active with Palestinians."[11] Especially the Israelis were intensely aware that their Jewishness grants them social and civil privileges in an unjust system, and that this makes them part of the problem. Their participation in the struggle for inclusive rights and freedom make them feel more liberated, authentic and empowered as opposed to their fellow citizens who just curse or deny the injustice. This meaning is intertwined with a profound sense of inner expansion. A former Zionist, for example, no longer looks at the Palestinians as the "other," but as part of the circle he belongs to. He was raised by upper middle-class Jewish-Israeli parents who were well connected to the cultural and the military elite, as well as the political system. He used to identify strongly with Zionism before understanding that he was part of an army, a state, and a social circle "involved in murdering innocent children," something "that goes through all the layers of justifications, rationalisation and compartmentation."[12] The disturbing discovery of being an implicit part of the killing of others that cut through all the layers of his loyal Zionist identity threw him into an emotional crisis. When he realized that his values were disconnected from his assumed reality, he decided to act. Over time he realized that his identity had changed, because the gap between himself and the Palestinians narrowed. Many of his previous connections were troubled, or had eroded since he started to campaign for the rights of Palestinians. But now, over and above his connection to the plight of the Palestinians, he derives gratification from experiencing a sense of belonging to a global circle of likeminded people. He views this expanded belonging as far bigger and more meaningful than what he had in his former social circle. He realizes that,

> thousands and thousands of human beings . . . have a world-view that I share . . . so many people from all over the world are caring about these things and they don't care just about the Palestinians. They care about the refugees in their own

countries and they care about the gap between rich and poor in their communities. These are the people that I love. I'm going to be connected to them. I want to be their friend and now I can be their friend, because I made a few decisions that put me on the side that I perceive now as the solution and not the problem. This is a huge sense of belonging that is bigger than the problems that you can have in one place or another.[13]

Like this man, the other respondents' relations, and their awareness, span national borders to reach out to other activists and other causes. They see themselves as part of an organized, global, non-violent movement of people from different religious orientations, countries, cultures, and other social strata who gather around the Palestinian struggle as the central issue while being mindful also of connections with other struggles. While prioritizing the cause over personal needs and demands, they are inspired by uniqueness, fluidity, and the interchange between people from different backgrounds. It is precisely in the confluence of various tributaries in a mutual struggle informed by shared values in the service of both their own cause and others that they experience the process as significant and meaningful. From this participation stems a profound sense of belonging, which in turn sustains their activism.

At the same time, they argued that when pluralism turns into a new dogma or is hailed as the only viable option, it once more turns into a form of exclusivism. They made it very clear that they value diversity (for example, in religion, culture, ethnicity, and other ways of relating to the same phenomena), but that they do not promote an absolute pluralism in which all and anything is acceptable. They remain *adamantly opposed to dogma* and do not think they know everything, or that truth is absolute. They set out to learn as they evolve and journey together. Yet they have very clear and firm frameworks from where they operate, such as their paradigms of humanism and feminism, their values, their religious traditions, and their rejection of Zionism's divisive exceptionalism, moral inconsistency and abusive domination. In their views, Zionism's false doctrine connects people throughout the world to Zionist Israel, but it is a connection that manifests as communal fear, exclusivism, superiority, land and resource theft, rigidity, an absence of empathy and a lack of imagination. In this kind of connectedness, people are perceived to move further and further away from personal integrity and free, safe, happy communities.

AN INSPIRING TOGETHERNESS IN A SHARED SPACE OF ACTIVISM

The support and nourishment of personal relations with other activists are deemed vital since it gives them the necessary energy and spirit to continue and it counters social alienation. An Israeli woman who mentioned her bond with a circle of mostly female activists, remarked, for example, that "there is always time for celebration, regrouping and going out to the next thing.... We always hug one another, and always support one another and I think that's a very feminist thing."[14] A younger Jewish Israeli woman spoke of "this feeling that we're all in this together even if we don't know each other very well. And you know, I've been really well accepted here, even though I'm a bit different."[15]

In South Africa, the communal value of co-struggling for Palestinian rights helps to break down the metaphorical walls between people from different orientations when they cooperate under trying circumstances. A South African Christian, for example, thinks that "for social cohesion in this society it's just such a good thing. I find myself in these spaces where It's just been so whole, you know. It just felt so good."[16] A Muslim woman I interviewed explained that my own experience of interrogation and detention at a border post staffed by the Israeli military helped to establish a link with her and other transnationals who underwent similar treatment by the Israeli military. The significance, she said, lies in how this experience of being made suspect because one values human rights, crosses over borders, cultures, and religions. One person recalled listening to fellow activists' presentations in parliament. What he remembered best was not what was said, but how it felt:

I remember that experience, sitting in that same Parliamentary precinct listening to you, listening to others and looking at the people around me. I mean where on earth do you get that experience where you have this sort of diversity of people? In fact, on that day we were speaking on Palestine, Cuba and Western Sahara. So we were talking three things.... I remember that particular morning [anonymous person] saying to me, "Wow, to sit in this context." For him it was something so special.... He was just so taken with this context. So I'm just finding myself meeting these amazing people actually.[17]

What the respondents described are experiences of privilege, discovery, inner and outer expansion, connectedness, belonging, love, trust, emotional safety, and an inspiring, uplifting coming together of people and ideas within—or despite of—racial, cultural, gender, religious, and national differences as they face discrimination and violence. It is an ethos that fosters healing and acceptance across conventional boundaries.

Yet such plural activist spaces can, from time to time, also be problematic. A woman who is a citizen of both South Africa and Israel, for example, explained that she was concerned when there were some anti-Semitic statements in public. At such times, she asks herself if she is careful enough regarding whom she works with. She, like the other respondents, were concerned about the abuse of religion and ideologies in obscuring, distracting, and manipulating public opinion and in promoting exclusivist power. The correction of such notions is a pertinent reason for activism for many.

INNER EXPANSION BY SHARING THE SHOES OF THE OTHER

Although the research respondents' experiences of connectedness in a divisive context nourish and inspire them in the course of their solidarity, these are unintended consequences and not primary motivations. It is by putting themselves in the shoes of the other and in their pursuit of justice and equality for the marginalized, and therefore in the process of finding alternatives to Zionism's exclusivist self-interest that "you feel warmth, you feel energy, you feel happiness of being together."[18] It is perceived as inspiring to sit with Palestinians, to listen to their stories and to be allowed to assist with their struggle. Thus, the very act of moving closer to the marginalised and being willing to engage with that which makes their lives miserable, turns into a profoundly enriching experience. The relation between motivation and meaning is not linear, but forms part of an expanding spiral. Put differently, their experiences of worthwhileness on its own do not motivate their activism and yet it enthuses them and it opens up new experiences and possibilities.

They express notions of courage, humility, and gratitude for deeply authentic experiences with the marginalized in the pursuit of creating a better dispensation. They may be tagged as this lefty, or this *toyi-toyier*,[19] or as supporters of terror, but their co-struggling with Palestinians, other Israelis, and internationals to end the systemic injustice and to campaign for inclusive human rights feels more safe, secure, empowering and energizing than the inner conflict they notice in Zionist friends and relatives. Despite challenges of personal discomfort such as feeling "naked in public";[20] verbal and physical attacks; the demands on their time, money, and energy; setbacks; and frustration, doubts, fears, cynicism, tension, and paradoxes they search for alternatives. The respondents are guided by their yearning for moral integrity.

An Israeli man recommends being an activist in the Palestinian struggle to everyone. It may be tough to step outside of the system of uncritical support for Israel. But, the act of becoming part of the Palestinian struggle unleashes an enormous power and energy like an atom that comes apart. It is "like a burst of energy. It's like a waterfall of motivation and empowerment" and if it is directed, one can "do huge and amazing things."[21] Another commented that once one starts to peel off the layers of disinformation, you then realize there is a lot to work with and that it is "a privilege" and "an honor" to live with Palestinians and to experience what Jerusalem can be."[22]

BEAUTY IN THE RUBBLE?

In this last section the discussion turns to how the awareness of death, desolation, and destruction amplifies aesthetics and hence the ability to see more than the obvious, and to go beyond the surface. It is neither an aspect that I asked about nor a dimension raised by everyone, so the points mentioned here were offered freely.

The first hint of aesthetics in the data corpus came from a former Muslim who is no longer religious. He spoke of "basic" but eternal human values in a poetic manner to express the significance of human life. It is his way of deciphering what is "good," what feels "soulful" and "beautiful" in human experiences. At the age of 19, this South African lived as a political refugee in countries with large numbers of other young political refugees, including Palestinians, all of whom fought for national liberation. As he spent time with Palestinians, his identification with their struggle turned into a deep bond or a "visceral tug" because of shared values such as trust, honesty, camaraderie, solidarity, and the value of submitting oneself to survival in a mutual struggle against colonialism. In reflecting on this time in exile, he fused time and space as he explained the close bond and values he continues to yearn for.

You weren't getting material benefit. It was bad for your health in so many different ways . . . Of course we had informers so the risks were there. Quite often it was a matter of life and death and you began to rely on individuals for survival and so these relations were not superficial. They were extremely profound and deep and issues of trust . . . of respect, of depending on those values, honesty, basic and profound things that I miss today. [. . .] Palestinians value those areas in the way we did.[23]

In another dimension of aesthetic meaning, a Christian described a spiritual togetherness and integration with God and the oppressed when in solidarity. For him,

> there is something of a—of a God presence within the struggles, and particularly when you've made a choice to stand with the oppressed. It is no longer an intellectual discussion that you are having about Palestine and all these kinds of things, but it's like I'm in the middle of this and I'm with these people who are oppressed and because God is with them God is with me also. There is this just this wonderful experience. I think it's difficult to explain, because it's difficult

to explain God in any case. But It's difficult to explain it to people who are not there as well. In other words, it's a "weird" thing, almost.²⁴

The "weirdness" he noted is about an unexpected, ironic, and an almost shocking sense of something more, something holy and perhaps even healing that elicits a sense of spiritual expansion that transcends earthly limitations. Therefore, that which is tragic and intolerable brings home also an intimate and an almost tangible awareness of the presence of God or the Ultimate Reality.

A Jewish South African who described himself as an atheist, in turn, spoke of the Palestinians' human ability still to be able to experience joy in the saddest of circumstances. He is touched by their ability to laugh despite their horror and pain. It inspires and challenges him to think differently as it is around a bigger truth. Hence, he pondered the power of imagination and the symbolic value of earthly reality in the context of images of Gaza where the people have been "bombed out" and lost their families and possessions, but still remain human. This paradox opens up a realm that allows him to think "there is something profound that I need to learn from that."²⁵

Without trying to relativize the decades-long catastrophic suffering and despair of the Palestinians, another South African recalled further images of grace and beauty juxtaposed by the rubble of bombed houses and hospitals, dilapidated infrastructure, death, and desolation. In this dread and horror he notices and feels inspired by the Palestinians' love of life. Their ability to still affirm joy in the midst of the most terrible circumstances signifies to him a resilient vitality that overshadow hatred and bitterness. This does not take away the immense suffering or his sense of urgency to make their plight known. However, this respondent witnesses a sense of awe about the beauty of life amidst ugliness. Quite often, he says, the Palestinians are sustained by their appreciation for the small things in life, their incredible sense of humor and their steadfast resistance.

> there is beauty and happiness in the midst of ugliness and brutality. That beauty and happiness revolves around those people who are fighting against the carriers of misery and of brutality and of ugliness. There is beauty in that. So this might sound horrible, but there is beauty in the Gaza Strip amidst the rubble and the poverty when people try and support each other with the little they have. There is beauty in a Nazi Concentration Camp when some of the condemned show ways of supporting each other. So in that sense I don't want to convey a notion that everything is doom and gloom. It never is.²⁶

This man (who used to struggle also against South African apartheid) articulated the wondrous option of not allowing state sanctioned destruction and devaluation to rob one's self-worth and humanity. The antithesis of crimes against humanity is the quest for the healing of life. There is also a tremendous beauty in those who are privileged in society and who make common cause with the oppressed, he added.

CONCLUSION

The respondents' compassion for the vulnerabilities and the humanity of the other, their willingness to engage with both the bright and the shadow sides of life and their critical discernment of what it means to be human steer them to advocate for an end to one of the biggest scandals of our time. In turn, quite unexpectedly, they themselves feel enriched.

The activists qualified notions of meaning and worthwhileness as gratifying, reflexive and relational. Their own transcendence of duality and division gave rise to experiences of expanded identity and an alternative reality. Two dimensions were noted.

In the first, the reciprocity is mainly between people, in service of the Palestinians and/or in relation to God. Fulfilment came through connections, from having gratitude, through growing in understanding and feeling expanded and liberated, sustained, energized and inspired. It was also associated with living with integrity, moving toward wholeness, healing, and with a sense of connection to something much bigger than being a person in a country participating in a particular cause. Their experiences of meaning and worthwhileness are mostly unexpected. These experiences that are inspiring and nourishing were not offered as reasons for why they became or remain activists. Experiences of meaning and worthwhileness spring from:

- feeling connected to and/or nourished by the support of, and love for, a wider circle of like-minded people with similar values and a shared passion for an ideal greater than limited self-interest;
- co-struggling for a better world that includes the rights and dignity of the Palestinians sensing closure, wholeness, and relief by feeling empowered, authentic, honest, and driven by truth;
- taking the chance for South African civilians from diverse backgrounds jointly to re-focus on their local socio-political-economic issues in addition to their solidarity with Palestinians. In this overlapping experiences the South African experience of pluralism and solidarity is renewed; and
- sensing gratitude for being allowed to be, and welcomed as, partners in the Palestinian struggle.

In the second, meaning and worthwhileness were experienced as aesthetics and hence as an inspirational, deeply nurturing, intangible reality that was acknowledged in the following aspects:

- basic, but eternal human values that express the significance of human life;
- a spiritual togetherness and integration with God and the oppressed when in solidarity;
- the power of spiritual imagination and the symbolic value of earthly reality;
- and images of humanity's grace and resilience juxtaposed by, and connected to, the ugliness of human suffering.

The respondents face the mutuality between disintegration and wholeness squarely. Without expecting it or searching for it, they gain access to the hermeneutics of meaning by seeing the dynamic links between life issues and between people, and in some cases also between themselves and a realm that they struggle to describe. They are consistent in valuing the humanity of both the oppressed and the oppressor in their attempts to narrow the gap between themselves and the other. For those who are religious, their attempts to narrow the gap between themselves and others is also an expression of their attempts to live as close as possible to the Other.

A Palestinian theologian and scholar, Mitri Raheb, once told me that if one goes to Palestine, "you'll feel that ultimate despair and ultimate hope are so close together."[27] Meaning as perceived by the respondents in the course of their activism is "about the unsolved paradoxes in life and the wisdom how to deal in a constructive manner and appropriate way with the 'and-and' of life."[28] Yet in allowing that which they seek through their activism to enter into their own beings, the activists' aspirations turn from projections into inspiring, enriching encounters that become the vehicles for the imagined, more humane future. It becomes possible to have moments of credible, deeply meaningful, and mutually nurturing connections with newly established global communities that transcend conventional boundaries, mono-identities and a single struggle. In short, their desired outcomes have already begun to take shape in the very act of a shared cause.

NOTES

1. Jeremy Sharp, "U.S. Foreign aid to Israel," Congressional Research Service, Report prepared for Members and Committees of Congress, last updated August 7, 2019, http://www.fas.org/sgp/crs/mideast/RL33222.pdf.

2. The hermeneutics of Christian Zionism can, but do not always, include an apocalyptic theology whereby Jesus will return to rapture Christian believers to heaven

before the end-time battle of Armageddon. It is assumed that God blesses those who bless Israel and that God has a special plan for the Jewish people. Christian Zionists believe they are faithful to God in their support of Israel and that the founding of the State of Israel in 1948 and the capture of Jerusalem in 1967 were the miraculous fulfilment of God's promises made to Abraham to establish the people Israel as a Jewish nation forever in Palestine.

3. Suraya Dadoo and Firoz Osman, *Why Israel?* (Johannesburg: Porcupine, 2013). Uri Davis, *Apartheid Israel.* (London: Zed, 2003). Hasan, Rumy, "The unitary, democratic state and the struggle against apartheid in Palestine-Israel." *Holy Land Studies: A Multidisciplinary Journal* 7, no. 1 (2008):81–94, ebscohost.com.ez.sun.ac.za/ehost/detail/detail?vid=18&sid=9497785b-e796–42d2–87b2–2b91aaba a317%40sessionmgr4003&hid=4201&bdata=JnNpdGU9ZWhvc3QtbGl2ZSZzY29 wZT1zaXRl#db=aph&AN=32772906. Naeem Jeena, *Pretending democracy.* (Johannesburg: AfroMiddle East Centre, 2012). Jihan Zakarriya, "Humanism in the autobiographies of Edward Said and Nelson Mandela: memory as action," *Third World Quarterly* 36, no. 1 (2015): 198–204, http://web.b.ebscohost.com.ez.sun.ac.za/ehost/detail/detail?vid=7&sid=ade8b120–3769–4511–8a2f-ca01f23e8a84%40session mgr198&hid=105&bdata=JnNpdGU9ZWhvc3QtbGl2ZSZzY29wZT1zaXRl#db=ap h&AN=100577790.

4. Marthie Momberg, "Why activists? A case-study into the self-perceived motivations of selected South Africans and Jewish Israelis in the Palestinian project" (PhD diss., Stellenbosch University, 2017), 89–282.

5. One person has citizenship from both countries. The numbers allocated to respondents (R1, R2, and so forth) do not necessarily reflect the sequence of the interviews. R1 to R9 and R21 were interviewed in person and R10 to R20 were interviewed via Skype. R1–R10 are South African, and R11–R20 are Jewish Israelis. R21 has citizenship of both countries. The interviews are available in the research project's hermeneutic unit and the endnotes indicate the numbering of paragraphs in ATLAS.ti. This software records the researcher's data handling decisions, and it offers a systematic, traceable process which allows others to check whether they too can reach the same findings with the same data.

6. Questions relevant to this process were, for example: Why is it this and not that? What do I see? How is it different from something else? Why is it expressed like this?

7. R12, personal interview with author, May 28, 2015, transcription in ATLAS.ti, 71–74.

8. R19, personal interview with author, June 16, 2015, transcription in ATLAS.ti, 47.

9. R7, personal interview with author, April 21, 2015, transcription in ATLAS.ti, 217.

10. R2, personal interview with author, April 16, transcription in ATLAS.ti, 43.

11. R19, interview, 77.

12. R19, interview, 20.

13. R19, interview, 73–77.

14. R13, personal interview with author, May 29, 2015 transcription in ATLAS.ti, 112.

15. R18, personal interview with author June 11, 2015, transcription in ATLAS.ti, 64.
16. R8, personal interview with author, April 23, 2015, transcription in ATLAS.ti, 83.
17. R8, interview, 84.
18. R19 interview, 76.
19. A dance that is often used during socio-political protests in South Africa.
20. R6, personal interview with author, April 21, 2015, transcription in ATLAS.ti, 126.
21. R19, interview, 92.
22. R12, interview, 81.
23. R1, personal interview with author, April 16, 2015, transcription in ATLAS.ti, 55–57.
24. R8, interview, 96.
25. R7, interview, 108.
26. R1, interview, 91.
27. Mitri Raheb, personal interview with author, June 8, 2014.
28. Daniël Louw, *Icons. Imaging the unseen. On beauty and healing of life, body and soul* (Sun Press, 2014), 12.

BIBLIOGRAPHY

Dadoo, Suraya, and Firoz Osman. *Why Israel? The anatomy of Zionist apartheid: A South African perspective*. Johannesburg: Porcupine, 2013.

Davis, Uri. *Apartheid Israel: Possibilities for the struggle within*. Londen: Zed, 2003.

De Vries, Rob, and Bert Gordijn. "Empirical ethics and its alleged meta-ethical fallacies." *Bioethics* 23, no 4 (2009):193–201.

Erakat, Noura and Radia Madi. "UN Committee 2012 Session concludes Israeli system tantamount to apartheid." *Jadaliyya* (2012). http://www.jadaliyya.com/Details/25970/UN-Committee-2012–Session-Concludes-Israeli-System-Tantamount-to-Apartheid.

Hasan, Rumy. "The unitary, democratic state and the struggle against apartheid in Palestine-Israel." *Holy Land Studies: A Multidisciplinary Journal* 7, no 1 (2008):81–94. ebscohost.com.ez.sun.ac.za/ehost/detail/detail?vid=18& sid=9497785b-e796–42d2–87b22b91aabaa317%40sessionmgr4003&hid=4201&bdata=JnNpdGU9ZWhvc3Qtbl2ZSZzY29wZT1zaXRl#db=aph&AN=32772906.

Jeena, Naeem. *Pretending democracy: Israel, an ethnocratic state*. Johannesburg: AfroMiddle East Centre, 2012.

Louw, Daniël. *Icons. Imaging the unseen: On beauty and healing of life, body and soul*. Stellenbosch: Sun Press, 2014.

Momberg, Marthie. "Why activists? A case-study into the self-perceived motivations of selected South Africans and Jewish Israelis in the Palestinian project." PhD diss., Stellenbosch University, 2017.

Pappe, Ilan. *The ethnic cleansing of Palestine*. London: Oneworld, 2013.

R1, personal interview with author, April 16, 2015.
R2, personal interview with author, April 16, 2015.
R6, personal interview with author, April 21, 2015.
R7, personal interview with author, April 21, 2015.
R8, personal interview with author, April 23, 2015.
R12, personal interview with author on Skype, May 28, 2015.
R13, personal interview with author on Skype, May 29, 2015.
R18, personal interview with author on Skype, June 11, 2015.
R19, personal interview with author on Skype, June 16, 2015.
Raheb, Mitri, personal interview with author, June 8, 2014.
Sharp, Jeremy, M. "U.S. foreign aid to Israel." Congressional Research Service, Report prepared for Members and Committees of Congress, last modified August 7, 2019, http://www.fas.org/sgp/crs/mideast/RL33222.pdf.
Tilley, Virginia. "Report: Israel practicing apartheid in Palestinian territories." *Human Sciences Research Council* (2009), http://www.hsrc.ac.za/en/media-briefs/democracy-goverance-and-service-delivery/report-israel-practicing-apartheid-in-palestinian-territories.
United Nations. *Rome statute of the international criminal court,* 2002. http://legal.un.org/icc/statute/romefra.htm.
Zakarriya, Jihan. "Humanism in the autobiographies of Edward Said and Nelson Mandela: Memory as action." *Third World Quarterly* 36, no 1 (2015):198–204. http://web.b.ebscohost.com.ez.sun.ac.za/ehost/detail/detail?vid=7&sid=ade8b120–3769–4511–8a2f-ca01f23e8a84%40sessionmgr198&hid=105&bdata=JnNpdGU9ZWhvc3QtbGl2ZSZzY29wZT1zaXRl#db=aph&AN=100577790.

Part IV

OCCUPYING LAND

Chapter Twelve

Occupation in North America
States, Rule of Law, Language, and Indians[1]
George "Tink" Tinker (Wazhazhe/Osage Nation)

Let's be clear. The place today called the united states of america (u.s.) is Occupied Territory. It is not occupied in the same structural way as, say, Palestine, yet at the same time there are remarkable similarities.[2] The underlying fundamental legal structure is articulated differently. For the state of israel, the legal doctrine is that curious addition to international law called the "right-of-return," a legal doctrine that has allowed a particular group of european religious refugees to take over Palestinian lands and homes with little moral compunction—following the genocidal decimation of historically marginalized and oppressed european jewish folk during world war II. The result is that the religious identity that connects these european folk gives them the international legal heft to enforce a military conquest and the occupancy of a foreign territory that was already occupied by others. That this gambit has worked so far is a tribute to the significant power state backing given to that religious migration of jewish zionism after the second world war.[3] To legitimize their occupation, of course, these refugees have come to tell a very different narrative than the one I outline here. Their narrative, rooted in the tragedy of the nazi holocaust, becomes one of the romance of return. Eurochristian folk in the u.s. tell themselves a persistent narrative of the romance of immigration and settlement—almost always relatively devoid of mentioning the Native inhabitants they physically and legally displaced—with genocidal force.

In the case of the united states, the legal foundation for occupation was provided by John Marshall in the 1823 supreme court case *Johnson v. M'Intosh*. It was likewise predicated on religious identity. According to justice Marshall, it was precisely the christian identity of the White, eurochristian invading force that gave them the moral and legal right to conquer and kill Native Peoples and to distribute Indian lands to these eurochristian (i.e., christian) "settlers."[4] Needless to say, the legal narrative foundation in both cases is wholly invented yet politically powerful. Like the state of Israel, the people of the united states have come to merely presume their right and to consider any Native objections to be not only superficial and immaterial, but also immoral and even illegal. The Rule of Law, however fabricated, provides a powerful narrative for making occupation normative. As Shawnee legal scholar Glenn Morris argues, commenting on this Marshall decision:

> Marshall himself quite simply invented the "legal principles" upon which he based his doctrine of settler dominion, in the process standing a large portion of existing international law on its head, and his successors have continued to treat these distortions as gospel right up to the present moment. (Churchill 2003:3)

It was in that moment of invention that Marshall invented the legal language of doctrine of discovery, or, as Lenape scholar Steve Newcomb would insist on calling it, the Doctrine of christian Discovery. Marshall's doctrine justified the eurochristian theft of Indian territory and the occupation of their lands as a moral christian legal principal.[5]

At the same time, Marshall's decision and his doctrine of (christian) discovery justified the whole eurochristian invasion and violent conquest of Indian Peoples and their lands. Predicated on roman catholic canon Law, Discovery was adopted into the largely protestant eurochristian legal code of the u.s. Along the way, a decade later, John Marshall found it necessary to re-imagine the very nature of American Indian communities. This was a move that required him to invent even further legal language, in order to assure the eurochristian moral conscience that Native Peoples were never real nations like those in eurochristian Europe. Rather, Indian folk were merely some sort of "domestic dependent nations" that came wholly under the authoritarian governance of the united states. The legal move here was from the right of conquest and the doctrine of discovery in 1823 to, finally, erasure of actual Native national sovereignty in 1831 (*Cherokee Nation v. Georgia*).

That has become the Law, yet Rule of Law is a language game as we can already see in my analysis so far. And we might add that the power brokers know as much. Even as the state uses the Rule of Law to thwart the aspirations of Native Peoples, for instance, the u.s. has persistently refused to accept the jurisdiction of international legal institutions like the World Court or the International Criminal Court—ostensibly as meddling in the internal affairs of a sovereign state. Thus, we must conclude either the u.s. is a rogue nation that stands outside of the Law, or international Law is only whatever the u.s. says it is—as it holds others to standards that it insists do not apply to itself. At the same time, the u.s. joins other colonialist states in strictly arguing that international Law cannot apply to the well-being of supposedly sovereign Peoples, i.e., Indigenous Peoples, whose land is claimed by some much larger organized state apparatus. That, we are told, is merely an internal affair in which no other international actor is permitted to intervene. This is particularly apparent in public discourses around the ongoing romance of "previously uncontacted tribes" in places like the jungle regions of Brazil. Brazil claims territory and ultimately occupancy, even if they stumble upon a community that had no prior knowledge of brazilian claims of occupancy but have lived on that land for several dozen generations or longer.[6]

In 1994, at the beginning of the UN "decade of indigenous peoples," I heard this statist rationale clearly articulated by the state of Ecuador's diplomatic representative (ladino/eurochristian). Essentially, this non-Native government official said, we love our indigenous folk and adore their quaint cultures; we just need to warn the other states of the UN against meddling in the internal affairs of our state—and its (largely ladino/eurochristian) government. So, Indigenous Sovereignty has become wholly an "internal affair" of the modern state that has swallowed up the Indigenous Nation and its territory.

A similar rationale worked for Bill Clinton in 1994. That autumn, we watched Clinton (the liberal democrat!) proudly host "*tribal* chairpersons" from "federally recognized *tribes*"[7] vociferously touting his respect for the "sovereignty" of those "tribal governments" and his attention to the "government-to-government" relationship between Washington and themselves.[8] Clinton was serving up a warmed-over Marshall doctrine of domestic dependent nations from 1831, reminding Indian leaders with a smile that they are less-than. Real Indigenous sovereignty would necessarily respect all international Treaties signed by Indian Nations with the u.s. and call for recognizing a Nation-to-Nation relationship with the u.s. government. Unfortunately, Mr. Clinton's rhetoric was met with a standing ovation from these "tribal" leaders.

It is a real postcolonial turn-around that National Native leaders today would come to accept that lesser status imposed on our Peoples by the power of colonial languaging, the Rule of Law. Native (tribal?) politicians, it would seem, have become self-satisfied with a mere reduction in the rate of military-enforced genocide, seeing the (equally genocidal) forced assimilation as increasingly inescapable as the Native experience of colonialist assimilation becomes more "normalized" and entrenched. They—but not all Indians by far—are giving in to what they perceive as the inevitable, going for the best deal they can get for their Nation at the moment, knowing full well that it is a distinct compromise.

The more explicit blood-and-guts violence, i.e., military terrorism, may have just become less immediately visible, yet violence is still in effect both as u.s. government policy and in the form of private armed militias—to wit, the militaristic response of the Dakota Access Pipeline (DAPL) to peaceful but forceful Indian resistance to their pipeline gambit. We experience it in the continued land loss and particularly in the loss of control over our territories or in the residual effect of intergenerational post-traumatic stress disorder on new generations of Native youth. In reality, the Rule of Law continues to increase the decline of Indian sovereignty, to erode what is left of Indian cultures, to make the survival of Native languages increasingly problematic, and to enhance the colonialist force for assimilation to a eurochristian cultural norm. One dramatic example is the proclivity for states like north and south Dakota to pass Laws in the aftermath of Native DAPL resistance at Standing Rock Lokota Reservation, making illegal any Native public protests of pipeline development projects (all too often on or around reservation land, and invariably over unceded Treaty territories) that deeply affect and threaten life on reservations.[9] The language usage here should also be noted in passing. States want to ban protest; Natives insist that they are not protesting but rather protecting what is theirs! Protest is meaningless when you have no legal status in the political systemic whole; resistance and protecting is everything.

So, we have arrived at the juncture in colonialism where the eurochristian narratives (including the narratives of Law) increasingly identify Native lands as american national properties (and Treaty lands as private property) and increasingly isolate Native resistance as a violation of eurochristian national (statist) interests.[10] This they accomplish with claims to american patriotism, along with the vilification of any who might impede "progress," "development," or the reestablishment of eurochristian privilege. On the other hand, the juncture finds a significant number of colonized Natives buying into that eurochristian narrative of american patriotism.

To capture something of this process, I want to argue that language, and particularly the language of Law, has been and continues to be used in order to enhance eurochristian control of American Indians and to systematically and systemically erase America's christian history of violence. Of course, it is used equally to control the larger eurochristian population themselves, but that has to await another treatment. I want to start, however, in a relatively strange place, with France and its own long history of colonialism; its occupation of Native territories around the world; its use of Law to enhance its colonial holdings and later to erase its culpability by reimagining its own romance narrative.

In 2005, in response to France wrestling with its own painful colonial past, the French Parliament passed a new law making it "mandatory to enshrine in its textbooks the country's 'positive role' in its far-flung colonies."[11] The parliament in Algeria, once one of France's most prominent colonial occupations, responded with justified outrage. It was only after 132 years of occupation in Algeria and after a bloody eight-year war, that France lost this prized colonial possession. To understand Algeria's outrage, we need only remember that only a decade after WWII, during the 1950s, France sustained an army force of up to 650,000 troops in Algeria, merely, as their political language spinners insisted both at the time and for several decades later, to "maintain order." By France's colonial (i.e., Legal) reckoning, Algeria at that time was actually part of France! Thus, the task was to maintain order; so linguistically it was styled as a police action, an internal affair—but with an inordinately high death rate. Only in 1999 had they finally changed their official languaging about the conflict and referred to the conflict as a "war." Yet, within a few years France's politicians decided to revise history again in order to remember the good times, to put a positive face on their oppression of the "*Wretched of the Earth.*"[12] By the Algerian National Liberation Front's (FLN) estimates after the war, the "police action" counted for an estimated 1.5 million deaths! And in 2005 the french parliament tried one more time to glorify the war in some romantic national memory in terms of its "positive role."

In similar ways it is this powerful but plastic use of language and its tendency to erase the past (and extinguish the land title) of the Native Other (i.e., Indigenous Peoples, American Indians, etc.) that begins to clarify the legal and narrative side of the colonial invasion, massacre, conquest, and occupation of Native north America. In the course of that history, the internationally vaunted (particularly by eurochristian states) Rule of Law is nothing more than a language system that can be and is arbitrarily manipulated by those with the power to make and change the narrative by which life is structured in their (artificially) bounded territory. As Steve Newcombe argues:

> By identifying federal Indian law as a system of language, I am attempting to heighten the reader's awareness that this 'system' is not hard or solid like a tree or a rock. Federal Indian law is comprised only of words and ideas."[13]

We might add here that legal discourse, like all other discourses, necessarily boil down to conceptual metaphors[14] which indeed escape Newcombe's notion of solidness. They only derive solidity as the language becomes more distant from everyday usage and finally becomes merely the technical language of Law, which gives the illusion of something solid—and does indeed confound most lay readers of Law. But in the final analysis the solid is always ephemeral when closely examined.

At the same time, the power of this invented language has become systemic—in that common usage means most speakers of the colonial language have become thoroughly conditioned to its discourse and equally accustomed to exercising the privilege that they presume comes with *righteous* conquest. And it is important to note that the illusion of moral righteousness encoded in this Rule of Law. It always claims some ethical high ground even as it is used to conceal immoral and unethical violence. It is deeply embedded in the eurochristian cultural whole to think of the self as righteous and to make every attempt to justify its history of violence. At the same time, that cultural whole and its legal discourse has made the move to justify the terrorism and violence initiated by righteous state governments—as opposed to *mere* terrorist violence. The Rule of Law becomes a cover for state exercized terrorist violence and at the same time provides a power base for condemning other terrorisms, and especially all acts of resistance (even those professing non-violent protest) toward colonial power, that threaten the state's supreme authority.[15]

Moreover, the use of Law and its social imaginary leads the whole of a eurochristian culture to imagine itself as non-violent and righteous. Even when the social whole may have in large part distanced itself from a direct religious identification with Christianity, the eurochristian culture of that social whole continues to hold deep cultural attachment to christian ideation. That, in turn, surfaces in a persistent habitual behavior of seeing the eurochristian corporate self as virtuous. The resulting self-image then imagines a romantic past that erases any culpable participation in unjust violence, particularly toward the Native inhabitants of the territory now occupied by these eurochristian usurpers of the land.[16] As a result, the acts of usurping are today nearly invisible to the current eurochristian occupiers of Native lands in north america.

From 2010 to 2012 I spent several months advising a national United Methodist task force on issues of methodist culpability in the Sand Creek Massacre that happened here in Colorado in 1864. The massacre (officially called such by three formal U.S. army and congressional investigations)[17] happened under the governorship of a famous methodist layman, John Evans, and under the u.s. army leadership of the Rev. Col. John Chivington, who had formerly been the district superintendent of methodist clergy in Colorado. It was an attack on a peaceful Cheyenne and Arapaho village located on treaty lands and under the supervision of the u.s. army post at nearby Ft. Lyons—a disgusting slaughter of women, children, and old people. One member of the task force, an academic colleague, was repulsed at the story when she heard it in 2010. She went on to ask me during an aside, "Tink, were there other incidents of this kind?" I was flabbergasted and at a loss for words initially. Finally, I replied, "Yes. All of them." In her own backyard of devastated western new york, I recommended reading Barbara Mann's book, heavily annotated from "revolutionary war" archival sources: *George Washington's War against Native America* (2005), which details Washington's war against civilians, bloody massacre after massacre with every intention of creating starvation that would result in Indians withdrawing from their prime agricultural lands. In his review of her book, Frank Cogliano avers,

> revelations of the depth, strength and sheer murderousness of America's past tend to hit euro-americans so hard that they lose consciousness, with many slipping into denial, minimization, or hysterical amnesia upon regaining their senses (2007: 261–63).

VIOLENCE QUA VIOLENCE, SCRIPTURE, AND GOD'S WILL

Early in the invasion of America, Law was not always invoked, even as Law was being invented at that coterminous moment as a tool to justify the occupying of Native Land. Sometimes pure violence was the starting point, merely justified by claiming divine will and, thus, claiming some Divine Law to support eurochristian genocide of Native Peoples. As always, the eurochristian invaders needed some rationale, so, again, the use of language was key. The earliest episcopalians and puritans invaded American Indian lands with an ideology that identified themselves as the "New Israel." Thus, the territory of Indian homes and communities became their own "promised land" given to them by their god. Indians were, *de facto*, the new Canaanites (the Palestinians of that day, perhaps) and were, therefore, to be systematically displaced one way or another, perhaps even under the hebrew bible mandate of "kill them all." This history alone makes it difficult for Indian people to adopt anything of the exodus story as a story of liberation (Warrior 1989:261–64). Yet it was this biblical narrative that justified the murder of Native Peoples for these eurochristians and rationalized their grand theft of Native land.[18]

So, in 1620, as the infamous pilgrims approached their beachhead, still 35 days from reaching the site that would become Plymouth colony, they made a little-remembered stop to replenish their supply of fresh water. Under the leadership of pilgrim military commander Captain Miles Standish, a platoon of "well-armed" pilgrims put ashore near the present-day location of Provincetown on Cape Cod. The Native Communities knew about english sailors and their proclivity for kidnapping Indian folk, so they withdrew into the woods, leaving the embers still hot in their fireplaces. The christians, calling it their god's beneficial graciousness, proceeded to discover and steal that village's entire winter cache of corn—leaving that Native Community, people they had never even met, to go hungry through the wintertime.[19] But at least the christians survived. While this was not yet the Rule of Law, it was their god's law and soon enough became fodder for the creation (the inventing) of the Rule itself. Surely christian lives are worth more than others; let's write that into Law so it's official![20] This attitude fuels the pilgrim slaughter of Natives at Wessagussett in 1622, and the combined puritan/pilgrim slaughter of Pequots at Mystic in 1637. Especially the latter is remembered for the eurochristians blatant attack on what they knew to be an unarmed Pequot village. Some 700 women, children, and old people were murdered on that day, prompting pilgrim chronicler and governor William Bradford to proclaim murder as a sweet sacrifice to their god, perhaps a burnt offering:

> It was a fearfull sight to see them thus frying in ye fyer, and ye streams of blood quenching ye same, and horrible was ye stinck & sente ther of; but ye victory seemed a sweete sacrifice, and they gave the prays therof to God, who had wrought so wonderfuly for them, thus to inclose their enimise in their hands, and give them so speedy a victory over so proud & insulting an enimie (Bradford 1637:425f).

God wanted blood, and that is what God got from His faithful puritan army—followed by christian praise and thanksgiving, especially a thanksgiving celebration and feast.

The english invasion of north american Native lands was not about gold, per se, but about land. Its appropriation had already been justified by Sir Thomas More in *Utopia* (1516): because the "natives did not 'use' the soil but left it 'idle and waste,' the English had 'just cause' [read here Rule of Law] to drive them from the territory by force" (Takaki 1992: 902). That theoretical legal case was argued by eurochristian thinkers who followed More, from Hugo Grotius and John Locke in the eurochristian 17th century through Emmerich Vattel in the next. Vattel's 1758 *The Law of Nations* was, needless to say, the law of eurochristian nations. Its only relevance to Native Nations was as a device to deprive us of our territories, to rationalize eurochristian occupation.

How can you just up and take over someone else's home? Easy enough if you can craft a narrative that says clearly that the Native Communities did not have a home there, that they were more like the animals that simply wander around the land. Of course, they knew there were people there. What they did was to craft legal language that insured that they did not have to take the Indigenous presence seriously because they had no eurochristian-like concept of land ownership, meaning that legally they could be swept away in favor of eurochristian occupation. In this way, *terra nullius* was used, particularly in Australia, based on the american occupation experience of the colonizer, as a doctrine to declare the land legally empty in spite of known facts to the contrary. Yet the eurochristian legal ideology of invasion used in Australia was crafted the century before in the eurochristian invasion of north America.

Winthrop, on board the puritan ship Arbela but not yet *en route*, already formally pronounced the legal dictum that native people in the land to which they were headed did not "so much own the land as roam it." John Winthrop, claiming Indian land for eurochristian occupancy, argued:

> The whole earth is that Lord's garden and he hath given it to the sons of men [that is, to christians invading from England] to increase and multiply and replenish the earth and subdue it. Why then should we stand starving here for the places of habitation...and in the meantime suffer a whole Continent as fruitful and convenient for the use of man to lie waste without any improvement (Takaki 1992: 910).

This narrative is confirmed repeatedly by the invaders. And almost immediately it is carved into liberal eurochristian discourse (and their Law) by no other than John Locke, the so-called father of democracy, in his chapter "On Property" in the *Second Treatise*: "Thus, in the beginning all the world was like America," namely, lacking the civilized notion of private property (1688: II: v: 49). Never having set foot in America, but vested by the Carolina Corporation with huge property ownership in the Carolinas, and Indian lands, Locke rationalizes english invasion and occupation along with the private ownership of property.[21] If Native Peoples had only registered their property deeds at the local county courthouses of their place of residency, then, perhaps, Locke and others would have respected them as fellow human beings and left them be. But occupancy is not ownership of property, hence, Natives are reduced to having no more of a property right than do animals that move through the forest, feeding as they travel (Tinker 2011: 49–60). Again here we have invented legal languaging that has come to function as second nature to eurochristian folk, and increasingly eurochristian colonialism has imposed it on the rest of the colonized world. Indian languages had no word for ownership. One cannot possibly own the land, grandmother, the earth! That is, until eurochristians transform our land into property, their property (Hall, 2010).

A century and a half after Locke, John Marshall, in his formative Supreme Court decisions, likewise announced that the Native inhabitants did not have a possessory right. That was closely followed only a half-decade later, with his political opposite and arch enemy, Andrew Jackson, echoing John Locke and Marshall, boldly announcing in his first state of the union address that Indian peoples had merely a "usufructuary" right to the land and certainly not "ownership." As we know, Jackson went on to forcefully remove whole communities of Native Peoples from their homeland to open up the vast and fertile southeastern territory to eurochristian occupancy—and his own immense personal profit.[22] Since the legislation was passed by the u.s. congress, it was indeed an act rooted in the phony sanctimony of the Rule of Law.

The occupation was on!—Legally rationalized, defended, entrenched, and finally celebrated in the romance narrative of the Rule of Law. Yet even with the Rule of Law on their side (on their side as their invention!), the invaders were left with some explaining to do. These were christian people who viewed themselves as defined by some moral code of conduct, even though their history was one distinctly peppered with violent war upon violent war, something that certainly did not abate with the invasion of America. How were these godly pretenders, eurochristian invaders, to explain their sudden accumulation of newfound wealth to themselves and to their progeny? How were they to explain their occupation of someone else's home as their own?

To make this legal claim demands the telling of a Lie (actually a set of lies). So, the invaders told themselves persistent lies about the Native Peoples they so willfully displaced, lies that continued from generation to generation, told to justify occupation. Indians were "nomads," "hunter-gatherers," but certainly *not* farmers or agriculturalists, which was Winthrop's claim before sailing and a colonialist favorite up to this day—even though Washington's generals' scorched earth tactics regularly destroyed Indian villages along with their massive stores of corn—two years' supplies, the record states.[23] So having satisfied themselves legally by their use of tortured language and lies about the Other, english christian men proceeded to help themselves first of all to those plots of land that Indian folk had already long cleared for their planting of corn that had created those plentiful supplies. Martin Marty wants to assure us that the puritan invaders did decide that the

> remnants of the smallpox-devastated Indians...had a natural right to as much land as they could improve, but no more. So the settlers went through the motions of buying the land, their consciences made clear when they saw how eager the natives seemed to be to sell (1984:64).

Of course, the colonialists' and Marty's memory of Natives eager to sell is already a romancing of the actual history. The Natives in this place called new England did not have words in their Native language for either "sell" or "property." So when the invaders or later colonialist historians say that Natives were eager to sell, that presumption begs the question about what was going on at that point in the invasion to invite that sort of colonizer conclusion. "Eager to sell?" Or was it "given little other choice than to 'sell'?"

The puritan renegade Roger Williams, after escaping to Rhode Island, gets closer to the truth—as Marty notes. Williams declared land and land ownership to be the puritan idolatry: For these new-england christian invaders, land was the false image, which had become "as great a God with us english as Gold was with the spaniards." The price of this pursuit of land pushed the puritans so far on their evangelical "errand into the wilderness," adds Marty, that battles became wars and wars led to massacres (1984: 64, 77). But Marty is too soft even at that, still trying to ease the pain and justify modern eurochristian occupation.

The eurochristian usurpers constantly framed their self-justification in terms of their manichaean theologies of good and evil (a concept unknown to Native Peoples at the time). They identified the sides of the invasion conflict in terms of their christian manichaeism as "no less than God and Satan," and that the colonies must "looke at the pequents, and all other Indeans as a common enimie, who though he may take occasion, of the beginning of his rage, from one parte of the English, yet if he prevaile, will surly pursue his advantage to the rooting out of the whole nation" (Bradford cited by Salisbury 1982: 221).

So begins the eurochristian myth of the savage and bloodthirsty Indian—in spite of the equally early criticism of Indian war-making. Namely, Henry Spelman's whining about Indian inability to take war seriously: They can fight for seven years and only kill one person! Yet eurochristians invented stories about Native to serve their needs to justify their own terrorism. To wit, new england puritan Richard Johnson's account that the American Indians were simply "cruel, barbarous, and most treacherous ... being most furious in their rage and merciless ... not being content only to kill and take away life but delight to torment men in the most bloody manner" (Takaki 1993:31). Yes, seven years at war and they only succeeded in killing one enemy, bloodthirsty. The rhetoric depends, it seems, on the political needs of the invader at any given time.

As we trace the shift from the ever-developing Rule of Law to the eurochristian public psyche, we see another characteristic tactic at play. Once the Rule of Law has established the Legality of occupation, the public psyche goes to work to ensure that it is a done deal. Most importantly, denial and erasure then become deeply embedded in the psyche of a public, especially among a eurochristian people who want desperately to see themselves as righteous and then naturally cast Native Peoples as their manichaean evil Other. Those with a more "liberal" sentiment tend a somewhat different direction. All too often they want the Native Other to mimic themselves, at least their best selves. In a slightly different tonality, I was struck with the deeply conditioned statist articulation of so many eurochristian "friends of Palestine" at a 2005 Bethlehem conference at which I spoke.[24] From all over Europe and north America, these "friends" persistently called for Palestinians to forgo violent resistance in favor of the new eurochristian icon of non-violence. Their criticism of Palestinian violence in Gaza and the West Bank could only, in my mind, recall the critique of Fanon. It was safe and comfortable liberals in

Europe, safe in their homes, who couched their support for Algerian People's fight against french occupation always in terms of their simultaneous critique of Algerian violence in terms of their own(new) liberal eurochristian idealism of non-violence. They had and continue to have the peaceful luxury of idealizing non-violence, says Fanon.

In the same way, the ideology of non-violence works for eurochristian folk when they are trying to diffuse the aspirations for freedom of oppressed Natives around the world and limit their options for resistance. Yet, that ideology gives way rapidly to a violent response should Natives in their midst actively resist progress on or around Native lands (e.g., non-ceded Treaty lands). For instance, big oil corporations and their banks were able to muster a well-armed militia at Standing Rock Reservation to violently beat back Native resistance to their Dakota Access Pipeline (DAPL) plan to dangerously tunnel their crude oil pipeline under the Reservation's major source of fresh water. The corporations' violent response was, needless to say, fully supported by the Rule of Law. In fact, when DAPL's private militia, with their cadre of trained and vicious attack dogs, proved insufficient, they privatized local and state police units who arrived on scene with military grade armaments, including heavily armored personnel carriers and water cannons. So, non-violence is a new eurochristian ideology imposed on the poor and oppressed, on Indigenous Peoples resisting continued occupation, but without hesitation, the powerful call on violence as an appropriate response to defend their invasion of Native lands, in 2016 and yet today.[25] What we have seen here then is the careful use of language and the codifying of law in order to distinguish between murder and justifying the use of violence in the eurochristian invasion of Native north America. Ultimately it is used to exonerate the dominant Self of a post-westphalian, eurochristian state over against the colonized, marginalized, but ever threatening, Other. So Indian Peoples were caricaturized by the advancing tsunami of White european land-grabbers as *hostiles*, or savages, lacking in intelligence, lazy, inept, devil worshippers, even as the eurochristian invaders invariably cast themselves in a romantic narrative of righteousness. Occupancy was a christian right and god-given. Even today, the denigrative description of Native Peoples helps contemporary eurochristian occupiers feign moral justification, always relying on the Rule of Law. That is, they make the rules, and that's the Law.

Indeed, the romantic narrative continues: The Natives morally deserved military conquest and massacre because they chose to defend their homes and homeland against a righteous [Justice Marshall says, christian] invasion. And to further soften the actualities, let us today call this invasion migration, or better yet immigration, or, even better, settler colonialism. After all, the superior armies, superior weapons, and the advanced war-making technologies must simply represent the hard-working, deeply religious, and deserving immigrants: to wit, Jefferson's ideal of a nation of yeoman farmers.[26]

Essentially, the u.s. has done and is doing what every eurochristian colonial power has done over the past 500 years to justify its theft of land in its presumed colonies and/or settled territories, and to justify the ensuing destruction of human communities that stood in the way. The colonized, of course, always stood in the way of the colonizer's greed for building their global wealth, but then the language was softened to cast the massacred as having stood in the *way* of progress, development, god's will, free trade, or whatever language will sell in the public arena of the colonizer at any given moment.

The brutal and bloody battle to occupy the north american continent takes almost 300 years for the initial land grab. But eurochristian conquest continues to this day with encroachments perpetrated by the likes of Dakota Access Pipeline, made famous by the Native resistance effort supporting the Standing Rock Sioux People, and the massive military industrial attack on the Athabascan Tar Sands in northeastern Alberta, lands still inhabited by (now severely damaged) Cree and Dene communities. While the christians (i.e., eurochristian folk) effectively used guns and germs to win the decisive gladiatorial contest with decisive military might across the continent, they have turned now to the Rule of Law to protect their occupation of Native lands and to narratives of romance to make it seem palpably moral to themselves. To that end, as they enjoy their repose on Native land, they have discovered a useful strategy of denial. That is, they have largely but intentionally forgotten their genocide of Native Peoples. Yet once each new beachhead was secured to solidify and reify their bloody conquest, they converted their words and stories to Law, the Rule of Law, so that their occupation of Native soil might be morally justified in their christian hearts, leaving themselves totally exculpable. And the words of the romance narrativists, academics, and historians, from Jerrod Diamond[27] to Perry Miller,[28] from Wallace Stegner[29] to Stephen Ambrose,[30] not to mention Jürgen Moltmann's privileged notion of hope,[31] and countless others, including the inevitable "state" historical societies committed to rationalizing eurochristian occupancy, continue to tell the historical eurochristian romance of "How the West Was Won."[32]

NOTES

1. The first section of the book: "On Violence;" especially notes his critique of the colonialist bourgeoisie and the colonized intellectual.

2. One of the more useful digital maps tracing the occupation is titled: "Invasion of America": http://usg.maps.arcgis.com/apps/webappviewer/index.html?id=eb6ca7

6e008543a89349ff2517db47e6. Palestine Portal has an analogous map of Palestine, titled "The Occupation": https://www.palestineportal.org/learn-teach/key-issues/settlements-and-the-occupation/. The comparison is useful in understanding the analogies of both situations.

3. Of course it should be noted that european jews fleeing the jewish genocide in europe were blocked from seeking refuge in power state territories like the u.s. or the u.k.

4. In building his legal case in the Johnson decision, Marshall clearly identifies the christian religion as key to legitimating the invasion, conquest, and occupation of Native Lands. He begins with the first english foray into north America:

> In this first effort made by the English government to acquire territory on this continent, we perceive a complete recognition of the principle which has been mentioned. The right of discovery ... is confined to countries 'then unknown to all Christian people;' and of these countries Cabot was empowered to take possession in the name of the king of England. Thus asserting a right to take possession, notwithstanding the occupancy of the natives, who were heathens, and, at the same time, admitting the prior title of any Christian people who may have made a previous discovery. [*Johnson v. M'Intosh*, 21 U.S. 543, 5 L.Ed. 681 (8 Wheat) 543 (1823): 576f.]

5. It is John Marshall in this decision who names and clearly defines the so-called doctrine of discovery which legally justifies christian violence in north America. See particularly, Steve Newcomb's fine analysis of Johnson in *Pagans in the Promised Land* (2008); also, Tinker's "Rites of Discovery: St. Junípero, Lewis and Clark" (2016): 97–100.

6. Colby and Dennett in *Thy Will Be Done* (1995), describe the collusion between evangelical missionaries and nation state governments in latin america during the 20th century. Evangelical missionaries were welcomed by many catholic heads of state because of their promise to teach Native communities the national language of the governments claiming state sovereignty over those Native territories. It was a very effective strategy to prime Native Peoples for conversion to the Rule of citizenship.

7. "Tribe" is a word characteristically used by eurochristians, especially eurochristian government folk, to identify but diminish american aboriginal Nations and Communities, to explicitly protect themselves from any uppity American Indian notions of equality with eurochristian folk and their governing structures. i.e., Genuine Indian Sovereignty. Indians are tribes, not Nations—in spite of the hundreds of international Treaties signed by the u.s. government and Native Nations.

8. One hears yet today the same "government-to-government" rhetoric voiced by current democratic candidates for the office of u.s. president. This languaging serves the same purpose as the use of the word tribe. The postcolonial trickster reality is that so many American Indians have bought into this use of language wholesale, especially those in National governments. So, the so-called "tribal chairpersons" roundly applauded Clinton's 1994 government-to-government speech in the Rose Garden.

9. Even as I am writing this, the widely reported news out of South Dakota is that the governor there has finally been forced to withdraw that state's versions of

such punitive and racially focused laws. "South Dakota to Drop 'Riot Boosting' Law Targeting Pipeline Protesters," *Democracy Now*, December 25, 2019: https://www.democracynow.org/2019/10/25/headlines/south_dakota_to_drop_riot_boosting_law_targeting_pipeline_protesters?fbclid=IwAR2NvUnjPxmcDY_Ic3ICCwhGC-GH3Il1GXOOaoTJOEDpzapd7e6VItMGA5U.

10. Indeed, Indian Reservations are in actuality "owned" by the u.s. federal government and held "in trust" on behalf of each (federally recognized) Native Nation (i.e., "tribe").

11. Elaine Ganley, "French Law Revising History Raises Ire of Algerians, Others," Associated Press, *Rocky Mountain News*, October 22, 2005: 32A.

12. This is the title of one of Franz Fanon's books about the Algerian struggle for freedom, along with his *Dying Colonialism*. Fanon, writing at the time of Algeria's war for independence against France's colonial power, reports the number of French troops involved in maintaining France's colonial control in Algeria. Fanon, *The Wretched of the Earth* (1963); and *Dying Colonialism* (1988). We should also note the persistent critique of French colonialism by pundits like Jean Paul Sartre, who among his useful other commentary, wrote the introduction to Fanon's *Wretched of the Earth*. One should also note Sartre's *Colonialism and Neocolonialism* (2001).

13. Steve Newcombe, "Pretension as the Rule of U.S. Indian Law," *Indian Country Today* June 13, 2003: reprinted online at: http://www.senaawest.org/ndnlaw/pretension.htm.

14. To that extent I agree with George Lakoff and cognitive linguistics. All language is metaphor.

15. In the eurochristian telling of the story, according to their "Rule of Law," Columbus was an appropriate perpetrator of violence as an official representative of a sovereign (eurochristian) state government—even a pre-westphalia monarchy. Indian peoples had no sovereignty—by definition. The eurochristian Rule of Law (indeed catholic canon law) made that clear in the legal precepts invented immediately after Columbus's first invasion of the Americas. A powerful spanish lawyer, Rodrigo Borgia, also known as Pope Alexander VI, published the so-called papal bull *inter caetera* (May 4th, 1493) only weeks after Columbus's return from his initial invasion. For a very useful analysis of *inter caetera*, see Newcomb, *Pagans in the Promised Land* (2008). It is this bull that underpins Marshall's main argument for his scotus opinion in *Johnson v. M'Intosh* (1823).

16. "Usurpers" is Albert Memmi's attempt at precision in referring to colonial occupiers in his famous *Colonizers and Colonized* (1956—with a 1999 expanded edition containing an introduction by Jean-Paul Sartre and afterword by Susan Gilson Miller).

17. See Clemmer-Smith et al. *Report of the John Evans Study Committee* (2014).

18. The biblical references are too numerous to catalog here. For a quick reference, see Deuteronomy 7:1f; 20:16ff., where the Israelites were to kill all the canaanite people who were living in the land; or the whole of the texts called "Judges" and "Joshua." Joshua is pictured as carrying out his god's command through the whole of canaanite territory.

19. We have one pilgrim's telling version of this criminality in William Bradford:

digging up, found in them diverce faire Indean baskets filled with corne, and some in eares, faire and good, of diverce collours ... tooke with them parte of ye corne, and buried up ye rest, and so like ye men from Eshcoll carried with them of ye fruits of ye land, & showed their breethren; of which, & their returne, they were marvelusly glad, and their harts encouraged...also ther was found more of their corne, & of their beans of various collours. The corne & beans they brought away

It is in this context Bradford exclaims:

And here is to be noted a spetiall providence of God, and a great mercie to this poore people, that hear they gott seed to plant them corne ye next year, or els they might have starved, for they had none, nor any liklyhood to get any till ye season had beene past. . . . (1620: chapter 10:99–100)

20. To wit: *Johnson vs. M'Intosh*, SCOTUS, 1823.
21. In service to the Carolina Corporation, John Locke wrote the first Law for the carolina colony: the *Carolina Constitution*.
22. Inskeep (*Jacksonland*, 2015) traces the ways Jackson used his military and political power to mark out Indian lands for his personal plunder, not unlike George Washington before him. Murder, conquest, subterfuge, and theft can be very profitable when one has the conquest power of the state behind him. For my tracing of Washington, see my "'Damn it, he's an Injun!' Christian Murder, Colonial Wealth, and Tanned Human Skin," *The New Polis*, January 21, 2019: http://thenewpolis.com/2019/01/21/damn-it-hes-an-injun-christian-murder-colonial-wealth-and-tanned-human-skin-tink-tinker-wazhazhe-udsethe/.
23. See Mann, *George Washington's War against Native America*, 2009.
24. "Shaping Communities in Times of Crisis: Land, Peoples and Identities," The International Center of Bethlehem, Palestine, November 6 to 12, 2005.
25. A really good book on the Standing Rock Resistance to the Dakota Access Pipeline is: Estes, *Our History Is the Future*, 2019. Two members of the press did cover the violence at Standing Rock—before the larger press was forced to begin paying attention: Amy Goodman (Democracy Now!) and Lawrence O'Donnell (MSNBC).
26. Jefferson's "Cause" was a society of small yeoman farmers. According to Jefferson, "the health of a society would be enhanced" by those who worked the soil, the yeomen, the "moral agents . . . the chose people of God." However, this vision would soon prove to be a "Lost Cause", because politically he needed the "Virginia Planters" and other "Southern constituents," i.e. slaveholders, "to reach his national goals." (Kennedy 2003:26–27, 42, 73).
27. Jared Diamond rightly notes the advanced war-making technologies that had been developed in christian Europe and gives an explanation of that development. On the other hand, he fails to report and even denies the advanced state of agriculture in the Americas and that 60–65% of our modern world's food production are post-colonial, post-1492, and american in origin. See *Guns, Germs, and Steel*, 1999.

Indeed, by Weatherford's measure (and many others) it was Indian technology, and particularly agriculture, that enabled eurochristian folk to generate the industrial revolution in Europe. The potato alone totally transformed the european economy after the sixteenth century. See *Indian Givers*, 1989. The one thing Diamond gets right in his highly flawed disaster of a book, is that euro-christian folk had far outpaced the Native Americas in that one crucial category—that of war-making technologies.

28. Perry Miller completely forgets that new-england was certainly not a wilderness before the pilgrim/puritan invasion. Indeed, the puritan christian "errand" was to eradicate the Native Peoples there in order to make way for puritan christian occupancy. This was indeed a religious experiment, but one that required the genocide of the Native "canaanite" Peoples, but for Miller, the genocide is efficiently erased. The romance Miller narrates was quintessential reading for many eurochristian american folk. See *Errand into the Wilderness*, 1956. This book was a standard textbook reading in virtually all north american protestant seminaries and schools of theology for some four decades after its publication.

29. See Cook-Lynn, *Why I Can't Read Wallace Stegner*, 1996.

30. For example: Ambrose, *Undaunted Courage*, 2013. A "gloriously told story," says one reviewer, this is pure romance that ignores the unadulterated fact that Lewis and Clark's Corp of Discovery was a military invasion intended to reify occupancy—in accordance with the Doctrine of christian Discovery. Note, also, David Plotz, "The Plagiarist: Why Stephen Ambrose Is a Vampire," *Slate*, (Januay 11, 2002): https://slate.com/news-and-politics/2002/01/why-stephen-ambrose-s-plagiarism-matters.html.

31. See Miguel A. De La Torre's superb critique of Moltmann's theology of hope as a clear expression of eurochristian privilege: *Embracing Hopelessness*, 2017.

32. George "Tink" Tinker, "How the West Was Lost: An Indian Take on the American Romance of the West," Chautauqua Institution, July 2014: posted on YouTube: https://www.youtube.com/watch?v=VkIRG9FvN3g.

BIBLIOGRAPHY

Ambrose, Stephen E. *Undaunted Courage: Lewis and Clark, Thomas Jefferson and the Opening of the American West*. New York, NY: Simon and Schuster, 2013.

Bradford, William. *Bradford's History of 'Plimoth Plantation' From the Original Manuscript: With a Report of the Proceedings Incident to the Return of the Manuscript to Massachusetts*. Ed. for eBook by Juliet Sutherland and Leonard Johnson. Salt Lake City: Project Gutenberg Literary Achieve Foundation, 2008 [1608–1648].

Churchill, Ward. *Acts of Rebellion: The Ward Churchill Reader*. New York, NY: Routledge, 2003.

Clemmer-Smith, Richard, Alan Gilbert, David Fridtjof Halaas, Billy J. Stratton, George "Tink" Tinker, and Nancy D. Wadsworth. *Report of the John Evans Study Committee, University of Denver*. Denver, CO: University of Denver, Office of Teaching and Learning, 2014: http://portfolio.du.edu/evcomm.

Cogliano, Frank. "George Washington's War on Native America" *The English Historical Review* Vol. CXXII, No. 495 (February 2007): 261–63.

Colby, Gerard and Charlotte Dennett. *Thy Will Be Done: The Conquest of the Amazon: Nelson Rockefeller and Evangelism in the Age of Oil*. New York, NY: HarperCollins, 1995.

Cook-Lynn, Elizabeth. *Why I Can't Read Wallace Stegner, and Other Essays: A Tribal Voice*. Madison, WI: University of Wisconsin Press, 1996.

De La Torre, Miguel A. *Embracing Hopelessness*. Minneapolis, MN: Fortress Press, 2017.

Emmerich de Vattel, Le droit des gens ou Principes de la loi naturelle appliqués à la conduit et aux affaires des nations et des sourverains. 2 Volumes. (Gallica, 1758), online at: https://gallica.bnf.fr/ark:/12148/bpt6k865729/f8.image.r=vattel.langEN; english translation: The Law of Nations, Or the Principles of The Law of Nature Applied to the Conduct and the Affairs of Nations and Sovereigns, Joseph Chitty, transl. (T. & J. W. Johnson, 1883).

Estes, Nick. *Our History Is the Future: Standing Rock Versus the Dakota Access Pipeline, and the long Tradition of Indigenous Resistance*. London, GB: Verso, 2019.

Fanon, Franz. *The Wretched of the Earth*. Translated by Richard Philcox. New York: Grove Press, 1961. https://www.democracynow.org/2019/10/25/headlines/south_dakota_to_drop_riot_boosting_law_targeting_pipeline_protesters?fbclid=IwAR2NvUnjPxmcDY_Ic3ICCwhGC-GH3Il1GXOOaoTJOEDpzapd7e6VItMGA5U.

Hall, Anthony J. *Earth into Property: Colonization, Decolonization, and Capitalism*. Montreal, CA: McGill-Queen's University Press, 2010.

———. *A Dying Colonialism*. Trans. By Haakon Chevalier. New York, NY: Grove Press, 1988.

Kennedy, Roger G. *Mr. Jefferson's Lost Cause: Land, Farmers, Slavery, and the Louisiana Purchase*. New York, NY: Oxford University Press, 2003.

Inskeep, Steve. *Jacksonland: President Andrew Jackson, Cherokee Chief John Ross, and a Great American Land Grab*. London, GB: Penguin Press, 2015.

Locke, John. "Second Treatise on Government: An Essay Concerning the True Original, Extent and End of Civil Government." *Two Treaties of Government*. London, GB: Whitmore and Fenn, Charing Cross, 1821 [1688].

Mann, Barbara Alice. *George Washington's War on Native America*. Westport, CT: Praeger, 2005.

Marty, Martin E. *Pilgrims in Their Own Land: 500 Years of Religion in America*. Boston, MA: Little, Brown & Company, 1984.

Memmi, Albert. *The Colonizers and the Colonized*. Boston, MA: Beacon Press, 1991 [1956].

More, Thomas. *De optimo rei publicae statu deque nova insula Utopia*. American edition: "Utopia." *The Essential Thomas More*. Trans. by John P. Dolan. Ed. by James J. Greene and John P. Dolan. New York, NY: New American Library, 1967 [1516].

Newcomb, Steve. *Pagans in the Promised Land: Decoding the Doctrine of christian Discovery*. Golden, CO: Fulcrum Press, 2008.

Salisbury, Neal. *Manitou and Providence: Indians, Europeans, and the Making of New England, 1500–1643*. New York, NY: Oxford University Press, 1982.

Sartre, Jean Paul. *Colonialism and Neocolonialism*. Trans. by Azzedine Haddour, Steve Brewer and Terry McWilliams. New York, NY: Routledge, 2001 [1962].

Takaki, Ronald. "The Tempest in the Wilderness: The Racialization of Savagery." *The Journal of American History* Vol. 79, No. 3 (December 1992): 892–912.

———. *A Different Mirror: A History of Multicultural America*. Boston, MA: Little, Brown & Company, 1993.

Tinker, George "Tink." "John Locke: On Property." *Beyond the Pale: Reading Christian Ethics from the Margins*. Ed. by Stacey Floyd-Thomas and Miguel A. De La Torre. Louisville, KY: Westminster John Knox, 2011.

———. "Rites of Discovery: St. Junípero, Lewis and Clark." *Yours, Mine, Ours: Unravelling the Doctrine of Discovery (special issue of Intotemak)*. Ed. by Cheryl Woelk and Steve Heinrichs. Winnipeg, MB: Mennonite Church Canada, 2016.

Warrior, Robert. "Canaanites, Cowboys, and Indians." *Christianity and Crisis* Vol. 49, No. 12 (September 11, 1989): 261–64.

Weatherford, Jack. *Indian Givers: How the Indians of the Americas Transformed the World*. New York, NY: Ballantine, 1989.

Chapter Thirteen

From Empire to Independent Composite Successor States

Postcolonial Political Theology in Melanesia

Richard A. Davis

This chapter seeks to deepen the understanding of the legacy of the formal colonization of the Melanesian Pacific, and by extension, to other postcolonial and colonial spaces, by looking at the modern states of the region through the lens of the empire. The transition from indigenous communities to empire to nation-state is one that has changed the societies of the pacific dramatically and forever. The way this historical narrative is usually told is that empires have gone and now the nations have become independent. The evolutionary understanding of this narrative is that progress has been made through the transition from empire to independent states. Yet, this transition left many ideas and practices in place. The ideas which justified empires have parallels or analogues in the ideas that justify the newly independent states. Even when these states "are ours" and we are ruled by "our people," the state maintains an imperial character, especially when it encloses a diverse mix of formerly independent peoples. Due to limited space, I cannot delve into questions about the neo-colonization of states in Melanesia or debates about whether states have any future in a changing world.

Drawing on critical political theory and history, I first provide an account of the typical narrative of the empire to nation. Second, I show that the narrative is incorrect, and that imperial ideology exists in all states. Third, and continuing along these lines, the theological justifications of empire have analogies in the theological justification of states. In conclusion, theologians wary of empires should also be wary of the imperial nature of even newly independent states.

NARRATING FROM EMPIRE TO NATION

The political decolonization narrative is typically this: following World War II, European empires around the world were defeated through a nationalist struggle against imperial powers resulting in declarations of independence and then the surrender of the occupying imperial power. The resulting decolonization process leads inevitably to an independent sovereign state that then governs itself by the will of the people and joins the family of independent sovereign nations on the global stage.[1]

There are several elements here. The first requires an occupying empire which governs a certain territory. This territory is imagined to be a homogeneous nation which has a coherent national consciousness. This nation asserts itself and struggles against the empire. Following decolonization, this nation develops its own state which democratically governs the now free nation. This is a common and comforting post-colonial narrative, even if sometimes the facts contradict it.[2] Given that "empire" is now a dirty word, formerly colonized peoples wish to narrate a story of decolonization that shows that their country and their ancestors were on the right side of history in battling empire. The narrative also serves to show how the empire is now completely gone from their independent nations, even though, as I show below, many of these post-colonial states are neo-empires of their own.

There are several problems with the narrative, and to examine them in detail requires being suspicious, not only of empire, but also of nations and states. Each empire and each nation-state are different, yet here I can only offer some remarks that might encourage looking at these particular instances in more detail. Adom Getachew's *Worldmaking after Empire* also wishes to challenge the predominant narrative of empire of the nation-state, but she challenges the idea that anticolonial nationalists mimicked the states of the imperial world.[3] By contrast, I propose that states themselves mimicked empires, but on a much-reduced scale.

Life in Pacific Island nations was very different before colonization. Islands and peoples with their own cultures and languages had no concept of nations and borders as we understand them now. The people lived in self-governing communities, without any political union.[4] The anti-imperial narrative often overlooks these precolonial polities. But by going back to the precolonial politics of the now independent societies we can see better what the impact of empire was and also the impact of the sovereign state on the people. In precolonial Melanesia, communities existed in great diversity (known from the incredible number of languages there). If we were to consult the records of the anthropologists and explorers of the contact era, we would see that the islands were self-governed and had hundreds or even thousands of separate self-governing communities.[5]

When the empires arrived, they gathered these communities into administrative units for the convenience of the empire.[6] These mini empires within empires grouped together diverse mixes of islands, cultures, and language. It was this imperial-driven binding of disparate peoples together under into a single unit that encouraged the later formation of national consciousness.[7] The Harvard political scientist Rupert Emerson observed that "the creation of nations themselves is in some instances, as in the Philippines and Ghana, to be attributed primarily to the bringing of diverse stocks under a single imperial roof. In this fashion inner unity has often been promoted by colonial rule."[8] The Catholic missionary sociologist Franco Zocca observed that "the unifying force of colonisation is undeniable, particularly in the very fragmented populations of Melanesia."[9] The results of this, Zocca notes, are found in reductions in fighting, the adoption of a common language (often in addition to their tribal languages), and preparation for statehood in a world "which at the present time believes only or mainly in the right of states and nations and 'legitimate governments,' not in any rights for peoples, and much less, for lesser minorities."[10] Another commentator on Melanesia wrote "The form and content of the contemporary nation-state were imported into the Pacific thanks to, and as the offshoot of, occupation by European powers."[11]

Another problem with this anti-colonial narrative is that it can distort political analysis, with blames for all social and economic problems of society coming to rest on the former empire. The independent state becomes associated with liberation because the process of state formation is by definition the process of national liberation. The newly independent state becomes an idealized source of national pride along with the symbols of the state, such as flags, uniforms, and other national projects, such as a national airline or shipping line. By implication, this means that the problems in Pacific societies have their source solely outside the country and in the legacy of European empires and their residual effects, such as colonized mindsets. Problems may also be attributed to globalization or neo-imperialism. In these ways, social problems are disconnected from the independent states and their rulers, who can deflect blame for their own failures onto the empires of the past and the neo-empires of the present. With this narrative firmly in place, problems like deep-sea mining, open-cast mining, tourism, and other exploitative or extractive industries come about without apparent involvement of the independent states and their present-day leaders. The fact that licenses and permissions are granted by states to overseas corporations is often overlooked, as is the endemic corruption of the leaders.

Questions can also be raised about the leaders of independence struggles and the later leaders of the newly independent states. The leaders of the independence movements, and therefore the new states, were those who were educated and shaped by former empires. Examples are easy to find. Gandhi, Nkrumah, and others from Asia and Africa.[12] In Melanesia it was the educated elites (often clergy) who took over the reins of the empire-created nation. In the case of Vanuatu, the new leaders included two clergymen educated abroad, Walter Lini and Sethy John Regenvanu. That these leaders were shaped by the West does not necessarily mean that they were ideologically captured by the West. But they had been immersed in the liberal and critical ideas of the West, which has varying influence on these men. They too have interests and a desire for power. While not too much can be claimed for the direct influence of this Western influence on these men, Rupert Emerson's assessment is that "The appearance of a Westernized elite is an indispensable part of the movement toward nationalism."[13] He goes on to say that it is in Western and Christian teachings that we find transmitted lessons revolutions for freedom and doctrines inconsistent with "race discrimination and economic exploitation."[14]

The new post-colonial states of the developing world did not simply come into being. The world they came into already had well-established states existing in a global order that they had created and fashioned to suit themselves. A state does not and cannot exist by itself. The very fact of its border means that the other states exist that may or may not respect that border. And a state must be recognized by other states to have legitimacy (although the sad case of Hawaii shows that this is a necessary, but not sufficient, condition for successful statehood). Any new state comes in a world of other states and their multi-lateral organizations that any new state is wise to recognize. This explains why new states become increasingly like the older established states. Along these lines, Adom Getachew wrote in *Worldmaking after Empire*, that since the height of imperialism, "at the turn of the twentieth century, Europe's political and economic entanglements with the rest of the world constituted a novel era of world politics that made it impossible to think [of] domestic politics in isolation from the ever-widening global interactions."[15] So to exist and survive as a newly independent state meant adapting to the world order that was slated in favor of the imperial states, or to remake the global order so that new states have a fighting chance for true independence.

Another factor in this post-colonial narrative is that the state as it is becomes the only way things can be. The states of the pacific have been prone to suppressing local people and minority voices. As with an empire, it is in the larger states that we see the most oppression of the minorities. Even though the Pacific region is notable for its differences, difference is suppressed by this narrative. To sustain newly won national unity, new states cannot afford to allow for the presence of separatists who wish to assert their local or ethnic diversity, putting at risk fragile national unity. The tangible representation of this is the suppression of succession movements in the Pacific. But as Stewart Firth observed: "Secessionists seek freedom from new forms of colonial domination created, ironically, by the decolonization process itself."[16] If succession movements further independence movements for self-determination, then their suppression illustrates an imperial moment by the state.

EMPIRES AND STATES

The standard post-colonial narrative is a narrative that doesn't always appreciate the history of the relationship between the imperial powers of Europe and rise of the state, with flow-on effects for the theory of states. Historian David Armitage, in his book *The Ideological Origins of the British Empire*, shows how the discourse of states and empires as distinct entities, obscures their similarities:

> The distinction between the 'internal' histories of (mostly) European states and the 'external' histories of (exclusively) European empires obscured the fact that those European states had themselves been created by processes of 'conquest, colonization and cultural change' in the Middle Ages.[17]

The formation of imperial states involved a historical process of conquering other people, subduing recalcitrant groups, colonizing (in the literal sense of "occupying") and changing culture, including the development of national languages. It should come as no surprise that states formed through such processes would seek to extend themselves through what we now call empires. But giving due attention to the details of empire shows that not all states or empires are equal, as Armitage points out in reinforcing his argument:

> it is notable that those European countries that accumulated the earliest overseas empires were also those that earliest consolidated their states; conversely, those weaker states that had not attempted extensive colonisation outside Europe—most obviously, Germany and Italy—only pursued imperial designs after they had acquired the marks of statehood in the later nineteenth or early twentieth centuries. Empires gave birth to states, and states stood at the heart of empires. Accordingly, the most precocious nation-states of early-modern Europe were the great empire states: the Spanish Monarchy, Portugal, the Dutch Republic, France and England—later, Britain.[18]

To fully understand the European empires and their successor states, it is not enough to study the empires as they appeared in the Pacific. One has to go back into the creation of the empire itself. This is important as the DNA, to use a biological metaphor, it passes on to the states it left behind in the continents of the Africa, Asia and the islands of the Pacific that will bear some resemblance to the original imperial design.

The new states of the Pacific were successor states, states which succeeded the empires of the region. Generally speaking, the states covered the same territory worked out by the imperial powers.[19] But some differences were made, as Stephen Henningham notes. The unified Colony of the Gilbert and Ellice Islands was split into Kiribati and Tuvalu. The United States Trust Territory was succeeded by four political entities: Marshall Islands, Federated States of Micronesia, Northern Mariana Islands, and Palau.[20] Some succession movements did not succeed. In the New Hebrides, the attempt by Jimmy Stephens to split the island of Espiritu Santo from the emerging state of Vanuatu failed and was suppressed with outside military help.[21] These boundaries and borders were completely arbitrary, as noted in many post-colonial criticisms, but more radical a critique can be made of borders of all, although these are not so obvious in the island states of the Pacific with the obvious and extreme example of the island of New Guinea with some of its peoples divided on the 141st meridian between Indonesia and Papua New Guinea.[22]

One of the legacies of the new state order, Henningham notes, is that among the recently independent states of the Pacific region,

> a marked reluctance exists to challenging the post-colonial statist order. Any tinkering with that order threatens the legitimacy of existing states, conflicts with the norm in international politics of non-interference in the internal affairs of other sovereign states, and could encourage a variety of dissident and secessionist tendencies within particular states.[23]

There are several obstacles to challenging this order. Firth notes that, by definition, new states "cannot themselves be colonizers" and notes that for new states threatened by succession movements this is a necessary doctrine, along with defining colonizers as "the old colonial powers."[24] Furthermore, according to Kabutaulaka, the political elites—which he and Ralph Pettman call "compradors;" in Papua New Guinea they have been called a "supertribe"[25]—of the new successor states in the Pacific owe their existence and positions to the new states as they are, and prefer to maintain the "colonially created boundaries."[26]

In other words, the states of the new nations will not, as imperial states and their empires before them, tolerate any succession or independence movements within their boundaries.[27] The state, as the empire before it, must remain intact and use force to ensure that it does. We can conclude this section with the observation of Étienne Balibar that, "In a sense, every modern nation is a product of colonization: it has always been to some degree colonized or colonizing, and sometimes both at the same time."[28]

THEOLOGIES OF EMPIRE AND THEOLOGIES OF STATES

Empires are so loathed these days that we no longer stop to consider in any detail the justifications and arguments that were given in support of them. This is lamentable, not because we wish to reestablish empires, but because we wish to avoid empires and things like empires that are based on imperial thought patterns. The foregoing narratives of the relationship between empires and nation-states is not only of interest to the social-scientist or historian. Theology also has interest here in how both empires and nations have been promoted and justified theologically.

When I teach political theology at the Pacific Theological College, one small assignment I set for the students is to have them read medieval justifications of empire and then ask them to take just one argument for the empire and criticize it. Arguments for empire are not sound arguments, and the student engages with them in learning post-colonial political theology. What proves revealing from this exercise is that arguments for empire resonate today, if not in the forms of empire, then in the forms of the organization of the contemporary state. Theological discussion on empires and states rarely discuss their analogous justifications. In post-colonial theology there is no justification for empires, while there are justifications for the independent state. However, past justifications given for the empire bear many similarities with present arguments justifying states. Here we wish to look into the theological justification of unified empires which developed in the middle ages, and then look at how these same arguments are deployed today in the justification of the modern state. The modern world is radically different to the middle ages, but in many ways developed and rearranged medieval thinking for the modern period. The analogous justifications shared between empires and states considered here are unity, security, justice, and the apparent immutability of political forms. With respect to Carl Schmitt, we might say that all significant concepts of the modern theory of the independent state are decolonized imperial concepts.[29]

One argument for empire is that it is based on the idea of unity. Unity was fostered by empire in practical ways, through the imposition of language. Indeed, the development of European states also involved the harmonization of homogenization of language. The development of French and German, for instance required the imposition of standards in language for administration of the kingdoms. Similar ideas of unity developed, as shown above, in the nationalism, which was necessary to foster anti-imperial independence movements in colonies.

Engelbert of Admont wrote an important treatise on empire entitled *On the Rise and End of the Roman Empire* (*De ortu, progressu et fine Romani imperii*). Engelbert, like many political writers before and since, argues that the human communities have peace as their end. He proceeds to write that "Peace . . . consists of two things, that is, concord among themselves and in not having discord with foreigners."[30] Concord or harmony comes through unity. Therefore, the end of human communities, being peace, is best served through unity, specifically unity of the "same fatherland, the same language, the same customs and the same laws, pleasing on another mutually."[31] This is the unity the nation gives to its communities. Then Engelbert asks whether kingdoms should be separate or united under one king (an emperor). He answers "yes," for three reasons: 1) in nature, beasts have the lion as their king and birds the eagle; 2) in a well-ordered multitude the many are subordinated to the few and then the one; and 3) the common good is better than an individual good and therefore the lesser good is subordinated to the greater goods—from the individual up to the imperial good.[32] This is extrapolated to politics, working from individuals subordinated to households, households to cities, cities to kingdoms, kingdoms to one empire. Hence empire, for Engelbert, is the best form of government. Likewise, in states, which locates all sovereignty focused in the power of the sovereign, whether in Parliament or in the King, finds an analogous single place of government.

Let's examine in some detail an argument against imperial unity. The argument comes from Augustine's *City of God* (IV.15) and argues that just as some houses stand separate happily outside a village, or that a village can stand alone apart from the city, a kingdom can stand alone from the empire.[33] Engelbert's reply to this counter-argument for empire is revealing of the justification of the state. This peace (the end of the state) is, in short, utopian. It demands that "kingdoms could conduct themselves perpetually toward one another as peaceful neighbours."[34] Since this is not possible in the present life, "it is better and more just for all kingdoms to be subject to one empire . . . to harmonize kingdoms among themselves and pacify the world."[35] How does this relate to the state? This ontology of violence, that violence is inevitable and part of the natural order of the temporal world, is a major justification for the state, at least since Thomas Hobbes. Just as the empire provides peace between nations, the state provides peace between individuals and communities and religions which would otherwise tear each other apart. To both imperialists and statists, it is not possible to live apart from the provider of social peace, either the empire or the state; to think otherwise is a utopian fantasy.

This notion of the protection against violence offered by political power is found in both empires and states. For empires in the medieval period, a central concept here is the *katechon*, as found in Paul's second letter to the Thessalonians: "And you know what is now restraining him, so that he may be revealed when his time comes. For the mystery of lawlessness is already at work, but only until the one who now restrains it is removed" (2 Th. 2: 6–7, NRSV). As Augustine pointed out, there have been many guesses and attempts at interpretation; with influential interpretations helping to win the text a certain importance. Dietrich Bonhoeffer follows many of the Church Fathers in seeing the restrainer as a political power.[36] Tertullian, for instance, saw the Roman Empire as having a role in arresting worldly afflictions ("Apology," §32). Adso of Montier-en-Der saw that the Antichrist could not gain ground as long as the Roman Empire had all nations under its control.[37] Carl Schmitt offers a small survey of similar interpretations in *The Nomos of the Earth in the International Law of the Jus Publicum Europaeum*.[38] Based on such ancient and medieval interpretations, Schmitt claims that this text and the notion of the restrainer was of capital importance in the Middle Ages.[39] He writes that "The empire of the Christian Middle Ages lasted only as long as the idea of the *katechon* was alive."[40] As Giorgio Agamben remarks, the ancient traditions of interpretation of this passage culminate "in the Schmittian theory that finds in 2 Thessalonians 2 the only possible foundation for a Christian doctrine of State power."[41] Bonhoeffer is just one theologian who justified the state on the basis of this passage. But its influence may extend into secular thought, as Agamben writes: "In a certain sense, every theory of the State, including Hobbes's—which thinks of it as a power destined to block or delay catastrophe—can be taken as a secularization of this interpretation of 2 Thessalonians 2."[42] The obvious biblical parallel to the state is its restraint of evil and sin by wielding the sword for the security of all (Ro. 13:3–4; 1 Pe. 2:14).[43] In short both empire and states provide protection against evil threats and this is justified theologically.

Another key criterion for the legitimacy of both state and empire is how power is attained and the purpose to which it is put.[44] If power is attained in a just way and used for justice, then it is just rule. In the common narrative, outlined at the beginning of this chapter, imperial rule was considered unjust and state rule which replaced was considered just. Why this distinction? Historically speaking, this is because the empire was imposed on subjected peoples, whereas state rules comes from the nation and is democratic in that it follows the organic will of a free people to determine their own destiny.

Engelbert acknowledges that Roman imperial rule looks unjust, but then examines the evidence for the three just ways by which the Romans acquired their empire. Firstly, through "armed justice" or just wars against its unjust and rebellious neighbors.[45] Secondly, through "testamentary disposition" or the gifting of territory by Kings grateful for the protection of Rome.[46] Thirdly, the Romans acquired territory and control by "voluntary subjection," which Engelbert says may follow subjection by a "warlike force," leading gradually to giving up one's own will and becoming "voluntarily obedient and subject."[47]

If we inquire into the origins of states we find similar arguments in place, that the origin of the state is just and the state must be rendered to. In the Pacific we see similar arguments with the just acquisition of state sovereignty. Arguably, Fiji's Deed of Cession (1874), which created "Fiji" and allowed Britain to add it to its colonies, could be an example of "testamentary disposition" by Fijian chiefs seeking the protection of the British.[48] In the Americas and beyond, the doctrine of discovery provided a rationale for discovering land which can be justifiably taken (Miller, et. al 2010). How many other states have myths of origin that paint a picture of just origins when the real picture from the subjected people is anything but? In the case of composite states, such as Vanuatu or Papua New Guinea, the territorial bodies were united unjustly by imperial powers and were then sustained in their colonial form by the new independent states.

One final similarity between the empire and the state worth mentioning is that in having been given a theological justification, they take on the aura of divinely ordained permanence or immutability. As states persist, they take on the appearance of being part of the permanent natural order, as the way things are or should be. Engelbert suggests that when things persist and happen regularly, they are either of natural or human or divine origin.[49] He concludes that political order is part of divine providence, meaning that it appears intractable. This applies not only to the empires of his time, but now to the states of ours. Being ordained by God, as many suggest of the state or empire, makes it not ours to change or even challenge. Yet throughout political history there have been many competitors and alternatives to the state. And there remain alternatives to this which are not infected by the taint of empire. This remains a challenge to political forms states, like empires, will not last forever.

CONCLUSION

In this chapter I wish to disrupt the simplistic post-colonial narrative of evolution from oppressive empire to liberating state. This narrative has been disrupted by political philosophers, but theology can also disrupt this by going into its own dark past of justifying empire and seeing how these arguments live on in the theological justifications of states that continue some of the functions of empire. Basil Davidson's narrative of the development of the African State, as just one example, shows that alternatives were available, and perhaps remain available, to the peoples of Africa. Adom Getachew also shows how alternatives to the state existed for decolonizing nations in the form of federalism.[50] Such alternatives, one might suppose, have also existed for the people of the Pacific who are grappling with the ongoing effects of empire, especially in the case of France and Indonesia, but also with successionist movements, such as in Bougainville and Malaita.

NOTES

1. Stewart Firth, "Decolonization" in *Remembrance of Pacific Pasts: An Invitation to Remake History*, Ed. by Robert Borofsky (Honolulu: University of Hawai'i Press, 2000) 317; Tracey Banivanua Mar, *Decolonisation and the Pacific: Indigenous Globalisation and the Ends of Empire* (Cambridge: Cambridge University Press, 2016) 5–6.

2. Krishan Kumar, "Nation-States as Empires, Empires as Nation-States: Two Principles, One Practice?" in *Theory and Society* Vol. 39, No. 2 (2010) 119–20.

3. Adom Getachew, *Worldmaking after Empire: The Rise and Fall of Self-Determination* (Princeton, NJ: Princeton University Press, 2019) 3.

4. This is the description of precolonial Papua New Guinea (Wanek 1996: 29).

5. Nwokolo, I. "Constitution Making and National Integration in a Plural Society" in *The Politics of Melanesia* Ed. by Marion W. Ward. Canberra, (AU: The Research School of Pacific Studies, Australian National University; Port Moresby: The University of Papua and New Guinea, 1970) 247.

6. Tarcisius Kabutaulaka, "Cohesion and Disorder in Melanesia: The Bougainville Conflict and the Melanesian Way" in *New Politics in the South Pacific*, Ed. by Werner vom Busch, Marjorie Tuainekore Crocombe, Ron Crocombe, Linda Crowl, Tony Deklin, Peter Larmour, and Esther Winimamaori Williams (Suva, FJ: Institute of Pacific Studies, University of the South Pacific, 1994) 65; Banivanua Mar, *Decolonization and the Pacific*, 41.

7. Sinclair Dinnen, "The Twin Processes of Nation Building and State Building" in *State, Society and Governance in Melanesia Bnreifing Note, No. 1*. (Canberra, AU: Australian National University, Department of Pacific Affairs, 2007) 3.

8. Rupert Emerson, *From Empire to Nation: The Rise to Self-Assertion of Asian and African Peoples* (Boston: Beacon Press, 1960), 3.

9. Franco Zocca, *Melanesia and Its Churches: Past and Present* (Goroka, PNG: Melanesian Institute for Pastoral and Socio-Economic Service, 2007) 50.

10. Ibid.

11. Edward LiPuma, "The Formation of Nation-States and National Cultures in Oceania" in *Nation Making: Emergent Identities in Postcolonial Melanesia*. Ed. by Robert J. Foster (Ann Arbor, MI: The University of Michigan Press, 1995) 43.

12. Rupert Emerson, *From Empire to Nation: The Rise to Self-Assertion of Asian and African Peoples* (Boston: Beacon Press, 1960) 17.

13. In Vanuatu, this elite was largely provided by the Presbyterian Church (Gardner 2013: 122–43). This is also true in Papua New Guinea (Wanek 1996:18); Ibid, 44.

14. Ibid, 53–54

15. Getachew, *Worldmaking after Empire,* 13.

16. Stewart Firth, "Decolonization," 318.

17. David Armitage, *The Ideological Origins of the British Empire* (Cambridge, GB: Cambridge University Press, 2000) 14.

18. Ibid, 15.

19. Barrie Macdonald, "Decolonization and Beyond: The Framework for Post-Colonial Relationships in Oceania" in *The Journal of Pacific History* Vol. 21, No. 3 (1986) 117.

20. Stephen Henningham, *The Pacific Island States: Security and Sovereignty in the Post-Cold War World* (Houndmills and London: Macmillan Press, 1995) 54.

21. Ibid.

22. Franco Zocca, *Melanesia and Its Churches,* 51.

23. Stephen Henningham, *The Pacific Island States,* 54.

24. Stewart Firth, "Decolonization," 319.

25. Alexander Wanek, *The State and Its Enemies in Papua New Guinea* (Richmond, GB: Curzon Press, 1996) 54–56.

26. Tarcisius Kabutaulaka, "Cohesion and Disorder in Melanesia," 65; Ralph Pettman, "The Solomon Islands: A Developing Neo-Colony?" in *Australian Outlook* Vol. 31, No. 2 (1977) 272.

27. Ralph Pettman, "The Solomon Islands," 270.

28. Étienne Balibar, "The Nation Form: History and Ideology" in *Race, Nation, Class: Ambiguous Identities*. Ed. by Étienne Balibar and Immanuel Wallerstein (London, GB: Verso, 1991) 89.

29. Carl Schmitt, *Political Theology: Four Chapters on the Concept of Sovereignty.* Tran. by George Schwab (Chicago, IL: University of Chicago Press, 2005) 36.

30. Engelbert of Admont, "On the Rise and End of the Roman Empire" in *Three Tracts on Empire: Engelbert of Admont, Aeneas Silvius Piccolomini and Juan de Torquemada,* Tran. by Thomas M. Izbicki with Cary J. Nederman. Sterling (VA: Thoemmes Press, 2000) 60.

31. Ibid, 63–64.

32. Ibid.

33. Ibid, 68.

34. Ibid, 75.

35. Ibid.

36. Dietrich Bonhoeffer, *Ethics*. Ed. by Clifford J. Green, Trans. by Reinhard Krauss, Charles C. West, and Douglas W. Stott (Minneapolis, MN: Fortress Press, 2009) 131–32.

37. Adso of Montier-en-Der, "Letter on the Origin and Time of Antichrist" in *Apocalyptic Spirituality: Treatises and Letters of Lactantius, Adso of Montier-en-*

Der, Joachim of Fiore, the Franciscan Spirituals, Savonarola. Ed. and trans. by Bernard McGinn (London, GB: SPCK, 1980) 93.

38. Carl Schmitt, *The Nomos of the Earth in the International Law of the Jus Publicum Europaeum*, Tran. by G. L. Ulmen (New York, NY: Telos, 2006) 60.

39. Ibid, 55–56, 87.

40. Ibid., 60.

41. Carl Schmitt, *Political Theology: Four Chapters on the Concept of Sovereignty*, 36.

42. Giorgio Agamben, *The Time That Remains: A Commentary on the Letter to the Romans*, Trans. by Patricia Dailey (Stanford, CA: Stanford University Press, 2005) 109.

43. Ibid., 110.

44. Engelbert of Admont, "On the Rise and End of the Roman Empire," 56.

45. Ibid, 54–55.

46. Ibid, 55–56.

47. Ibid, 56.

48. John D. Kelly and Martha Kaplan, *Represented Communities: Fiji and World Decolonization* (Chicago, IL: University of Chicago, 2001) 126.

49. Engelbert of Admont, "On the Rise and End of the Roman Empire," 67.

50. Nwokolo also discusses, and rejects, the possibilities of a federal constitution for New Guinea (1970:263–65); Adom Getachew, *Worldmaking after Empire*.

BIBLIOGRAPHY

Adso of Montier-en-Der. "Letter on the Origin and Time of Antichrist." *Apocalyptic Spirituality: Treatises and Letters of Lactantius, Adso of Montier-en-Der, Joachim of Fiore, the Franciscan Spirituals, Savonarola*. Ed. and trans. by Bernard McGinn. London, GB: SPCK, 1980.

Agamben, Giorgio. *The Time That Remains: A Commentary on the Letter to the Romans*. Trans. by Patricia Dailey. Stanford, CA: Stanford University Press, 2005.

Armitage, David. *The Ideological Origins of the British Empire*. Cambridge, GB: Cambridge University Press, 2000.

Balibar, Étienne. "The Nation Form: History and Ideology." *Race, Nation, Class: Ambiguous Identities*. Ed. by Étienne Balibar and Immanuel Wallerstein. London, GB: Verso, 1991.

Banivanua Mar, Tracey. *Decolonisation and the Pacific: Indigenous Globalisation and the Ends of Empire*. Cambridge: Cambridge University Press, 2016.

Bonhoeffer, Dietrich. *Ethics*. Ed. by Clifford J. Green, Trans. by Reinhard Krauss, Charles C. West, and Douglas W. Stott. Minneapolis, MN: Fortress Press, 2009.

Davidson, Basil. *The Black Man's Burden: Africa and the Curse of the Nation-State*. London: James Currey, 1992.

Dinnen, Sinclair. "The Twin Processes of Nation Building and State Building." *State, Society and Governance in Melanesia Bnreifing Note, No. 1*. Canberra, AU: Australian National University, Department of Pacific Affairs, 2007. http://hdl.handle.net/1885/141454.

Emerson, Rupert. *From Empire to Nation: The Rise to Self-Assertion of Asian and African Peoples.* Boston, MA: Beacon Press, 1960.

Engelbert of Admont. "On the Rise and End of the Roman Empire." *Three Tracts on Empire: Engelbert of Admont, Aeneas Silvius Piccolomini and Juan de Torquemada.* Tran. by Thomas M. Izbicki with Cary J. Nederman. Sterling, VA: Thoemmes Press, 2000.

Firth, Stewart. "Decolonization." *Remembrance of Pacific Pasts: An Invitation to Remake History.* Ed. by Robert Borofsky. Honolulu: University of Hawai'i Press, 2000.

Gardner, Helen. "Praying for Independence: The Presbyterian Church in the Decolonisation of Vanuatu," *The Journal of Pacific History* Vol. 48, No. 2 (2013):122–43.

Getachew, Adom. *Worldmaking after Empire: The Rise and Fall of Self-Determination.* Princeton, NJ: Princeton University Press, 2019.

Henningham, Stephen. *The Pacific Island States: Security and Sovereignty in the Post-Cold War World.* Houndmills and London: Macmillan Press, 1995.

Kabutaulaka, Tarcisius. "Cohesion and Disorder in Melanesia: The Bougainville Conflict and the Melanesian Way." *New Politics in the South Pacific.* Ed. by Werner vom Busch, Marjorie Tuainekore Crocombe, Ron Crocombe, Linda Crowl, Tony Deklin, Peter Larmour, and Esther Winimamaori Williams. Suva, FJ: Institute of Pacific Studies, University of the South Pacific, 1994.

Kelly, John D., and Martha Kaplan. *Represented Communities: Fiji and World Decolonization.* Chicago, IL: University of Chicago, 2001.

Kumar, Krishan. "Nation-States as Empires, Empires as Nation-States: Two Principles, One Practice?" *Theory and Society* Vol. 39, No. 2 (2010):119–43.

LiPuma, Edward. "The Formation of Nation-States and National Cultures in Oceania." *Nation Making: Emergent Identities in Postcolonial Melanesia.* Ed. by Robert J. Foster. Ann Arbor, MI: The University of Michigan Press, 1995.

MacDonald, Barrie. "Decolonization and Beyond: The Framework for Post-Colonial Relationships in Oceania." *The Journal of Pacific History* Vol. 21, No. 3 (1986):115–26.

Miller, Robert J., Jacinta Ruru, Larissa Behrendt, and Tracey Lindberg. *Discovering Indigenous Lands: The Doctrine of Discovery in the English Colonies.* Oxford, GB: Oxford University Press, 2010.

Nwokolo, I. "Constitution Making and National Integration in a Plural Society." *The Politics of Melanesia.* Ed. by Marion W. Ward. Canberra, AU: The Research School of Pacific Studies, Australian National University; Port Moresby: The University of Papua and New Guinea, 1970.

Pettman, Ralph. "The Solomon Islands: A Developing Neo-Colony?" *Australian Outlook* Vol. 31, No. 2 (1977): 268–78.

Schmitt, Carl. *The Nomos of the Earth in the International Law of the Jus Publicum Europaeum.* Tran. by G. L. Ulmen. New York, NY: Telos, 2006.

———. *Political Theology: Four Chapters on the Concept of Sovereignty.* Tran. by George Schwab. Chicago, IL: University of Chicago Press, 2005.

Sider, Ronald J. *Just Politics: A Guide for Christian Engagement.* Grand Rapids, MI: Brazos Press, 2014.

Tertullian. "Apology." *Tertullian: Apologetical Works and Minucius Felix: Octavius.* Trans. by Rudolphus Arbesmann, Emily Joseph Daly, and Edwin A. Quain. Washington, DC: Catholic University of America Press, 1950.

Wanek, Alexander. *The State and Its Enemies in Papua New Guinea.* Richmond, GB: Curzon Press, 1996.

Zocca, Franco. *Melanesia and Its Churches: Past and Present.* Goroka, PNG: Melanesian Institute for Pastoral and Socio-Economic Service, 2007.

Chapter Fourteen

Palestine, Zionism, and Global Struggle

A Jewish American's Journey

Mark Braverman

I was born in 1948, within a month of the declaration of the State of Israel, into a traditional Jewish family in the United States. Like virtually every other identifying Jew of my generation, I embraced the Zionist narrative as a romantic, compelling story of heroism and redemption. The story of my emancipation from Zionism parallels the gradual awakening of the West to the reality of Israel, not as a democratic, egalitarian haven, but as a settler colonial state pursuing a brutal program of land theft and ethnic cleansing. This awakening has taken the form of solidarity with the Palestinian struggle by other liberation movements, economic and diplomatic sanctions on the part of governments, and increasing mobilization of the churches of the world in opposition to the violation of Christianity's values of justice and compassion. For the Jewish community, the realization is growing that our story today is no longer about what has been done to us. Rather, it is the story of what we are doing to another people.

In 1948, the State of Israel was established by the Zionist movement. The military conflict that followed provided the opportunity for the military forces of the new state to carry out a program of conquest and dispossession that had been planned for decades. By the 1949 ceasefire, three quarters of a million Palestinians had been expelled, their descendants now numbering over four million. Palestinians remaining inside the de facto borders of Israel were consigned to second-class citizenship. Since the conquest by Israel of the West Bank, Gaza, and the Golan Heights in 1967, the annexation and colonial settlement of remaining Palestinian lands has continued, in violation of international law and with the diplomatic and financial support of the world powers. Palestinians in those territories live under various levels of military and administrative restriction on movement, commerce, and growth. The result is that an apartheid situation exists in the territory of historic Palestine.

The appeal of the Palestinian people for the restoration of their homeland and their human rights has brought this issue to the attention of the world at large through successive and persistent waves of resistance, including the 2005 call for Boycott, Divestment and Sanctions,[1] and to the churches on a global and ecumenical level through calls from the Christians of Palestine (e.g., 2007,[2] 2009,[3] 2017[4]). In December 2019, Palestinians and international supporters gathering in Bethlehem called attention to the increasingly brutal and aggressive nature of Israeli actions against the Palestinians, including the murderous suppression of the March of Return in Gaza, the increase in illegal settlement and annexation of Palestinian lands, and, in the words of the conference statement, "three more appalling developments: U.S. recognition of Jerusalem as the capital of Israel, the U.S. Secretary of State's announcement that the U.S. government no longer deems West Bank settlements to be 'inconsistent with international law,' and the State of Israel's recent adoption of the Nation State Law [declaring Israel to be the nation state of the Jewish people and officially relegating the rights of non-Jews to secondary status] which clearly reveals that *de facto* apartheid has become *de jure* apartheid."[5]

A JEWISH AMERICAN'S JOURNEY

The period following World War II and the establishment of the State of Israel in 1948 saw the most dramatic shift in Jewish identity in almost 2,000 years. The destruction of the Second Temple in Jerusalem by Rome in 70 CE marked the end of Jewish theocracy in Palestine and Judaism's transformation from a territorially-based cult to a worldwide religious community. Rabbinic Judaism, as it came to be called, defined Jewish identity as obedience to the one God, observance of prayer, rituals governing everyday life, and commitment to an ethical code, uncoupled from physical locality and temporal power. The synagogue liturgy that developed over the millennia did include images of Jerusalem and a yearning for a return to Temple worship. But these motifs, while vivid, were symbolic and not connected to an actual program of return and restoration, until they were called into service by the Zionist movement at the end of the 19th century. Perceived as being in conflict with Rabbinic Judaism, the ethnic nationalist program that was political Zionism was rejected by the major Jewish denominations. Nevertheless, the project was energetically pursued by the Zionist movement, which, although adopting biblical language, was entirely secular in its leadership and ideology. The archaic ideology and hermeneutic of modern Zionism, which transposed the biblical (and non-historical) narrative of conquest and hegemony into a contemporary right of land possession, did not infiltrate and eventually overtake mainstream Judaism until the actual establishment of the State of Israel.

And so it was that I was raised in the potent combination of Rabbinic Judaism and political Zionism that had become the norm for Jews across the theological and denominational spectrum after the creation of the Jewish state. The State of Israel was not a mere historical event. As the "Prayer for the State of Israel," added to the Jewish prayer book in 1948 reads, Israel is "the first flowering of our redemption." We had secured our safety and restored our dignity by having a country of our own and an army to defend it—and we petitioned for the protection of both in that same prayer. Commitment to the newly established State of Israel was an essential component of Jewish identity, inseparable from religious observance and adherence to the ethical and ritual codes. I first visited Israel as a boy of 17, and I fell in love with the young state. My Israeli family—religious Jews—warmly embraced me. But even as I embraced them in return, I heard the racism in the way they talked about "the Arabs." It was the way that white people talked about blacks in the pre-civil rights Philadelphia of my childhood. I began to understand that something was wrong with the Zionist project—but my attachment to Israel and to Zionist fundamentals stayed strong. After college, I lived for a year on a kibbutz, ignoring the implications of the pre-1948 Palestinian buildings repurposed as the communal dining hall and social center, and the abandoned olive groves on the edges of its vast apple orchards.

Returning to the U.S., my concerns about Israel increased in direct proportion to the pace of illegal settlement-building in the territories occupied in 1967. Still, I held to the Zionist narrative: The occupation, although lamentably abusive of human rights, was the price to be paid for security. Then I went to the West Bank. Traveling in Israel and the occupied Palestinian territories in the summer of 2006, I experienced first-hand the crimes committed against the Palestinian people and the deeply damaging effect of the role of colonizer on Israeli society. I witnessed the separation wall snaking through the West Bank on stolen land, the checkpoints, the network of restricted roads, the massive, continuing construction of illegal Jewish settlements and towns, the vicious acts of ideological Jewish settlers, and the effect of militarization and ongoing conflict on Israelis, especially the young. I came to realize that the project to establish Jewish hegemony over the territory of historic Palestine, besides being morally indefensible and a violation of international law, would never satisfy the yearning of my people for safety and security. My liberation from Zionism—as an identity, a political persuasion, and a theology—did not happen overnight. I had accepted unquestioningly the Zionist narrative about the founding of the state ("a land without people for a people without a land") and the self-perceptions that came with it. Over the years, however, I became increasingly disturbed by the demonization and othering of "the Arabs," as we called them. I grew more and more uncomfortable with the exceptionalism and the sensibility of triumphalist victimhood which infuses our liturgy and which, along with the redemptive vision of the State of Israel, seemed intended to define me: "Thou hast chosen us from among all the peoples." "In every age a tyrant arises to destroy us."

It was grace that, in my middle age, brought me to Palestine to encounter this purported enemy. Even more than the shock of witnessing the injustice against the Palestinians, it was the welcome I received from this generous, hospitable, persistent, and proud people that changed me. Like Jacob reunited with Esau, when I met these sisters and brothers on the other side of the wall that had been built to separate us, I saw the face of God. I met the Palestinian Christians, who introduced me to the Palestinian of 2,000 years ago, whose example of resistance they followed. The story of a Jew fiercely faithful to the core of his tradition, taking aim directly at the Jewish establishment that had betrayed that tradition by throwing in with empire, spoke strongly to me as a Jew horrified and heartbroken by what was being done in my name and what was laying waste to the justice tradition in which I was raised.

Contrary to the charges of some of my co-religionists, I do not seek the destruction of the State of Israel. I am not, as they imply, naïve about the persistence of anti-Semitism. Rather, I feel deep concern for the future of the state and profound sadness for my friends and family in Israel. Their predecessors, who had come to Israel out of idealism or in flight from persecution, did not know that the dream of a socialist haven they had been promised involved a carefully planned program for the ethnic cleansing of an indigenous people. They did not know that their children and grandchildren would be raised in a toxic brew of fear and racism that would poison their society and condemn them to neverending conflict and increasing isolation from the community of nations. I feel very much like two other Jews, the prophet Jeremiah and, eight centuries after him, Jesus of Nazareth, standing before Jerusalem and weeping for the self-inflicted destruction to come. If questioning Zionism and the very concept of a Jewish state makes me an exile from mainstream Judaism, so be it. I have joined the growing ranks of Jews who actively question the actions of Israel that purport to advance the cause of Jewish survival. My exposure to the consequences of political Zionism, and my encounter with Palestinian society and especially the Christians of Palestine, changed my relationship to Israel forever.

Returning home to the U.S. from the West Bank in 2006, I was eager to share what I had seen. But the organized Jewish community did not want to hear what I had to say. My message of support for Palestinian rights and criticism of Israel's policies put me beyond the pale of what was acceptable.

But then the unexpected happened—the doors of churches were flung open. Christians were eager to hear a Jew talk about justice for Palestinians as a moral imperative and the path to peace. They received my message with what I can only describe as gratitude because, almost without exception, they felt that, as Christians, they could not actively take on the Palestinian cause. They knew that, as followers of Jesus, they were duty-bound to respond to the cry of the oppressed. But in the case of Israel and Palestine, they could not act accordingly, first because they had been told that the Jewish people were owed a state because of their history of suffering, and second, because they felt responsible for having caused that suffering. In addition, there was a powerful theological component. In conversations with Christian clergy and seminary professors, I learned that, for Christians, a new theology had grown up after World War II as part of the project to atone for church anti-Semitism. This revisionist theology exalted the Jews as God's chosen people and supported the Jewish quest for safety and self-determination in the form of the establishment of a Jewish homeland. In this reversal of age-old Christian doctrine, the Jews were no longer condemned to wander the earth. In fact, we had been reinstated as God's elect—the original covenant between God and Abraham was in force, and with it the promise of a particular piece of territory. Christianity's effort to correct its historic anti-Judaism is laudable. But the support for Zionism that came with this theology has put generations of theologians and clergy—not only in the West but in the global South as well—on a slippery slope of endorsing a racist and exceptionalist ideology that goes against the most fundamental principles of Christianity. Faced with the evidence of Israel's violations of those precious values, Christians are now facing a significant challenge.

CHALLENGING CHRISTIAN ZIONISM

The good news is that owing to the work of Palestinian theologians and the Western theologians who have followed their lead, this challenge is being met. Since the turn of the century, a body of theological work has emerged that brings important implications for church renewal, interfaith relations, and political, economic and social justice not only for Palestine, but also for the world at large. Palestinian theologians, beginning with Naim Ateek[6] and Mitri Raheb,[7] have countered the dominant Western narrative of a primary Jewish right to the land as well as the theology that has supported this claim. Prior to the appearance of this work, the hermeneutic of dominance and colonialism that had been advanced to support the modern Jewish homeland project had gone unchallenged in the West, with the exception of a few voices.[8] In the aftermath of the Nazi period, Zionism has exerted a powerful pull on Christian theology and sensibility, drawing from the deep well of Christian Zionism, its roots reaching back to the English Reformation.[9] Christian Zionism is characterized by a reading of the Bible in which the identity of the ancient Israelites is transferred directly to the contemporary Jewish citizens of Israel and indeed, to all Jewish people. For some, the State of Israel is seen as the beginning of the fulfillment of End Times prophecies.[10] Christians who do not subscribe to this eschatology nevertheless accept Jewish privilege with respect to the land, out of nostalgia for a biblical Israel and guilt about the persecution of Jews throughout the millennia. For these Christians, to support the cause of Palestinian liberation through word or action is to abandon support for the Jewish state as a vehicle of repentance and to betray the postwar program of reconciliation with the Jewish people.[11] Even progressive Christians who do not explicitly or knowingly subscribe to Christian Zionism are reluctant to criticize Israel, and may even accuse those advocating for Palestinian rights as lending support for anti-Semitism or being anti-Semitic themselves.

Since the publication in 2009 of the Kairos Palestine "Moment of Truth: A Word of Faith, Hope and Love from the Heart of Palestinian Suffering," however, a shift in attitude has begun to appear. Also known as "Kairos Palestine," the document, written by Palestinian clergy, theologians, and civil society leaders, presents the "signs of the times" of a brutal and worsening occupation that is the continuation of a program of ethnic cleansing that began with the declaration of the State of Israel in 1948. It articulates a theology that requires resistance to the evil of occupation: "resistance with love as its logic." Naming the Israeli occupation a sin, Kairos Palestine calls out to the international community, reserving its final appeal for the church itself: "What is the international community doing? What are the political leaders in Palestine, in Israel and in the Arab world doing? What is the Church doing?"[12] The release of this document produced an outpouring of statements of support from church-related groups on every continent, and where relevant, acknowledgments of complicity with and responsibility for Palestinian suffering.[13] A global Kairos network has been created under the leadership of the Kairos Palestine organization, located in Bethlehem.[14]

A THEOLOGY OF LAND: THE BIBLE THROUGH PALESTINIAN EYES

The biblical narrative of chosen people and land promise has been used throughout modern history as justification for settler colonialism, ethnic cleansing, and chattel slavery. The question of the land has captured the attention of the church globally and ecumenically. In 2008, American theologian Harvey Cox cautioned attendees at the World Council of Church's Palestine Israel Ecumenical Forum conference on "Promised Land" with this question:

> What do we really mean by "promised land?" How has the term been hijacked and used for various political reasons, when maybe that is not the significance of the texts at all? Ancient Israel is often confused with modern Israel. They are not the same. We can talk about an integral relationship which must be there theologically between Christians and the Jewish people. Jesus was Jewish; the whole background of Christianity comes from the Jewish people, but the Jewish people and the modern State of Israel, though they overlap in certain ways, are not the same, and therefore we have to be thoughtful and self-critical about how that theme is dealt with.[15]

In advancing the urgent need for a "new hermeneutic of liberation," Palestinian theologian Mitri Raheb takes issue with theology that is done "independent from geo-political analyses."[16] For Raheb, this bears on the question of how individual and collective identity are formed. Raheb's analysis leads us back to the birth of the church as a community based on resistance to tyranny and the move from the tribal to the universal: "It might be easy to read the Old Testament as a collection of narratives on land, peoples, and identity," writes Raheb, "but what of the New Testament? The whole New Testament is a collection of narratives that challenge the then-existing exclusive national and religious narratives. The New Testament introduces a new lens; instead of identifying with one people over against the others, which is the traditional way of forming one's identity, it calls people to reflect on the entire process of identification as misleading."[17] Raheb enjoins us to read the Bible through the eyes of the Palestinians. In so doing, he takes us back to the ministry of that Palestinian of 2,000 years ago. Jesus introduced his paradigm-shattering vision on the day he initiated his ministry, when he crossed the ethnic and cultural barrier by elevating the examples of the widow in Sidon and the leper in Syria. That transgression, as recounted in Luke chapter four, unleashed murderous rage against him. It is not an overstatement to say that the story of that first Sabbath in Nazareth introduces the central issue that drove Jesus's entire ministry, crystalized in the question asked and answered by Jesus: "Who is my neighbor?"

Raheb brings the question into the present day: "After almost half a century of Israeli occupation of Palestinian land, Western theologians have been unable to see that the empire is at work in Israel itself . . . the State of Israel as a modern expression of empire."[18] Raheb writes that "Western and increasingly Asian theologians . . . ascribe to the myth of a Judeo-Christian tradition. This myth of the Judeo-Christian tradition is unequivocally part of imperial theology that sees and believes itself as supreme."[19] Raheb's analysis raises issues of critical importance for the forging of a new perspective for Christians confronting the crime of the dispossession of the Palestinian people. The myth of the Judeo-Christian tradition serves three purposes: (1) it glosses over the critical differences between the two traditions with respect to particularity vs. universality, (2) inasmuch as it has been invoked in the attempt to renounce or undo supercessionism, it serves Christian penitence over church anti-Judaism, and (3) it allows Christians to hold on their own exceptionalism by granting theological legitimacy to the exceptionalism inherent in the Old Testament narrative of divine favor and privilege bestowed on one particular ethnic group or nation. The Christian project to atone for anti-Semitism has, ironically, served not to bring the Good News of God's love for all humanity, but to prop up Christian particularity by projecting it back on to the Jews and then hitching a ride on it. Christians are "guests in the House of Israel," declared American theologian Clark M. Williamson, in an expression borrowed from Karl Barth.[20] "Christianity," wrote theologian Paul M. van Buren, "must refer to Judaism in order to make sense of itself. This is in the service of the church's reversal of its position from that of anti-Judaism to an acknowledgement of the eternal covenant between God and Israel."[21] Thus, postwar Western theology has taken God's house, and, in a betrayal of Pentecost, made it smaller and exclusive, and granted Christians rent-free occupancy in perpetuity. In the penitential project to purge Christianity of its anti-Semitism and to reconcile with the Jewish people, Christians have avoided what should have been the key issue faced by the Christian world in confronting the ovens of Auschwitz: Christianity's own exceptionalism and triumphalism. Instead, the issue is sidestepped by substituting Christian particularity with an even more potent Judeo-Christian triumphalism—and its language is Zionism.

HARD CHOICES: CONFRONTING THE SHADOW

Christians in the West today are in a bind. They are caught between the desire to preserve the work of over 70 years of interfaith reconciliation, and their mounting awareness that all is not right with the Jewish national homeland project. To be in such a bind is not comfortable—but the times call for hard choices. Because of the well-intentioned desire to atone for Christian anti-Judaism, Christians, individually and institutionally, have been muzzled from principled criticism of Israel's human rights violations. This is a disaster for Christianity and for world peace. Never before has it been so urgent for Christians to hold fast to their faith in pursuing the gospel imperative to stand up for the oppressed in pursuit of justice for the Palestinian people. The Kairos document shines the brightest when it talks about the universal mission of the land. Christianity's spiritualization and universalization of the land is the clearest example of how the new faith that arose in Palestine two thousand years ago came to fulfill the prophetic message of social justice.

The intractable nature of the conflict in Israel-Palestine and the particularly destructive forms that the struggle has taken demand that both Christians and Jews examine their beliefs, assumptions, and behaviors. There are lessons here for both groups. As Jews, we can lay claim to a long tradition of support for human rights—but our support for the human rights of oppressed and persecuted people rings false as long as Israel pursues policies that deny justice to the Palestinian people and thwart progress toward peace. Psychoanalyst Carl Jung termed the unacknowledged, unexamined aspects of individual and group character the "shadow." Our Jewish shadow is our sense of specialness and entitlement, reinforced by millennia of persecution and marginalization. We understand this aspect of our cultural identity all too well—but instead of realizing how it has led us into error and the betrayal of our values of fairness and compassion, we have allowed it to grant us license to do that very thing. If we honor our tradition and desire a future of security and dignity for the citizens of the current State of Israel, we must confront the evidence of our shadow in action: the glorification of military power, houses demolished, land taken, an entire people humiliated through collective punishment, and fundamentalist settlers acting out the will and design of a racist and expansionist government. We deny this reality at our peril. For their part, Christians must be ready to acknowledge how they have actively or passively enabled the injustice. To the extent that Christians, on personal and institutional levels, avoid the issue out of personal discomfort or a misguided "sensitivity" to the past suffering of Jews, or allow themselves to be guided by a theology that supports Jewish exceptionalism, they will be disempowered from taking the actions they would otherwise pursue in their humanitarian missions and social justice work.

THE CHALLENGE TO THE CHURCH

I recall a workshop held in Johannesburg on Israel and Palestine organized by the South African Council of Churches. It was attended by clergy and church officials from across the denominational spectrum, most of them with little knowledge about the situation. I remember vividly the words of a bishop of a South African apostolic church. Having just heard the testimonies of South Africans who had worked for Palestinian human rights as participants in the

World Council of Churches' Ecumenical Accompaniment Program, and Palestinian theologians on the subject of the gospel's message of the universal mission of the land, the bishop declared, "we need to re-read our Bibles!" More heartening still, he and many others in the room were asking the question, "How can we bring this back to the people in our churches and communities?" But even more significant was the next question asked by this same bishop: "How do we meet their objections that by questioning the actions of the State of Israel, *we are going against the Word of God*?" This is the challenge facing the churches today—and the stakes are very high.

There is a moral, political, and theological case to be made for a critique of biblical scholarship and hermeneutics with respect to Zionism, and the attitudes, beliefs, and habits governing support for Israel's colonialist policies, not only in Palestine, but in its relations with other countries. The dispossession of the Palestinian people and the growing power of Zionism as a theologically-informed ideology has implications that extend beyond one particular human rights struggle. It links to local struggles throughout the world and participates in the advancing process of dispossession, economic plunder, and militarism facing the world today. Delegates to an international conference in Johannesburg on the 30th anniversary of the South African Kairos document stated that "Palestine is a microcosm of global empire, a critical site of reflection that can bring experiences in other locales into sharper focus. Palestine does not eclipse other situations around the globe but instead intensifies the need for greater interconnection and mutual engagement."[22] From the mid-20th century on, churches have played a decisive role in liberation struggles at local and global levels.

In the case of Palestine, however, an almost universally accepted reading of the Bible with respect to land, promise, and peoplehood has been used to legitimize Israel's project to erase Palestinians' history, identity, and presence in their land. In addition, myths about Israel's vulnerability, informed by Islamophobia, have served to justify Israel as a special case needing protection and loyalty. Church institutions at the highest levels conform to and often actively participate in national governments' alliances with Israel, including support of Zionist-sponsored religious pilgrimages to the Holy Land. This has become increasingly critical for churches throughout the African continent, as Israel strengthens its alliances with churches in its stepped-up pursuit of diplomatic and economic ties and its export of arms and security technology. The rapid rise of Zionism in Africa as both theology and political ideology and how it connects to the rise of global powers, investment interests, and various struggles in other parts of the world are of great concern. In short, the case of Israel and Palestine serves as a focused lens for global issues such as colonialism, occupation, racism, religious fundamentalism, power abuse, militarism, and violence, as well as double standards in theologies and in the application of international law.

Happily, there are signs that the churches are mobilizing and organizing in response to the Palestinian call. A global network of organizations has emerged, standing in solidarity with Palestinian Christian organizations such as the Jerusalem-based Sabeel Ecumenical Liberation Theology Center, the Bethlehem-based Kairos Palestine, and Diyar Consortium in Bethlehem. Local, national, and denominationally-based groups throughout the world have established connections with human rights, healthcare, educational, and fair trade organizations throughout Palestine. The support provided by this network includes financial assistance, education and awareness-building, promotion of Kairos theology, and support for direct action for Palestinian rights. The Palestinian call for Boycott, Divestment, and Sanctions (BDS) has been endorsed and actively supported by many of the organizations comprising this network. BDS is steadily gaining momentum. The Southern African provincial synod of the Anglican Church (ACSA) has adopted the BDS boycott of Israel. ACSA represents Anglican Christian communities in southern African countries including South Africa, Namibia, Mozambique, and Angola. After years of heated internal controversy, Protestant denominations in the United States and elsewhere have officially endorsed BDS, with more to follow.

Post-supersessionist Christian thinkers have rejected the age-old dogma that set up Christianity as the superior faith, with Judaism as, in Catholic priest and author James Carroll's words, "the shadow against which Christianity could be the light."[23] But in doing so, Christians have thrown the baby of the radical universalism of Pentecost out with the bathwater of the church's anti-Judaism, which was an essential part of the early church's strategy to gain favor with the Roman Empire. If, as post-supersessionist Christian thinkers are suggesting, we are to revisit the momentous events of the first century CE, to this Jew it is clear what questions Jews and Christians must be asking themselves: What was Jesus saying to the power structures of his time—priestly, monarchical, and imperial? What was the nature of the parting between the Jews of the time and those who came to be called Christians? We must be very clear, therefore, about the purpose of the interfaith dialogue we undertake. We must call to account those Christian theologians who, in the service of "interfaith reconciliation," and in an effort to rehabilitate Judaism from Christian denigration, have supported Jewish land in Palestinian territory claims on theological grounds.

To allow the powerful system of Zionist beliefs to go unchallenged is to support the continued violation of the most fundamental and sacred principles of Christianity. The biblical land promise has been called into the service of

Zionism as a political and theologically-based ideology, breathing new life into the racist, colonialist Christian Zionism birthed in the English Reformation. Ideological support for Zionism feeds into globalism, a system which, in the words of three prominent liberation theologians, "is not a benign and neutral process . . . Globalism is driven by a powerful minority of individuals, corporations, politicians and other patriarchal constellations pursuing their self interest in the guise of 'development' and 'progress,' serv[ing] the agenda of empire without regard to the consequences for living beings and the planet.[24] When we unpack Zionism, we are open to the reality of the neoliberal global order—a level of consciousness, set of attitudes and view of humanity and human relations that threatens human civilization and the Earth itself.

Anti-Semitism is real and must be recognized when it manifests. But we live in a different context than the one that emerged in the aftermath of World War II. We have passed from the post-Holocaust era and have entered the post-Nakba era. Nakba—catastrophe—is the word that the Palestinians use to describe the dispossession of 1948 and the ethnic cleansing and incremental genocide that continues to this day. The churches have been called to answer for their theological, institutional, and, it is not a stretch to say, political support for the historic and ongoing crimes against the Palestinians. They have been called by those in their ranks, who, willing to pay the cost in opposition from high places and name calling from colleagues from within and outside the church, have worked tirelessly to bring their churches to confession and action. Far from being anti-Semitic, working for justice for the Palestinians is an act of love toward the Jewish people. It is time to do for Israel what the world did for South Africa—through economic and cultural pressure, liberate both oppressor and oppressed from the evil of apartheid in our time.

NOTES

1. "Boycott, Divestment, and Sanctions," https://bdsmovement.net/, accessed April 19, 2019.

2. World Council of Churches, "The Amman Call," https://www.oikoumene.org/en/resources/documents/wcc-programmes/public-witness-addressing-power-affirming-peace/middle-east-peace/the-amman-call, accessed April 16, 2019.

3. Kairos Palestine: "Moment of Truth: A Word of Faith, Hope and Love from the Heart of Palestinian Suffering," accessed April 16, 2019, http://www.kairospalestine.ps/index.php/about-us/kairos-palestine-document.

4. "Open letter from The National Coalition of Christian Organizations in Palestine (NCCOP) to the World Council of Churches and the ecumenical movement," https://www.palestineportal.org/news-center/nccop-open-letter-wcc/, accessed April 16, 2019.

5. Kairos Palestine 10th Anniversary Conference Statement & Call to the Church, https://www.kairospalestine.ps/index.php/resources/statements/kairos-palestine-10th-anniversary-conference-statement-call-to-the-church, accessed December 16, 2019.

6. Naim Ateek, *Justice Only Justice: A Palestinian Theology of Liberation,* (Maryknoll, NY: Orbis Books, 1989).

7. Mitri Raheb, *Faith in the Face of Empire: The Bible Through Palestinian Eyes* (Maryknoll, NY: Orbis Books, 2014).

8. Donald E. Wagner, *Anxious for Armageddon.* (Scottsdale, AZ: Herald Press, 1995); Rosemary R. Ruether, and Marc H. Ellis, eds., *Beyond occupation: American, Jewish, Christian and Palestinian Voices for Peace.* Boston, MA: Beacon Press, 1990): Michael Prior, *Zionism and the State of Israel, a Moral Inquiry* (London and New York: Routledge, 1999).

9. Donald E. Wagner, *Anxious for Armageddon*; Stephen Sizer, *Zion's Christian Soldiers? The Bible, Israel and the Church* (Downer's Grove, IL: Intervarsity, 2007); Robert O. Smith, *More Desired than Our Owne Salvation: The Roots of Christian Zionism* (Oxford: Oxford University Press, 2013).

10. Sizer, *Zion's Christian Soldiers? The Bible, Israel and the Church.*

11. Marc Ellis. *Toward a Jewish Theology of Liberation: The Challenge of the 21st Century* (Waco, TX: Baylor University Press, 2004) 43.

12. Kairos Palestine: "Moment of Truth"

13. Mark Braverman, *A Wall in Jerusalem* (New York: Jericho Books, 2012).

14. "Global Kairos," http://www.kairospalestine.ps/index.php/about-us/global-kairos, accessed April 19, 2019.

15. Bern Perspective, https://www.oikoumene.org/en/resources/documents/wcc-programmes/public-witness-addressing-power-affirming-peace/middle-east-peace/bern-perspective, accessed April 22, 2019.

16. Mitri Raheb, *The Biblical Text in the Context of Occupation* (Bethlehem: Diyar. 2012) 26.

17. Mitri Raheb, *Faith in the Face of Empire*, 71–72.

18. Ibid., 93.

19. Ibid., 65.

20. Clark M. Williamson, A *Guest in the House of Israel: Post-Holocaust Church Theology* (Louisville, KY: Westminster/John Knox: 1993).

21. Paul M. Van Buren, "The Jewish People in Christian Theology: Present and Future," in Darrell J. Fasching, ed., *The Jewish people in Christian preaching* (Lewiston, NY: Edwin Mellon Press: 1984) 19–33.

22. Kairos 30th Anniversary Statement: Dangerous Memory and Hope for the Future. https://kairossouthernafrica.wordpress.com/2015/08/20/kairos-sa-30th-anniversary-conference-statement/. Accessed December 17, 2019.

23. James Carroll, *Constantine's sword: The Church and the Jews,* (Boston: Houghton Mifflin, 2001) 109.

24. (Allan A. Boesak, A. J. Weusmann, & Charles Amjad-Ali, eds., *Dreaming a Different World. Globalisation and Justice for Humanity and the Earth. The Challenge*

of the Accra Confession for the Churches. (Evangelisch Reformierte Kirche, Germany and the Uniting Reformed Church in Southern Africa, 2010) 4.

BIBLIOGRAPHY

Ateek, Naim. *Justice Only Justice: A Palestinian Theology of Liberation,* Maryknoll, NY: Orbis Books, 1989.

Bern Perspective, https://www.oikoumene.org/en/resources/documents/wcc-programmes/public-witness-addressing-power-affirming-peace/middle-east-peace/bern-perspective, accessed April 22, 2019.

Boesak, Allan A., J. Weusmann, and Charles Amjad-Ali, eds. *Dreaming a Different World. Globalisation and Justice for Humanity and the Earth. The Challenge of the Accra Confession for the Churches.* Evangelisch Reformierte Kirche, Germany, and the Uniting Reformed Church in Southern Africa, 2010.

"Boycott, Divestment, and Sanctions," https://bdsmovement.net/, accessed April 19, 2019.

Braverman, Mark. *A Wall in Jerusalem,* New York: Jericho Books, 2012.

Ellis, Marc H. *Toward a Jewish Theology of Liberation: The Challenge of the 21st century.* Waco, TX: Baylor University Press, 2004.

"Global Kairos," http://www.kairospalestine.ps/index.php/about-us/global-kairos, accessed April 19, 2019.

Kairos 30th Anniversary Statement: Dangerous Memory and Hope for the Future. https://kairossouthernafrica.wordpress.com/2015/08/20/kairos-sa-30th-anniversary-conference-statement/. Accessed December 17, 2019.

Kairos Palestine 10th Anniversary Conference Statement & Call to the Church, https://www.kairospalestine.ps/index.php/resources/statements/kairos-palestine-10th-anniversary-conference-statement-call-to-the-church, accessed December 16, 2019.

Kairos Palestine: "Moment of Truth: A Word of Faith, Hope and Love from the Heart of Palestinian Suffering," http://www.kairospalestine.ps/index.php/about-us/kairos-palestine-document, accessed April 16, 2019.

"Open letter from The National Coalition of Christian Organizations in Palestine (NCCOP) to the World Council of Churches and the ecumenical movement," https://www.palestineportal.org/news-center/nccop-open-letter-wcc/, accessed April 16, 2019.

Prior, Michael. *Zionism and the State of Israel, a Moral Inquiry,* London and New York: Routledge, 1999.

Raheb, Mitri. *The Biblical Text in the Context of Occupation.* Bethlehem: Diyar, 2012.

———. *Faith in the Face of Empire: The Bible Through Palestinian Eyes.* Maryknoll, NY: Orbis Books, 2014.

Ruether, Rosemary R. and Marc H. Ellis, eds. *Beyond occupation: American, Jewish, Christian and Palestinian Voices for Peace.* Boston: Beacon Press, 1990.

Sizer, Stephen. *Zion's Christian Soldiers? The Bible, Israel and the Church,* Downer's Grove, IL: Intervarsity, 2007.

Smith, Robert O. *More Desired than Our Owne Salvation: The Roots of Christian Zionism*. Oxford: Oxford University Press, 2013.
Van Buren, Paul M."The Jewish People in Christian Theology: Present and Future." In *The Jewish People in Christian Preaching*, edited by Darrell J. Fasching, 19–33. Lewiston, NY: Edwin Mellon Press, 1984.
Wagner, Donald E. *Anxious for Armageddon.* Scottsdale, AZ: Herald Press, 1995.
Williamson, Clark M. *A Guest in the House of Israel: Post-Holocaust Church Theology* Louisville, KY: Westminster/John Knox, 1993.
World Council of Churches, "The Amman Call," https://www.oikoumene.org/en/resources/documents/wcc-programmes/public-witness-addressing-power-affirming-peace/middle-east-peace/the-amman-call, accessed April 16, 2019.

Chapter Fifteen

The Re-Reading of the Exodus Narrative

An African Perspective

Sindiso Jele

INTRODUCTION

The exodus narratives present the details on how the oppressed people of 'God' were liberated from Egypt.[1] It provides a portrait of a 'God' who hears his people as they cry out to 'Him'; and then acts accordingly. The people of God are identified as the sons of Israel and Israelites.[2] Such a specific identification makes this chapter raise questions on the exclusion of other people, especially those who are not Israelites. Such question of suspicion sees the exodus narratives as designed to provide a theological legitimacy on Israelian colonization of Canaan (Transjordan land). As such, it calls for re-reading within the African history who experienced colonization and continue to be economically colonized by the conceptual West.

The re-reading of the exodus within the narratives of the African colonisation is to reject the wholesale interpretation of the exodus narratives as liberation motifs. It is to argue that such reading amounts to one-sided theological reflection that fails to account for the experience of the local people. The experience of the local people in colonial time is defined with genocide, loose of identity, and land grabbing. In order to argue against this one-sided reading of the exodus, this chapter sees the Israelites as the colonisers and Canaan as the colonized land. In this case, Africa is identified with Canaan and European colonizers with the Israelites. In order to achieve this, the chapter looks at Africa as the context of the discourse, and considers the colonization of Africa as the point of departure. This chapter advocates that the re-reading of the exodus must be done with the African lenses in order to expose the one sidedness of the narratives and how the locals have suffered genocide and demonization of their religion. Therefore, the chapter concludes with the call for the rejection of the wholesale reading of the exodus that does not include the narratives of the indigenous people. This chapter arises out of the suspicion for the over emphasis of the 'let my people go' as a liberation motif, arguing it overshadows Israelites as colonizers and occupiers, thus requiring interrogation.

AFRICA AS THE CONTEXT AND LOCATION OF THE DISCUSSION

This chapter intends to argue that in as much as the exodus motifs have provided the points for departure for the liberation theologies, it is not innocent of having provided the same to the colonial regimes. When the Dutch,[3] who have colonised Cape Town (then Cape Colony, South Africa), were pushed out by the British who were to be the new colonisers, they evoked the spirit of the exodus. General Piet Retief is quoted having said:

> we complain of the unjustifiable odium which, under the name of religion, has been cast upon us by interested and dishonest persons. . . . We are now leaving the fruitful land of our birth, in which we have suffered enormous losses and continual vexation, and are about to enter a strange and dangerous territory; but we go with a firm reliance on an all-seeing, just, and merciful God, whom we shall always fear and humbly endeavour to obey.[4]

The reading of the General Retief declaration seems to suggest to the reader the role of religion and how it can be invoked to legitimatize. The statement seems to call for God's attention to the Retief's community as they journey away from the British colonizers. The only challenge I have with General Retief is that he gives the impression that he must be considered as one of the indigenous people of Cape Colony. He may be correct in terms of the birth place, but not as an indigenous person of the land. He is also theologically correct: God is all-seeing, just, and merciful. These are the attributes of the God of creation—not of the selected few—the God who can be invoked by the local people who were also under the fear of the 'strange and dangerous people,' to use General Retief's words in reverse. The God of the exodus and the theology which legitimates it, as invoked by General Piet Retief and his people, is void of the cries of the indigenous people that subsequently suffered in the hands of General Retief himself. The discussion as to who colonised who and why, also provides the point of departure in the re-reading of the exodus within the African context.

The scientists and explorers were interested in Africa's wildlife and natural resources. While on the other hand, European missionaries wanted to convert the Africans to Christianity, which was influenced by the Western way of life and culture. Such a worldview contributed to the understanding that Africans did not have a way of life—no religious policy and governance philosophy to follow. Bennie Van der Walt argues that the exodus to Africa was for the hunt of the riches.[5] In that case, I add it cannot be likened to the Hebrew Bible exodus story, where the Semites of Joseph were economic asylum seekers in Egypt and who were later oppressed when they became a threat to the local politics and economy. This hunt for wealth and cheap labour to support the European economy led to colonisation. The conference to orderly colonise Africa was called. I will liken it to the Joshua conference whereby the land beyond the river Jordan was parcelled to the tribes of Israel.

During this Berlin conference 1884, Africa was not invited. Without making a parallel, this becomes the replica of Joshua 13:1–7: "I will drive all these peoples out as the people of Israel advance. You must divide the land among the Israelites, just as I have commanded you to do. Now then, divide this land among the other nine tribes and half of the tribe of Manasseh, for them to possess as their own."[6] This was a conference which later defined the identity of Africa, i.e., Anglophone, Francophone and Lusophone.

UNDERSTANDING COLONIALISM AS A POINT OF DEPARTURE

Bulhan argues that in its classic form, colonialism was about European invasion, occupation and exploitation. It was not limited to material and cultural exploitation; it has to do also with "European self-aggrandizement to compensate for gnawing doubts on the wholeness and integrity of the self." This means that colonialism must be understood as both economic, political, cultural and psychological invasion of the indigenous people by the outsider.[7] This chapter aligns itself with the Bulhan's argument, especially on the questions that can be hypothetically raised: How much political, sociological and religious trauma has colonisation had on the local people? How far have the local people understood and how far is their voice recorded in the colonial history?

Van der Walt, looking at colonialism in retrospect, argued that there is need to understand why the colonisers came to Africa.[8] I suppose it must be the same with what the re-reading of the Exodus must go through. Some argue that they came for the cheap labor, and harvesting of the resources (wealth, milk and honey). It must also be argued that they were also interested in the expansion of the conceptual Western or white supremacy, even missiological, there is an understanding that it was about taking the gospel to the heathen land. In this case the term heathen is taken to mean 'people without faith or without a God.' The imperial thinking is that if 'you are not subscribing to my religion' you don't have a religion. Similarly, occupation and colonisation speak of civilizing the uncivilized.

Banana argues that the '. . . European Churches often shared the same attitude of superiority towards the beliefs, values, customs and traditions of the peoples of the lands being colonised.'[9] This was done by and through the demonization of the indigenous people; a reflection found in the exodus too. The indigenous were described as barbaric, heathen, and people of pagan rituals, therefore any theology born out of the re-reading of the exodus and seeking to address the repeat of the colonization must not avoid confronting oppression, slavery by any name, economic and political injustices especially on the local people.[10] Therefore, re-reading Exodus within the understanding that colonisation points to the truth on how religion can be used to invoke the industrial looting of the 'milk and honey' resources, including the human resources through the slavery of the local people. The flat bedding in the definition of colonisation exposes the void of the stories of the indigenous people in the exodus narrative, which later become the thesis of this chapter.

EXODUS: THE RE-READING

A number of scholars have tried to re-read or contextualise the exodus narratives. Fernandez, arguing from the point immigration, looks at exodus narratives. His reading of the exodus suggests that Filipinos, when they migrated to America, were on their journey to the promised land which became their Egypt. This reading sees the exodus in reverse, people going back to Egypt.[11] Such a proposed project would not work for Africa as it would be bringing back colonialism that is characterised with oppression, exploitation and genocide. To suggest that Africans were not killed by genocide as they were to be used as slaves is an unforgivable insult to the painful history of Africa where they suffered under colonial rule which found some theological backing from the exodus narratives. This chapter thus rejects such insensitive reading. Whether there is now milk and honey in Egypt, the re-reading of the exodus must not take the people back there. Therefore, the Fernandez proposal 'Exodus-towards-Egypt: Filipino-Americans' struggle to realize the 'promised land' in America' in Africa may not work.

The other interesting voice in the re-reading of the exodus narratives is that of Cheryl A. Kirk-Duggan. She argues that those who read (re-read) exodus must do so from the lenses of the oppressed and the marginalised, I add from the lenses of the indigenous people. In doing so, those who read the exodus would be confronted with and by the stories of genocides, enslavements, and freedom.¹² Her thesis is that all the stories in the exodus narrative must be listened to and be heard, and must form part of the pack of the exodus narratives. This will help in transforming the heart of the oppressor; and the liberation of the oppressed to be realized.

But it is the thesis of Allen Robert Warrior that influences the African perspective's re-reading of the exodus. His point of departure is to identify the exodus motifs with the indigenous people of America. The Indians must be identified with the Canaanites of the Exodus who were already in the land promised to the Israelites. I align with his thinking that:

> " . . . the story of the Exodus is an inappropriate way for the Native American to think of liberation . . . "¹³ and so is for Africa. This reading is reflective of Africa's situation then (colonial times) and even now with the colonisation of the mind. He further argues that the reading (re-reading) of the exodus narratives must not be separated from the history that accompanied and informed them. The mistake people normally make when they re-read the exodus for the political actions 'let my people go' is to separate the narratives from the historical realities littered with genocide, and the stealing of the human dignity and identity.

The political call becomes incomplete in the sense that it doesn't say the people must be massacred or oppressed or land stolen from, but to go and share and never look down on the local people's identity and religion, for that forms their identity. Warriors' thesis therefore is that the voice of the local people is overlooked. Their experience in exodus narratives cannot be identified with triumphal theology of the Israelites, but the liberation theology developed from the lives of the local people. The chapter seeks to challenge the programme or prophetic announcement which seems to leave out those at the margins. The re-reading of the Exodus therefore must help those on the margins to have their cry heard by the God of the oppressed. It must deny God of the exodus of Israelites, who commands genocide and cultural and religio-social supremacy, which gives in to apartheid as was the case with South Africa and Palestine.

My approach to the re-reading of the exodus narratives is to use hermeneutics of suspicion as a model. Rita Felski argues that the hermeneutics of suspicion is the commitment to unmasking 'the lies and illusions of consciousness;' it is the style of interpretation which circumvents obvious or self-evident meanings in order to draw out less visible and less flattering truths.¹⁴ Felski further claims that hermeneutics remain a path not taken in Anglo-American literature and I add that it is less used in the reading of the Exodus narrative. If it was used it would have helped to unmask the absence of the narratives of the local people behind those of the Israelites.

The other point to note in that re-reading is about the optics, how we see things. As the topic suggest, the re-reading is done from the African perspectives. In this case, it looks at the audience of the book and why it was written. Exodus was the record of the events which dealt with the Israel's deliverance from Egypt and how Israel developed to a nation. And thus, the sequence would be Egypt, desert, trans-Jordan world, killing the indigenous people and distributing their land among the twelve tribes of Israel. As such, there is no academic offence in re-reading the narratives to see whether God still speaks to human history, and from whose ears are we hearing God's voice! Does an agent with and for those on the margins, the victims of the economic exploitation and political bullying get reflected in the traditional reading of the exodus?

The two exilic stories—Assyrian exile 720 BCE[15] and Babylonian 582 BCE[16] may also be read to suggest Israel was not prepared to live with other civilisations; if they were to, those people must be prepared to accept the supremacy of the Israel religion and culture and even the political formation. To accept that thinking may suggest other civilisations and people are the children of a lesser God, but I disagree.

RE-READING OF THE EXODUS: A MISSIOLOGICAL RESPONSE

Chammah J. Kaunda argues that the mission of God in the world is a mission of life as antidote against violence and injustice.[17] This chapter takes the understanding of the world as inclusive of Africa during and after the time of colonialism. In that sense, the reading of the exodus as it is in catechumen classes does not speak to the situation of Africa. The missiological response is a challenge to the African readers to reject the over emphasized liberation motif which leaves out the survivors of the invaders as was and continues to be the case with Africa. The missiological response is an intentional prophetic resistance of the continued brutality and economic exploitation of the indigenous people under the disguise of civilization of the heathen and uncivilized world.

Can God be found in lives and experiences of the local people (Canaanites) in the exodus narratives? This is a very urgent question for those schools of thought which want to over emphasise the liberation motifs of the Israelites by leaving out the Canaanites. The brief summary of the exodus within the missiological stand point is that God redeemed Israel—that cannot be denied. But it cannot be true that other people were saved too. The universalisation of the salvation plan is by interpretation and can be taken as apologetic theology which seeks to cover the thought that God sanctioned colonization and the accompanying genocide. In trying to solve this challenge of the re-reading of the exodus, Christopher J. Wright calls for political and spiritual interpretation of the exodus. The spiritual interpretations seek to link the exodus to the death of Jesus on the cross. The link is that, in the exodus Israel, was redeemed from slavery and in Jesus Christ the people are redeemed from sin.[18] This thinking, with which I agree, argues that the exodus missiological outcome is not what it affirms. In as much as those narratives have a lot of biblical support, Wright argues they are not biblical enough. Paralleling the deliverance to slaves and salvation from sin is not convincing, it fails to answer the question of 'whose sin.' And thus, fails to see exodus from the Africa perspective. It is therefore missiological and scandalous to spiritualize exodus, especially when read with the African lenses. Such an act airbrushes the socio-economic and political dimension of that historical event. These were the core of the exodus. But even though I agree with Wright, I still have to find the socio-economic and political realities of the local people being intentionally included them in the salvation agenda of the exodus as recorded in the Hebrew Bible, not as the enemies, but as the created being who as Kaunda argue,[19] not by extension, have the cries that the created God must listen to and hear.

Wright further argues that there is another school of thought which argues for the political interpretation of the exodus. The school of thought is based on God's interest in justice and God's stance against exploitation.[20] But it must be appreciated that God had a specific relationship with Israel and God was particular in God's dealings, such persuasion puts other people less close to God, and that is the position of the Exodus as it is in the Hebrew Bible. John R. Stott puts it well:

> the special relationship which God had established between himself and his people Israel.[21] . . . God rescued his people from Egypt in fulfilment of his covenant with Abraham, Isaac and Jacob and in anticipation of its renewal at Mount Sinai.[22] He made no covenant with the Syrians or the Philistines, nor did his providential activity in their national life make them his covenant people.[23]

The other people, local or otherwise, were not part of the exodus salvation agenda as recorded in the Hebrew Bible. Their inclusion in the narration was to show how the indigenous' politics and religion were a threat or contamination to the socio-religious life of the Israelites. Missiological response builds on the understanding that discernment is critical and radical, and thus must go to the roots, for this thus justifies the re-reading of the Exodus motifs. As such, they will be able to join in the *missio Dei*. Therefore, there is need for a new theological grammar. The missiological response calls for the development of the more responsive missiological grammar which will help people to discern the will of God and help them to unmask the empire who is now like them and among them.

The re-reading of the Exodus accepts that God acts in history, and the exodus narratives can be read and re-read over time and space. In the process, if they are not relevant in needing to be spelt out, the re-reading acknowledges the fact that scripture speaks to one situation and can be rejected by the other communities. The re-reading is Christian, the example of Jesus of Palestine reading the book of Isaiah 61:1–2 where he left out: *'the day of revenge will come.'*[24] The synagogue elders were surprised by why Jesus, a Jew, does include in his reading the scripture that spells out the racial supremacy, but Jesus left it out: Is. 61:2. . . . *'That the time has come When the LORD will save his people And defeat their enemies. . . . 5 My people, foreigners will serve you. They will take care of your flocks and farm your land and tend your vineyards.'*

The other point to note in the re-reading of the exodus is that African civilisation differs from the Jewish civilisation. In as much as the Jews were oppressed in Egypt, as the African were by the Europeans, it would be naïve to deny the fact that Israelites were colonisers of the land on the other side of the river Jordan, and the Africans were the indigenous of the colonised land. The lesson must be drawn also for those who got their liberation from the colonizers. Be careful how you use the scriptures, avoid the repetition of using scripture to legitimatise and create super races or tribes and dominance, or even having new oppressors. This reinforces the rejection of the wholesale reading of the exodus.

The African re-reading of the exodus narratives as liberation motifs looks at the sequence of the events. The exodus narratives during the time of Moses and Joshua were that the people were free to occupy while the African liberation wars were fought to force-back oppression and regain the 'stolen' land and identity. So, the Africans reading must identify themselves with Canaanites, whose land was taken and whose religion was demonised. The re-reading accepts that theology is the story of the people's interaction with God and naming Him within their experience. The stories of the indigenous people must be unique, not be used to complete the redemption equation of the Israelites. Therefore, it will be difficult to have one individual story which squarely captures the experience of the world without forcing one's ideology on other people, thus technically occupying them.

There seems to be a pattern in how the exodus and colonisation of Africa are structured:

Step 1: The occupiers bring the mentality of political and religious superiority. This is done by demonizing other religions and political set-ups. The correct and divine accept political ideology is as the one of the conceptual West.

Step 2: There's a sense in which the occupier tries to kill all the indigenous people of that land. In other words the re-reading of the exodus shows that it is also a narrative of genocide. The process of the genocide includes the destroying of their identity and culture, and bringing the culture and the religion of the coloniser. In the exodus, this is done under the instruction of God.

Step 3: There seems to be a striking similarity whereby the occupier grabs the land of its 'milk and honey,' that is its riches of land in the form of natural resources and the exploitation of the people. This reduces the local people to second class citizens in their own land.

In the summing up of this discussion I borrow what Banana said about the Methodist church in Zimbabwe: that the church was the reluctant accomplice of the colonialism. The effect of colonialism of Africa is expressed in the form oppression, slavery, and economic and political injustices. Banana further argues and I agree that 'the European churches often shared the same attitude (with the colonisers) of superiority towards the beliefs, values, customs and traditions of the people of the land being colonised.'[25] This is the pattern we find in the re-reading the Exodus.

This chapter argues that the reading of the exodus in the Africa context suggests that the African of the colonial time and now need to identify their stories with Palestinians, not with the Israelites and the Egyptians who are recorded as the oppressors and exploiters. The Israelites of the exodus time are now the occupier of the local people's land, the land of the Palestinians and demonization of the local religion. Such theological mandate of the exodus would not serve the African interest.

CONCLUSION

This chapter argued that the wholesale reading of the exodus, especially when read from the African perspective, is one sided. It does not capture the story of the indigenous people who suffered genocide, loses of identity, land and the demonization of their religion and culture. This chapter further argued that the structure of the exodus is reflected in that of the colonization of Africa, and therefore, the re-reading is the rejection of the wholesale reading of the exodus. The Israelites must be identified with the colonizers and Africans must identify themselves with the Canaanites. This must be the hermeneutical point of departure in the African reading of the narratives and the subsequent development of the theology thereafter.

NOTES

1. Africa or African in this chapter intentionally refers to the black people of the Black ancestry (Kaunda 2015:1), and I use the same understanding and conviction.

2. Ex 1:1–22; 2:23–25.

3. The Dutch settlement history in South Africa began in March 1647 with the shipwreck of the Dutch ship *Nieuwe Haarlem*. The shipwreck victims built a small fort named 'Sand Fort of the Cape of Good Hope.' They stayed for nearly one year at the Cape. And this led to the subsequent colonisation of the Cape colony.

4. George McCall Theal, *The History of the Immigrant Boers in South Africa* (London, GB: Swan Sonnenschein, Lowrey, & Co., 1888), 61; cf J. Du Plessis, *A History of Christian Mission in South Africa, Cape Town* (Cape Town, SA: C. Struik Publishers, 1965), 108.

5. Bennie Van der Walt, *Understanding and Rebuilding Africa: From Depression Today to Expectation for Tomorrow* (Potchefstroom, SA: Institute for Contemporary Christianity in Africa, 2008), 5.

6. Joshua 13:6–7.

7. Hussein A. Bulhan, 'Stages of Colonialism in Africa: From Occupation of Land to Occupation of Being' in *Journal of Social and Political Psychology* Vol. 3, No. 1 (2015) 240.

8. Van der Walt, *Understanding and Rebuilding Africa*, 5.

9. Canaan Sodindo Banana, *Politics of Repression and Resistance: Face to Face with Combat Theology* (Gweru, ZI: Mambo Press, 1996), 7.

10. Ibid, 6.

11. Eleazar S. Fernandez, 'Exodus-toward-Egypt: Filipino-Americans' Struggle to Realize thePromised Land in America' in *Voice from the Margins; Interpreting the Bible in the Third World*. Ed. by R.S. Sugirtharajah (New York: Orbis Books, 2006), 295.

12. Cheryl A. Kirk-Duggan, 'Let my People Go! Threads of the Exodus in African American Narratives' in *Voice from the Margins; Interpreting the Bible in the Third World*. Ed. by R.S. Sugirtharajah (New York, Orbis Books, 2006), 312.

13. Allen Robert Warrior, 'A Native American Perspective: Canaanites, Cowboys, and Indians' in *Voice from the Margins; Interpreting the Bible in the Third World*. Ed. by R.S. Sugirtharajah (New York: Orbis Books, 2006), 21.

14. Rita Felski, 'Critique and the Hermeneutics of Suspicion' in *M/C Journal: A Journal of Media and Culture* Vol. 15, No.1 (2012) 1.

15. 2 Ki 15:29.

16. Jer 52:20 and 2 Ch 36:20.

17. Chammah J. Kaunda, 'Reconceptualizing eucharist as subservient ritual. A missiological response to public violence in Africa' in *Scriptura* Vol. 114 (2015) 2.

18. Christopher J. Wright, *The Mission of God: Unlocking the Bible's Grand Narratives* (Westmont, IL: Intervarsity Academic Press, 2006), 276.

19. Kaunda, 'Reconceptualizing eucharist,' 2.

20. Wright, *The Mission of God,* 281.

21. Cf Amos 3:2.

22. Ex 2:24, 19:4–6.
23. John R.W. Stott, *Christian Mission in the Modern World* (London, GB: InterVarsity Classics Falcon, 1975), 96.
24. Is 61:2b.
25. Banana, *Politics of Repression,* 7.

BIBLIOGRAPHY

Anderson, Bernhard W. *The Living World of the Old Testament, 4th Edition.* Boston, MA: Addison-Wesley, 1975.

Banana, Canaan Sodindo. *Politics of Repression and Resistance: Face to Face with Combat Theology.* Gweru, ZI: Mambo Press, 1996.

Bulhan, Hussein A. 'Stages of Colonialism in Africa: From Occupation of Land to Occupation of Being.' *Journal of Social and Political Psychology* Vol. 3, No. 1 (2015): 239–56.

Du Plessis J. *A History of Christian Mission in South Africa, Cape Town.* Cape Town, SA: C. Struik Publishers, 1965.

Felski, Rita. 'Critique and the Hermeneutics of Suspicion.' *M/C Journal: A Journal of Media and Culture* Vol. 15, No.1 (2012): http://journal.media-culture.org.au/index.php/mcjournal/article/viewArticle/431.

Fernandez, Eleazar S. 'Exodus-toward-Egypt: Filipino-Americans' Struggle to Realize the Promised Land in America.' In *Voice from the Margins; Interpreting the Bible in the Third World,* edited by R.S. Sugirtharajah. New York, Orbis Books, 2006.

Kaunda, Chammah, J. 'Reconceptualizing eucharist as subservient ritual. A missiological response to public violence in Africa.' *Scriptura* Vol. 114 (2015):1–12.

Kirk-Duggan, Cheryl A. 'Let my People Go! Threads of the Exodus in African American Narratives.' In *Voice from the Margins; Interpreting the Bible in the Third World,* R.S. Sugirtharajah. New York: Orbis Books, 2006.

McCall Theal, George. *The History of the Immigrant Boers in South Africa.* London, GB: Swan Sonnenschein, Lowrey, & Co., 1888.

Stott, John R.W. *Christian Mission in the Modern World.* London, GB: InterVarsity Classics Falcon, 1975.

Van der Walt, Bennie. *Understanding and Rebuilding Africa: From Depression Today to Expectation for Tomorrow.* Potchefstroom, SA: Institute for Contemporary Christianity in Africa, 2008.

Warrior, Allen Robert. 'A Native American Perspective: Canaanites, Cowboys, and Indians.' In *Voice from the Margins: Interpreting the Bible in the Third World,* R.S. Sugirtharajah. New York: Orbis Books, 2006.

Wright, Christopher, J. *The Mission of God: Unlocking the Bible's Grand Narratives.* Westmont, IL: Intervarsity Academic Press, 2006.

Conclusion

Mitri Raheb and Miguel A. De La Torre

Occupation is a synonym for empire. Empires per definition need to keep crossing borders, occupying adjacent and foreign land, expanding territories, exploiting their resources, and subjugating peoples and nations. For their expansion they need resources and bodies, but they need also legitimacy. Empires exercise dominion through hard military power as well as soft power. Waging wars needs more than hardware. Ideology, theology, media, and culture provide empires with the software needed for a smooth operation. In this context, the Bible has been used to justify colonialism, occupation, and discrimination.

What the chapters in this book clearly show is that occupation is a global phenomenon that is not limited to time and space. It is true that most of the essays in this book reflect contexts of occupation related to 19th–20th century European colonialism: mainly British, Dutch, and American. Yet, several contexts of occupation in East-Asia, by China and Japan, are dealt with as well. European colonialism emerged with a European Christian context, but, as the examples of Israel and Indonesia show, occupation knows no religious boundaries. Judaism, Islam, Hinduism, Buddhism, or any religion can be utilized to legitimize the occupation of foreign lands and peoples. No region or religion is thus immune.

If occupation is synonymous with empire, so is resistance. Occupation provokes resistance. Oppression is never accepted by the occupied. To exist in a context of occupation is to resist. Resistance though takes diverse forms and inspires diverse methods. The occupied resist sometimes with force, sometimes with tricks, and often through art and literature. While occupying forces aim to erase the identity of the occupied, indigenous culture becomes an important vehicle for resistance. The different chapters in this book testify to such rich expressions of resistance.

One can study the phenomenon of occupation and resistance from a political or socio-economical perspective, and such analyses are vital and important to understand the context in its entirety. Yet, the essays in this book were written mainly by theologians. If empires employ soft power to subjugate people, occupied people resort to theology to liberate their own people. The Bible becomes a battle ground used by occupiers as a tool for colonization and by the occupied as a tool for liberation. The God of the Exodus and the God of Joshua become two different points of reference. God stands here against God. In fact, empires provoke questions about God. Empires behave like God. They are omnipotent, they have the final say about the life and death of the occupied bodies and souls. They have so much might that it constitutes right, and they often claim divine right. Their religious establishment provides them with legitimacy, while on the other hand, prophets question their right and legitimacy. Both do it in the name of God. Occupied people wonder where god is and why is he so silent. They struggle to find meaning for life under occupation. They search for narratives and cultural expressions to sustain them.

The entire bible emerged out of contexts of occupation: Assyrian, Babylonian, Persian, Greek, and Roman. Diverse texts of the bible were written in the context of occupation or exile. Several texts were written in prison, other texts had to be written in an apocalyptic language as underground literature to trick the empire. It is no wonder that the theme of liberation is found throughout the Bible like a red thread. In this sense, the scripture has to be read as resistance literature.

> The Phrase 'resistance literature,' according to Barbara Harlow in her book of the same name, was developed by Palestinian writer Ghassan Kanafani to describe the literature of that people. It presupposes a people's collective relationship to a common land, a common identity, or a common cause on the basis of which it is possible to distinguish between two modes of existence for the colonized, 'occupation' or exile.' This distinction also presupposes an 'occupying power' that has either exiled or subjugated . . . the colonized population and has, in addition, significantly intervened in the literary and cultural development of the people it has dispossessed and whose land it has occupied.[1]

In this sense, one has to understand the chapters in this book as belonging to the genre of resistance literature. The writers question the logic, rationale, theology, and epistemology of the empire. They dare to question the legitimacy and normativity of the empire. Such a task has never been as important as it is now. The rise of populism, religio- and ethno-nationalism, and authoritarian regimes is frightening. In fact, it is very difficult to recognize our world anymore with Trump in the US, Johnson in the UK, Modi in Indian, Putin in Russia, Xi Jinping in China, Erdogan in Turkey, and Netanyahu in Israel. They all have their own colonial ambitions, but what they have in common is a religious ideology that provided them with legitimacy and votes. They question the world order that developed in the aftermath of the Second World War and have no problem in violating International Law and human rights standards, while shrinking the space reserved for civil society. It's a gloomy time and the light at the end of the tunnel is out of sight. Yet, this new world constellation makes things clearer than ever before. The empire is no longer shy to remove the mask.

There is no country left today that doesn't feel the heat of one empire or another. The peoples and nations affected today by imperial policies have reached a record. It's therefore high time for resistance. It's high time to connect the dots, to map the global web of occupation, and to hear the voices of subaltern from the different corners of the world. This book comes thus at the right time, shedding light on a crucial issue that is relevant today to the global South like never before. Our hope is that this book will provide readers with new insights, analyses, and paradigms to understand the new context and faces of empire. For all those struggling in a context of occupation, we hope that this book will give them the needed strength to continue their journey of prophetic witness and their creative resistance by utilizing theology as a tool for the liberation of lands, peoples, minds, and bodies.

NOTE

1. Steven Salaita, *Holy Land in Transit: Colonialism and the Quest for Canaan*. Syracuse, NY: Syracuse University Press, 2006, 16.

Index

activist, 2, 67, 98, 99, 101, 106, 123, 153, 155, 156, 157, 160, 162, 163, 164, 167
alienation, 20, 153, 159, 163
ambiguity, 36, 133
Amungme, 121, 123, 126
ancestors, 9, 48, 87, 196
animal(istic), 52, 89, 100, 111, 120, 124, 125, 182, 183
another world, 3, 51, 87
anti-statism, 4
anticolonial, 196, 197. *See also* decoloniality
apartheid, 70, 131, 139, 154, 155, 159, 166, 211, 212, 222, 231
apathy, 155
architecture, 28, 38, 39, 44, 45
asylum, 99, 229

barbarism, 10, 83
barrier, 54, 55, 56, 57, 95, 217. *See also* boundaries
BDS (Boycott, divestment and sanctions), 154, 221, 222
Black people: bodies, 14, 105, 105, 110–13; blackness, 108, 109.
blind(ness), 30, 31, 61, 71
border(line), 7, 8, 23, 24, 52, 55, 60, 82, 95, 99, 100, 101, 110, 134, 162, 163, 196, 198, 200, 211, 239

boundaries, 3, 44, 53, 54, 55, 56, 57, 59, 95, 110, 163, 168, 200, 239
Brexit, 2, 19–34
brutality, 11, 15, 16, 17, 105, 166, 232

Canaan(ites), 4, 66, 70, 71, 72, 181, 227, 231, 232, 234, 235
capitalism, 11, 133
celebration, 89, 118, 163, 182
Charleston 9, 105, 112
checkpoints, 213
chosen people, 67, 68, 72, 81, 215
city gate, 37–47
civilization, 2, 8, 10, 53, 80, 222
class, 3, 9, 10, 53, 54, 55, 80, 87, 107, 125, 131, 149, 150, 161, 211, 232, 235; classism, 12, 106, 108, 113
coloniality, 28, 80; colonizer, 1, 2, 8, 12, 14, 15, 38, 39, 44, 71, 80, 82, 85, 86, 132, 144, 182, 184, 187, 200, 213, 228
communism, 11, 52
complicity, 4, 7, 9, 16, 61, 159, 216
conquest, 41, 61, 67, 69, 71, 73, 80, 83, 175, 176, 179, 180, 186, 187, 199, 211, 212
creolization, 86
cultural stratification, 90

243

decoloniality, 80; decolonization, 3, 4, 18, 118, 131, 132, 196, 199
deep-sea mining, 197
demilitarized zone (DMZ), 3, 59–60. *See also* military demarcation line (MDL)
democracy, 52, 55, 134, 139, 183
desegregation, 111
despair, 15, 159, 166, 168
development, 28, 33, 66, 81, 108, 114, 148, 149, 178, 187, 199, 201, 202, 205, 212, 222, 235, 140
dignity, 29, 33, 123, 150, 151, 155, 156, 167, 213, 219, 231
disablement, 166
discipleship, 26, 33
discriminate, 69, 88
discrimination, 54, 69, 80, 108, 114, 120, 156, 159, 163, 198, 239
dispossession, 18, 159, 211, 218, 220, 222
doctrine of (Christian) discovery, 71, 176, 188, 204
dogma, 86, 162, 221
Dome of the Rock, 62–65
domination, 1, 7, 46, 79, 80, 105, 108, 162, 199
dualism, 159

ecotheology, 123
empowerment, 164
energy, 54, 56, 124, 125, 126, 162, 164
epistemology, 106, 107, 240
erasure, 1, 4, 28, 153, 176, 185
esperanza, 9
ethnic diversity, 162, 199
Eurocentric, 1, 2, 4, 7, 8, 9, 11, 12, 13, 14, 15, 17
Eurocentrism, 9, 14, 15, 17, 18, 80
Eurochristian, 4, 175–87
expansion, 55, 70, 81, 114, 154, 163, 164, 166, 229, 239
exceptionalism, 153, 154, 162, 218, 219
exploitation, 21, 54, 80, 81, 99, 107, 108, 109, 114, 133, 198, 229, 230, 232, 233, 235

fake, 20, 23
fantasy, 21, 24, 26, 27, 29, 203
feet washing, 150
feminist, 108, 113, 162
firearms, 98
folklore, 79
fundamentalism, 15, 220

Gaza, 160, 166, 185, 211, 212
gender, 4, 106, 108, 113, 131, 149, 157, 163
genocide, 8, 81, 177, 181, 187, 188, 222, 227, 230, 231, 232, 234, 235
geocide, 125
geontopower, 3, 117, 121, 122, 123, 125, 126
geotheology, 3, 117, 124, 126
global south, 131, 241
globalization, 4, 131, 133, 149
guerilla, 148

"Hai Tanahku Papua," 118
happiness, 160, 161, 164, 166
Haram, 62, 64, 65
hermeneutics, 268, 220, 231
heroism, 153, 211
Holocaust, 70, 71, 73, 74, 153, 154, 175, 222
Holy Saturday, 10
homeland, 2, 37, 38, 46, 62, 67, 69, 71, 91, 120, 139, 154, 183, 186, 212, 215, 218
homeless, 66
hope, 4, 8, 9, 10, 11, 12, 14, 15, 18, 33, 44, 46, 51, 52, 59, 70, 98, 117, 68, 87, 216, 241. *See also esperanza*
hopelessness, 10, 12, 15, 18
households, 202
hybridity, 3, 46, 47, 79, 86, 88, 90

idealism, 186, 214
imagination, 3, 11, 33, 37, 51, 52, 59, 60, 63, 162, 166, 168, 180
immanence, 108, 109, 110
inculturation, 61

indigenous, 1, 2, 12, 13, 17, 32, 48, 70, 71, 72, 73, 79, 80, 81, 82, 83, 84, 85, 86, 89, 90, 119, 177, 179, 186, 195, 214, 228, 229, 230, 231, 232, 233, 234, 235, 239
indignity, 1
injustice, 10, 12, 24, 153, 157, 160, 161, 164, 214, 219, 230, 232, 235
integrity, 158, 179, 160, 162, 167, 229
intercultural theology, 149
interfaith, 119, 215, 218, 221
intersectional, 108, 113
intifada, 65, 57
Islamophobic rhetoric, 65
island, 3, 28, 33, 37, 38, 39, 40, 44, 83, 91, 118, 134, 136, 143, 184, 196, 197, 200

joder, 2, 7, 14, 15, 17
jodiendo, 15, 16, 17, 18
José Martí, 12
justice, 8, 9, 10, 31, 38, 46, 47, 51, 98, 99, 107, 109, 112, 114, 131, 149, 150, 151, 159, 161, 164, 201, 203, 204, 211, 214, 215, 219, 222, 233

Kairos, 72, 216, 219, 220, 221
Kanwar, Amar, 148–49

land theology, 67, 70, 71, 72, 73, 74
landless, 66
landscape, 40, 41, 123, 124
language, 19, 21, 23, 24, 37, 44, 46, 56, 61 62, 65, 84, 88, 111, 120, 133, 134, 175, 176, 177, 178, 179, 181, 182, 183, 184, 186, 187, 196, 197, 199, 201, 202, 212, 218, 240
Latinx, 9, 12, 15, 16, 17
let my people go, 24, 228
liberation, 1, 4, 8, 9, 13, 19, 21, 23, 26, 33, 38, 46, 53, 64, 73, 74, 91, 106, 10, 159, 165, 179, 181, 197, 211, 213, 216, 217, 220, 221, 222, 228, 231, 232, 234, 240, 241
lynchings, 105

make love, 98
market, 23, 28, 32, 85, 118
martial law, 37
media, 148, 156, 159, 160, 239, 248
metacolonialism, 80
metanarrative, 11, 25
migrant, 71, 98, 99, 100, 119, 186
migration, 23, 100, 139, 175, 186
militarization, 159, 213
military, 30, 39, 40, 52, 53, 57, 61, 64, 65, 67, 68, 69, 95, 118, 122, 131, 132, 133, 134, 136, 143, 148, 153, 154, 161, 163, 175, 177, 181, 186, 200, 211, 219, 239
military demarcation line (MDL), 52, 53, 57, 59, 60. *See also* DMZ
minjung, 134, 139
morning star, 118
Motherly Spirit, 3, 117–26
Moyen, Donatus, 143–47
mural, 38, 39, 41, 42, 136, 144–47
myths, 45, 107, 154, 155, 185, 204, 217, 218, 220
mythologies, 14, 20

nakba, 222
nationalism, 19, 21, 31, 33, 99, 132, 148, 154, 198, 202, 240
native, 61, 67, 70, 71, 73, 82, 83, 86, 87, 91, 100, 119, 120, 175–87, 231
neoliberal(ism), 1, 7, 12, 15, 125, 126, 222
nirvana, 158
non-violence, 185, 186

ontology, 110, 158, 202
oppression, 1, 2, 4, 8, 10, 13, 21, 29, 45, 54, 74, 108, 109, 133, 153, 154, 156, 160, 179, 198, 230, 234, 235, 239
othering, 24, 214
outcasts, 153

pale, 214
Palestine, 4, 61–74, 153–68, 175, 185, 211–22, 231, 234

Papua (West, New Guinea), 3, 4, 117–26, 131, 133, 143–47, 45, 200, 204
pedagogy, 106, 108
persecution, 153, 154, 214, 216, 219
perversion, 106
plantains, 12, 13, 14
popular culture, 106, 107, 148, 149
populism, 19, 240
possession, 16, 39, 44, 82, 89, 166, 179, 188, 212
poverty, 11, 14, 15, 18, 55, 99, 134, 143, 166
praxis, 10, 12, 14, 15
primitive, 39, 84, 119, 120
promised land, 3, 66, 71, 72, 73, 74, 217, 230, 231
propaganda, 38, 40, 41, 133
property, 83, 108, 109, 110, 178, 183, 184
protest, 16, 17, 111, 133, 178, 180
punishment, 100, 109, 219

Qing 37, 39, 44

race, 4, 80, 82, 84, 87, 88, 108, 109, 110, 131, 149, 198, 234; racism, 3, 32, 81, 90, 108, 111, 112, 113, 117, 119, 120, 121, 125, 133, 213, 214, 220; racist, 9, 105, 106, 215, 219, 222
rebellion, 88, 95, 120. *See also* resistance
reconciliation, 3, 131–51, 154, 216, 218, 221
redemption, 11, 211, 213, 234
refugees, 14, 95, 98, 99, 154, 161, 165, 175
religious pluralism, 3, 79, 246
resistance, 3, 12, 13, 79, 85, 90, 118, 126, 131–51, 155, 166, 178, 180, 185, 186, 187, 212, 214, 216, 217, 232, 239, 240, 241
restoration, 53, 212

right-of-return, 175
rule of law, 105, 175–87

sacrality, 107
salvation history, 11, 71
Santería, 14, 86
savage(s), 119, 185, 186
scandal, 100, 167, 233
segregation, 105, 111, 113. *See also* race
settlement, 20, 28, 29, 70, 73, 121, 175, 211, 212, 213; settlers, 4, 29, 62, 64, 65, 69, 70, 71, 72, 73, 74, 79, 82, 118, 119, 132, 139, 154, 176, 184, 186, 211, 213, 216, 219
sexual abuse, 14; exploitation, 81, 107, 108; trafficking, 105, 113
sexism, 12, 106, 108, 113
shadow, 1, 9, 32, 167, 218, 219, 221
shrine, 41, 63, 64, 65, 85
silence, 105, 149, 155, 157
simulacrum, 45, 46
sitz im leben, 61, 64
skeletons, 97
slavery, 81–85, 87, 89, 90, 105, 111, 113, 134, 216, 230, 233, 235; slave trade, 28, 81, 82, 84, 85, 86, 90
Snowpiercer, 3, 53, 54, 56, 57
solidarity, 15, 18, 46, 101, 119, 156, 159, 164, 165, 167, 168, 211, 221. *See also* unity
software, 239
Song-Dam, Hong, 133–39, 149
sovereignty, 73, 105, 110, 119, 148, 176, 177, 178
Standing Rock, 178, 186, 187
Stopforth, Paul, 139–43, 149
strangers, 9, 69
subaltern, 2, 23, 149, 241
subjugate, 2, 7, 240
superiority, 8, 21, 80, 81, 82, 83, 119, 162, 230, 234, 235
supremacy, 2, 3, 9, 12, 13, 17, 105, 106, 107, 108, 109, 110, 113, 114,

229, 231, 232, 234. *See also* white supremacy, race

Temple Mount, 62–65
terra nullius, 182
theological innocence, 65, 74
Theys Eluay, 118
token, 13, 107
tourism, 197; tourists, 41
trade posts, 132, 139
traitors, 153
transmigration, 118, 119, 143
trauma, 3, 131, 133, 134, 136, 148, 151, 229
trickster, 2, 14, 17, 188
triumphalism, 218

unification, 59
unity, 197, 199, 201, 202

vassalage, 19
victim (victimhood), 19, 21, 23, 24, 96, 101, 112, 114, 134, 139, 149, 150, 151, 214, 232
violence, 7, 10, 11, 53, 59, 66, 80, 81, 84, 85, 113, 114, 148, 156, 163, 177, 178, 180, 181, 185, 186, 202, 203, 221, 232
vocation, 20, 31

water, 32, 52, 57, 89, 95, 121, 124, 136, 137, 138, 181, 186
wealth, 11, 15, 28, 55, 121, 184, 187, 229
white supremacy, 2, 3, 9, 12, 13, 17, 105–10, 113, 114, 229
whiteness, 108, 109, 110
wholeness, 31, 47, 160, 167, 168, 229
wilderness, 91, 100, 119, 185
wine, 12, 13, 14, 81
womanism, 108. *See also* sexism
wretched, 12, 179

xenophobic, 99. *See also* white supremacy

Yoruba, 14, 87, 89, 90

zaria, 161
Zionism, 71, 73, 153, 154, 155, 161, 162, 164, 168, 175, 211–22

About the Contributors

Mark Braverman is executive director of Kairos USA, an ecumenical organization of churches in the U.S. founded in response to the Kairos call of the Palestinian Christians. He serves on the Theology Working Group of Global Kairos for Justice. He is research fellow in systematic theology and ecclesiology at Stellenbosch University in South Africa.

Richard A. Davis is a senior lecturer in the Department of Theology and Ethics at the Pacific Theological College in Fiji. Originally from Aotearoa New Zealand, he earned his PhD from the University of Edinburgh on a Council for World Mission scholarship, graduating in 2013. Davis publishes and teaches across the fields of systematic theology and ecumenical ethics, with a special focus on Christian social ethics and political theology.

Wanda Deifelt is professor of religion at Luther College in Decorah, IA. She is originally from Brazil, where she held the Chair of Feminist Theology at Faculdades EST, in São Leopoldo. She is an ordained pastor of the Evangelical Lutheran Church in Brazil and has served as theological advisor for several ecumenical organizations, including the World Council of Churches, the Lutheran World Federation, and the Latin American Council of Churches. Her research and publications address contextual and liberation theologies, gender studies, reproductive rights, ecumenical and interreligious dialogue, and embodiment.

Miguel A. De La Torre is a scholar-activist tenured as professor of social ethics and Latino/a studies at Iliff School of Theology in Denver, Colorado. Since obtaining his doctorate in 1999, he has published over thirty-five books, five of which won national awards. He served as the 2012 president of the Society of Christian Ethics. And wrote the screenplay for the documentary *Tails of Hope and Terror* (https://www.trailsofhopeandterrorthemovie.com/).

Stacey M. Floyd-Thomas is the E. Rhodes and Leona B. Carpenter Associate Professor of Ethics and Society at Vanderbilt University Divinity School. She is also past-executive director of the Society of Christian Ethics, co-founder of the Society of Race, Ethnicity and Religion, and co-founder and current executive director of the Black Religious Scholars Group. Her research in Christian social ethics focuses on race, gender, and class as it confronts the challenges of religious pluralism, social justice, and the political world and compels constructive ethics to make liberationist discourse more viable. Her concern for what she calls "the why crisis" of faith is exemplified in her numerous articles, book chapters, two book series, and seven books.

Toar Hutagalung received his master of arts in theological research (MATR) from Andover Newton Theological School. He holds his bachelor of science in theology (S.Si.Teol.) from Jakarta Theological Seminary, where he taught for two years. He continues his doctoral studies at Garrett-Evangelical Theological Seminary with a focus on postcolonial/decolonial studies.

Currently, he is the chair of association of [young] Indonesian Theologians and the coordinator of Asian/Asian American Center at Garrett-Evangelical Theological Seminary.

Sindiso Jele is a Zimbabwean now based in South Africa, where he is an ordained minister of the United Congregation Church of Southern Africa (UCCSA). Holding the PhD in missiology, he currently works as the CWM Africa Mission Secretary. He presented two conference papers on political and economic injustice under the Southern African Missiological Society (SAMS).

Junghyung Kim is an assistant professor at Presbyterian University and Theological Seminary, Seoul, South Korea. He earned his PhD. at Graduate Theological Union, Berkeley. In addition to a theology of peace anticipating the unified Korea, his current theological interests focus on reconstructing the doctrine of creation in response to the climate crisis and reformulating a theology of work and rest in light of technological renovations.

Luciano Kovacs is currently serving as Presbyterian Church (USA)'s area coordinator for Middle East and Europe. Previously, he worked as World Student Christian Federation North America Executive and Global Director for Advocacy and Solidarity. His *Laurea* dissertation from the University of Turin, Italy, "A gender critique of R.K. Narayan's novels," was part of his specialization in literature of English-speaking countries. His studies included courses in the UK, Ireland, Scotland and Germany. Kovacs studied acting at HB Studio in New York City and produced six Off-Off-Broadway plays at the Jan Hus Playhouse in New York City. He has written poetry, short stories, and one novel. He is currently writing his second one.

Volker Küster is professor of comparative religion and missiology, Johannes Gutenberg-Universität Mainz, Germany. Küster explores the interconfessional, intercultural and interreligious dimensions of Christian faith by employing methods such as hermeneutics, aesthetics, communication theory, postcolonial critic, and globalization theory. Perspectives of culture, religion, race, class, gender, and inclusion are involved in this multi-axial approach. His research in contextual and intercultural theology evolves along two lines: *dialog, conflict, and reconciliation* and *visual art and religion*.

Su-Chi Lin received her PhD at Graduate Theological Union (GTU) in Berkeley. Since 2017, she has offered courses on the arts at Taiwan Graduate School of Theology and Christ's College Taipei. She is the author of *Spaces of Mediation: Christian Art and Visual Culture in Taiwan*.

Marthie Momberg, a post-doctoral fellow at Stellenbosch University's Discipline group for systematic theology and ecclesiology and the Beyers Naudé Centre for Public Theology, has postgraduate qualifications in literature, education, and theology. Her interdisciplinary praxis has always been driven by a personal quest for empowered and dignified lives. In her earlier career, her work in strategic business consulting, branding, and corporate communication has received numerous regional and international industry awards.

Mitri Raheb is the founder and president of Dar al-Kalima University College of Arts and Culture in Bethlehem. The most widely published Palestinian theologian to date, Dr. Raheb is the author of 20 books in eleven languages, including: *Faith in the Face of Empire: The Bible through Palestinian Eyes* and *The Cross in Contexts: Suffering and Redemption in Palestine*. A social entrepreneur, the work of Dr. Raheb has received wide media attention and numerous international awards.

John McNeil Scott is from Ireland. He serves as principal of the Scottish United Reformed and Congregational College, a centre for theological education in Glasgow, Scotland. As well as his home country and Scotland, he has studied, lived and worked in England, Taiwan, and the United States. He completed his doctoral studies with Chicago Theological Seminary.

George "Tink" Tinker (wazhazhe / a citizen of the Osage Nation) is emeritus professor of American Indian Cultures and Religious Traditions. He taught for thirty-four years at Iliff School of Theology and volunteered for a quarter century as director and spiritual leader of Four Winds American Indian Council in Denver, an urban Indian political and spiritual support organization closely related to Colorado AIM. He was recently awarded the 2019 Walter Wink Scholar Activist prize for his work.

www.ingramcontent.com/pod-product-compliance
Lightning Source LLC
Chambersburg PA
CBHW061710300426
44115CB00014B/2626